Analysing Exemplary Science

Analysing exemplary science teaching:

theoretical lenses and a spectrum of
possibilities for practice

Edited by Steve Alsop, Larry Bencze and Erminia Pedretti

Open University Press

Open University Press
McGraw-Hill Education
McGraw-Hill House
Shoppenhangers Road
Maidenhead
Berkshire
England
SL6 2QL

email: enquiries@openup.co.uk
world wide web: www.openup.co.uk

and Two Penn Plaza, New York, NY 10121–2289, USA

First published 2005

A catalogue record of this book is available from the British Library

ISBN 0 335 21311 1 (pb) 0 335 21312 X (hb)

Library of Congress Cataloging-in-Publication Data
CIP data applied for

Typeset by YHT Ltd, London
Printed in the UK by Bell & Bain Ltd, Glasgow

Contents

List of contributors   ix
Foreword: Exemplary practice as exemplary research   xv
   William F. McComas
Acknowledgements   xxi

INTRODUCTION
Creating possibilities   1
Steve Alsop, Erminia Pedretti and Larry Bencze

PART 1
Accounts of exemplary practice   13

Account 1 Kidney function and dysfunction: enhancing understanding
   of the science and the impact on society
   Keith Hicks   15

Account 2 Episodes in physics
   George Alex Przywolnik   23

Account 3 Recollections of organic chemistry
   Josie Ellis   29

Account 4 The science classroom of tomorrow?
   Richard Rennie and Kim Edwards   32

Account 5 Science with a human touch: historical vignettes in the
   teaching and learning of science
   Karen Kettle   38

Account 6 Exploring the nature of science: reinterpreting the Burgess
   Shale fossils
   Katherine Bellomo   46

Account 7 Motivating the unmotivated: relevance and empowerment through a town hall debate
Susan A. Yoon   53

Account 8 Mentoring students towards independent scientific inquiry
Alex Corry   63

Account 9 Learning to *do* science
Gabriel Ayyavoo, Vivien Tzau and Desmond Ngai   71

Account 10 Practice drives theory: an integrated approach in technological education
James Johnston   84

PART 2
Account analyses   93

Analysis 1 Challenging traditional views of the nature of science and scientific inquiry
Derek Hodson   96

Analysis 2 Developing arguments
Sibel Erduran and Jonathan Osborne   106

Analysis 3 STSE education: principles and practices
Erminia Pedretti   116

Analysis 4 Conceptual development
Keith S. Taber   127

Analysis 5 Problem-based contextualized learning
Ann Marie Hill and Howard A. Smith   136

Analysis 6 Motivational beliefs and classroom contextual factors: exploring affect in accounts of exemplary practice
Steve Alsop   146

Analysis 7 Instructional technologies, technocentrism and science education
Jim Hewitt   160

Analysis 8 Reading accounts: central themes in science teachers' descriptions of exemplary teaching practice
John Wallace   171

Analysis 9 Equity in science teaching and learning: the inclusive science curriculum
Léonie J. Rennie   183

Analysis 10 School science for/against social justice
Larry Bencze   193

PART 3
Possibilities, accounts, hypertext and theoretical lenses   203

Reflection 1 Voices and viewpoints: what have we learned about
   exemplary science teaching?
   Erminia Pedretti, Larry Bencze and Steve Alsop   205

Reflection 2 Integrating educational resources into school science praxis
   Larry Bencze, Steve Alsop and Erminia Pedretti   217

References   227
Index   243

List of contributors

Steve Alsop is Associate Dean in the Faculty of Education, York University, Ontario, coordinating research and continuing professional development. Previously he directed the Centre for Learning and Research in Science Education [CLARISE] at the University of Surrey Roehampton, England, where he now holds the position of senior honorary research fellow. Steve has taught in primary and secondary schools in London, England. His research interests include affective, cognitive and epistemological issues in science education, science teacher education and internationalization. Recent publications include: *Teaching Science* (with Hicks, 2001) and *Beyond Cartesian Dualism: Encountering Affect in the Teaching and Learning of Science* (in press).

Gabriel Ayyavoo (BSc, BEd, MEd) is currently a science instructor at the Ontario Science Centre in Toronto. He has 18 years' experience as a science teacher in Singapore and Canada. Much of his work involves promotion of student-driven science projects. Among his various activities, he is the Toronto regional coordinator for students' participation in the Canada Wide Science Fair.

Katherine Bellomo has been a science educator for 25 years. She has taught science in a variety of high schools in Ontario and has been a department head and curriculum consultant for a large urban school board. Currently she teaches in the pre-service (BEd) programme at the Ontario Institute for Studies in Education of the University of Toronto where she is also a doctoral candidate. She has an interest in the challenges that teachers face as they construct the biology curriculum, with a focus on social justice issues, for a diverse student population.

Larry Bencze (BSc, MSc, BEd, PhD) is an associate professor in science education at the Ontario Institute for Studies in Education of the University of Toronto. Prior to this, he worked as a secondary school science teacher for 11 years and a science consultant for a school district. Larry's research programme involves development and studies of students' opportunities to be engaged in realistic contexts of knowledge building in science and technology, along with relevant pedagogical considerations.

Alex Corry (BSc, BEd, MEd) is currently a vice-principal in a secondary school in Markham, Ontario. Prior to that he worked for several years as a teacher of science and has served as a science department head for two different school districts in Ontario. He has been, and continues to be, a major proponent of student-led science project work. As a school administrator, his current work is focused around instructional leadership, building community capacity and assessment and evaluation practices.

Kim Edwards is Head of Middle School and Acting Deputy Principal for Pastoral Care at Presbyterian Ladies' College, Western Australia. She has been teaching for 20 years, nine of which have been devoted to science teaching in the middle school. In 2002 she was jointly awarded the International Association of School Librarianship award for 'Most Innovative Practice for School Libraries' for the development of the 'Bloom's Thinking Strategy' teacher and student resource package. This is a framework for encouraging higher level thinking and learning in the classroom. She continues to explore ways of using technology in the classroom to assist in differentiating the curriculum and enhancing student learning.

Josie Ellis excelled at advanced level sciences and English at Elliott School in London. She is currently an undergraduate reading English at a University in the UK. She continues to bridge the 'two cultures' with a particular interest in science and the media.

Sibel Erduran is a lecturer in science education at the University of Bristol. She received her PhD in science education from Vanderbilt University, MS in Food Chemistry from Cornell University and BA in Chemistry from Northwestern University. She taught high school chemistry in Cyprus, and had research and teaching experience at the University of Pittsburgh and King's College, University of London. Her research interests include cognitive and epistemological issues in science education.

Ann Marie Hill (PhD, Ohio State) is Professor of Education and Coordinator (Technological Education) at Queen's University, Kingston, Ontario. She has been a visiting scholar at Melbourne (Australia), Waikato (New Zealand), Leeds (UK) and UBC (Canada). She presents at international conferences and is known internationally for publications on technological and technology education that deal with design, creativity, authentic leaning environments, project-based leaning, community-based projects, curriculum and teacher education.

Jim Hewitt is an associate professor in the Department of Curriculum, Teaching and Learning at the Ontario Institute for Studies in Education, University of Toronto. His research focuses on the educational applications of computer-based technologies, with a particular emphasis on discursive processes in collaborative learning environments. Dr Hewitt's recent publications include studies of telementoring, thread development in asynchronous distance education courses, sociocultural supports for knowledge building in elementary science classrooms, and applications of multimedia case studies in teacher education programmes.

Derek Hodson has more than 30 years' experience in science education in schools and universities in the United Kingdom, New Zealand and Canada. He is currently Professor of

Science Education at the Ontario Institute for Studies in Education of the University of Toronto, Director of the Imperial Oil Centre for Studies in Science, Mathematics and Technology Education, and Managing Editor of the *Canadian Journal of Science, Mathematics and Technology Education*. His research interests include the history, philosophy and sociology of science, multicultural and antiracist science education, science curriculum history and action research.

Keith Hicks is Head of Science at Elliott School which is a large comprehensive school in London, England. He has worked in the field of initial teacher education for many years and has an interest in assessment and constructivist learning in science. Keith has been involved in a series of research projects and co-edited the text *Teaching Science* (with Alsop, 2001).

James Johnston (Diploma in Technical Education, BA, BEd, MEd) is a technological education teacher at Frontenac Secondary School in Kingston, Ontario, and an adjunct lecturer at the Faculty of Education, Queen's University, Ontario. James is a strong advocate of subject integration and the application of learning using a student-centred, project-based learning model. His personal philosophy could be summarized as a 'practice drives theory' approach to education.

Karen Kettle has been an educator in Durham Region, Ontario for 21 years. She has served as a high school science and geography teacher as well as a programme consultant. She has recently completed a three-year secondment to York University Faculty of Education and is looking forward to teaching at Port Perry High School. Her passion is student leadership.

Desmond Ngai is currently studying for a science degree at the University of Toronto. When he was in high school, he won the prestigious gold medal at a major biotechnology fair. He also was a medalist at the Canada-wide Science Fair and was ranked third at the International Science and Engineering Fair.

Jonathan Osborne is a professor of science education at King's College London where he has been since 1985. Prior to that he worked as an advisory teacher and a teacher of physics in inner London. He has an extensive record of publications and research in science education in the field of primary science, science education policy, the teaching of the history of science, argumentation and informal science education. He was a co-editor of *Beyond 2000: Science Education for the Future* (1998), an ESRC fellow on their Public Understanding of Science Programme, an adviser to the House of Commons Science and Technology Committee on their report on science education produced in 2002, and has been a member of the Board of the North American Association for Research in Science Teaching. His first degree is in physics, he has a masters degree in astrophysics and a PhD from King's in education.

Dr Erminia Pedretti is Associate Professor of Science Education at the Ontario Institute for Studies in Education of the University of Toronto. She is also Associate Director of the Imperial Oil Centre for Studies in Science, Mathematics and Technology Education. Her research interests include: science, technology, society and environmental education, action research, teacher professional development and learning science in non school settings.

Recent publications include studies of issue-based exhibitions and learning in science centres and development and implementation of multimedia case studies in teacher education programs.

George Przywolnik has over 20 years' experience in science education and is a leading teacher at a private school in Western Australia. His interests include peer instruction techniques such as the modelling method and whiteboarding, and computer-based teaching and learning.

Dr Léonie Rennie is Professor of Science and Technology Education in the Science and Mathematics Education Centre at Curtin University of Technology in Western Australia. She is also Dean, Graduate Studies at the University. Léonie's research interests relate to gender, learning and assessment in science and technology, in both in-school and out-of-school settings.

Richard Rennie was a science teacher in secondary schools for 37 years; the last 19 at an independent girls school in Perth, Australia where the SCOT Project described in Account 4 was carried out. Richard is now setting up a science discovery centre that uses historic light and sound technology in educational and entertaining programmes.

Howard A. Smith (PhD, Toronto) is Professor of Education at Queen's University, Kingston, Ontario. He has held university appointments at Stanford, Bologna (Italy), Indiana, Deakin (Australia) and Parané (Brazil). He is known internationally for publications on nonverbal communication in teaching, human learning and the semiotics of education. His most recent book, *Psychosemiotics*, was published in 2001.

Dr Keith S. Taber is a lecturer in science education in the Faculty of Education at the University of Cambridge, UK. He is the Physics Education Tutor, and works with trainee teachers and research students. Dr Taber is an associate editor of the journal *Chemistry Education: Research and Practice*, and Chair of the Royal Society of Chemistry's Chemical Education Research Group. His main research interests are in various aspects of learning in science. He moderates an email discussion list (http://uk.groups.yahoo.com/group/learning-science-concepts), and writes a column of 'Reflections on teaching and learning physics' for the journal *Physics Education*.

Vivien Tzau (BSc) is currently a law student at Queen's University, Kingston, Ontario. When she was in high school she gained extensive experience in science fairs and biotechnology fairs. One of her projects involved studies of effects of organic sulphur compounds on breast cancer cells.

John Wallace is Professor of Science Education at Curtin University of Technology in Perth, Western Australia. His research interests include science teacher learning, case methods in science teacher education and school reform. His most recent (co-edited) books are *Dilemmas of Science Teaching: Perspectives on Problems of Practice* (with W. Louden, 2002) and *Leadership and Professional Development in Science Education: New Possibilities for Enhancing Teacher Learning* (with J. Loughran, 2003).

Susan Yoon has worked as a science educator in several capacities including public school science teacher and pre-service instructor over the past 11 years. Her doctoral work at the University of Toronto primarily focused on understanding cognitive and social processes involved in the study and application of complex systems in educational settings. She is currently completing a post-doctoral fellowship at the Massachusetts Institute of Technology where she uses complex systems science as a framework for investigating knowledge development both with students in classrooms and teachers in professional development networks.

Foreword:
Exemplary practice as exemplary research

William F. McComas

Introduction

Regrettably, educational research is rarely taken as seriously as it should be by the very institutions and individuals the researchers hope to impact. This reality is debated, dissected and bemoaned every time scholars discuss their work. On reflection, however, perhaps we who are engaged in educational research are partially to blame for the lack of influence of our endeavours. We frequently focus our investigations on questions that are more interesting to the research community itself than to the schools and practitioners that represent the focus of our studies. Furthermore, many empirical investigations examine large groups of teachers or students and, as a result, report typical practices and average levels of achievement that shed light on the problems but do little to suggest solutions.

Such approaches are not wrong or misguided because occasionally useful implications for practice do arise. However, given the terse nature of scholarly writing and the limited manner in which results of such studies are disseminated, it is easy to see why many schools, teachers and other educational leaders ignore and even criticize the reports and recommendations from the research community.

Needless to say, the production of new and valid knowledge through any means should not be constrained, but at the same time we must not be seduced into thinking that pure research is always more valuable than applied. Perhaps it is time to consider the utility of the middle ground in which scholars and teachers together produce, evaluate, synthesize, comment on and make practical recommendations as a team. This is clearly the rationale inherent in *Analysing Exemplary Science Teaching: Theoretical Lenses and a Spectrum of Possibilities for Practice*.

This book is both unique and useful. From its focus on exemplary practices, to its organizational scheme, to the interplay of science education experts and expert science teachers, there are few texts that will appeal to each of the community of scholars, science teaching methods instructors and classroom teachers looking for ways to examine and introduce best practices. The text before us continues to extend the important line of research into exemplary practices with a compelling look into the classrooms of ten gifted science teachers.

Looking for excellence

The domain of study that forms the foundation of this book cuts across the divide that usually separates pure science from applied with its focus on the examination of exemplary practices. The past few decades have seen the genesis of a cottage industry in such investigations in a wide variety of settings ranging from chess playing to business practices. Such studies reject the utility of examining large groups of average practitioners to focus on small groups of highly effective individuals. Any bookstore will have on its shelf titles such as *The Five Practices of Exemplary Leadership* (Kouzes and Posner 2003), *In Search of Excellence* (Peters and Waterman 1984) and *The 7 Habits of Highly Effective People* (Covey 1989). The potential utility of such works is obvious, even if they are wide-ranging synthetic analyses rather than reports of original scholarship, although many are both. It would be hard to imagine any publisher or reader showing much interest in *The Twenty-seven Practices of Ineffective Leaderships*, *In Search of Mediocrity* or *The 200 Habits of Average People*. It is possible to learn something from studying what does not work, but the positive approach is far more interesting and enlightening. The list of books featuring an analysis of exemplary practices continues to grow and has extended to include economics, German women writers, middle schools and parenting, to name just a few such domains. A personal favourite features an analysis of the exemplary husband, a book that most men would probably rather their wives not read but likely recognize that they themselves should.

While the examination of 'best practices' in science education has not been as robust and ongoing as one might hope, various initiatives over the past several decades have helped to share some useful and interesting insights, and in doing so, provide a clear rationale for continuing and expanding such studies. One of the first and most extensive examinations of exemplary practices was the Search for Excellence in Science Education (SESE) sponsored by the US National Science Teachers Association (Penick and Yager 1983, 1986). This effort began with criteria for excellence established by the earlier Project Synthesis (Kahl and Harms 1981), itself a detailed analysis of a multitude of studies and recommendations regarding the current state and future desired nature of science instruction. Criteria used in the SESE were established for

> specific age groups, such as middle/junior high or K-6; standard academic disciplines, such as biology and chemistry; and interdisciplinary areas, such as energy education, science as inquiry, and science/technology/society. In each area the Search identifies hallmarks of excellence in terms of goals, curriculum, instruction, evaluation and teacher qualifications.
>
> (NSTA 1987: 4–5)

The SESE culminated with a multi-volume set of case studies of excellence each in a particular area such as biology, physical science, elementary science and other domains, accompanied by a set of generalizations and recommendations generated by the final cross-case analysis. The impact of SESE was immediate. For the first time it was possible to know that recommendations made by science education experts could be put into practice in real world classrooms; the case studies provided proof of this assertion.

In Australia, a related project, a search of Exemplary Science and Mathematics (ESME) (Tobin and Fraser 1987) grew out of the SESE project. The ESME investigators asked educators to nominate outstanding teachers of science and mathematics and to defend their choices. Nominated teachers were reviewed by researchers and then studied by teams of investigators. As in SESE, the goal of ESME was to construct case studies of these individuals based on reviews of interviews, lessons, curriculum materials, tests and other student work. Their results have been widely reported (Tobin and Garnett 1988; Tobin and Fraser 1990) and have helped to define the state of exemplary practice in science education.

At this same time, researchers in other disciplines such as mathematics (Driscoll 1985) engaged in similar projects perhaps leading Berliner (1986: 9) to state what has since become the mantra of exemplary practice researchers, 'the study of expert teachers can provide useful case material from which we can learn'. How true. A review of the literature in this area shows that this line of research continues although perhaps not at the same large scale level as with the SESE and ESME projects. In recent years the exemplary practice model has been applied to help define the state of best practices in laboratory instruction (McComas 1991), mathematics teaching (Roulet 1998), art education (Little 1993) and effectiveness in working with particular groups of students (Olson 2001), to name but a few. These studies nicely blend both theoretical perspectives with the quest for practical applications and, in doing so, both define a new hybrid domain of study while potentially enhance teaching and learning in specific curriculum areas and school settings in ways not immediately possible with other research formats.

Even the current US National Science Education Standards (NSES) (National Research Council 1996) takes a 'best practices' approach. Of course, content standards such as those contained in the Standards have long been used to define the goals for instruction in one discipline or another, but the NSES go further. In addition to comprehensive discussions of the content that should frame the focus of school science teaching, we are also provided with extensive descriptions of the desired state for the professional development programmes for science teachers, assessment, science programmes themselves and science education systems. These recommendations are drawn from the growing literature defining high quality practices in these various domains.

Using *Analysing Exemplary Science Teaching*

As the editors themselves describe, this book is designed almost like hard copy hypertext. Such a claim made for a paper document may seem impossible in reality, but it is accurate. This book is a sort of interactive discourse between educators and researchers resulting in a set of case studies that both exemplify high quality teaching as they are described and analysed by the accompanying expert opinions with their related empirical support.

In the first part of the book we meet science teachers like Keith, Richard, Karen, Susan, Alex, James and George, to name a few. In their own words we are invited into their classrooms to experience and examine some remarkable practices. We learn about the importance of objects in the teaching of kidney function, the kinesthetic teaching of astronomy, modelling in chemistry, and how the locus of control shifts to students when they have appropriate technological support. We see students who come to understand scientists as humans first and researchers second, to examine the dynamics of an unresolved problem regarding the evolution of early animals, to debate the pros and cons of a bioethical dilemma, to experience a science apprenticeship, to consider the importance of mentoring and to explore the utility of blending science with technology as students use a mousetrap as a power source rather than for its intended purpose.

In Part 2, the science education experts – each with a unique lens or frame of reference – have written a commentary on the same set of cases. Such an approach is rarely used but is applied here with great skill. We are afforded the opportunity to consider each of the exemplary cases from a slightly different viewpoint thus providing an incredibly rich overall view of the individual instances of high quality science teaching. In addition, the expert commentaries provide a cross-case analysis of the set of exemplary practices, each offered from the writer's unique perspective.

The individual perspectives these experts bring to bear include a focus on the nature of science, the role of argumentation in science teaching, science-technology-society and environment (STSE) education, science learning as a conceptual development endeavour, and the issue of providing context for science learning through real world problems and hands-on methods. We are also invited to consider these cases from a view of the affective domain, from a technological vantage point, from the lens of teaching itself and from considerations of equity, inclusion and social justice. In reading these diverse commentaries we get the benefit of a range of scholarly perspectives all looking from slightly different starting points at the same case material. There is no single 'right' answer provided here nor can there be; each of the perspectives is as valid as the next and that is exactly the point. Science teaching is a complex act and exemplary teaching is even more so. It requires these multiple vantage points to fully conceptualize and describe the rich vignettes provided as case studies in this remarkable book.

In one of the cleverest elements of the book, the science education experts have commented on these high quality teaching practices by adding notes to each account linked with reference codes to their own individual narratives. These notes call out particular pedagogical, psychological or practical aspects that define high quality teaching. Readers can flip back and forth between the accounts in the front of the book and the commentaries at the back to note the shared elements of excellence that are applied and noted within and between the case studies. Such commonly cited elements include issues related to the development of inquiry skills, the role of apprenticeships, language in the practice of effective science teaching, the importance of providing concrete examples in the science classroom, the notion that all learning is embodied and many other such issues. One could easily extract just these marginal comments from the book and apply them as a set in guiding discussion in a preservice science teaching methods class, an inservice teacher enhancement discussion group or by an individual teacher for personal improvement and reflection. It is very likely that readers of this book will find profitable and interesting ways to use them that those involved in its development could not now predict.

Final thoughts

Some have criticized the notion of exemplary practice as indefinable and it is reasonable to note, as Roth (1998) does, that the subtle nature of quality teaching makes such analysis difficult. I agree with Roth and with John Wallace who in this volume says that 'exemplariness is a tricky concept, defying a formulaic definition ... what one ... may see as exemplary another may not' (p. 181). Not everyone looking into the classroom of a reputed master science teacher will be equally impressed all the time, but we have long known that some teachers are simply more personable, professional, innovative, engaging and ultimately effective than others. Just ask their students who are the ultimate consumers with their years of hard-won experiential data.

We should avoid the postmodernists and proponents of political correctness who would have us believe that all practices are equally valid. We should reject asking the question, 'who are we to say what is a best practice; how could I know that one way is the most effective way?' Certainly, in an arena as varied as the school classroom in a domain as complex as science teaching there can be no one best practice. However, if we allow that there are small groups of procedures and orientations that are more effective than others in science practice and pedagogy, we can feel quite justified in calling such practices exemplary. I salute all those involved in this remarkable book for their courage in following this line of research and for their skill in producing a truly innovative approach to the analysis of science instruction. They have made a useful and interesting contribution to the literature in this area and in doing so are helping further to defend the rationale that it makes more sense to study best practices if one wants to impact and enhance teaching rather than simply describe it.

References

Berliner, D.C. (1986) In pursuit of the expert pedagogues, *Educational Researcher*, 15(7): 5–13.

Covey, S.R. (1989) *The 7 Habits of Highly Effective People*. New York: Simon and Schuster.

Driscoll, M. (1985) *A Study of Exemplary Mathematics Programs*. Chelmsford, MA: Northeast Regional Exchange.

Kahl, S. and Harms, N.C. (1981) Project synthesis: purpose, organization and procedures, in N.C. Harms and R.E. Yager (eds) *What Research Says*, Volume 3. Washington, DC: National Science Teachers Association, pp. 5–11.

Kouzes, J.M. and Posner, B.Z. (2003) *The Five Practices of Exemplary Leadership*. New Jersey: Wiley and Sons.

Little, B.E. (1993) Expert teachers in the productive domain: selected factors in exemplary art teaching at the secondary level (doctoral dissertation, University of Georgia, 1993), *Dissertation Abstracts International*, 55(01A): 4647.

McComas, W.F. (1991) The nature of exemplary practice in laboratory instruction: a case study investigation. Unpublished doctoral dissertation, University of Iowa, Iowa City, IA.

National Research Council (1996) *National Science Education Standards*. Washington, DC: National Academy Press.

NSTA (National Science Teachers Association) (1987) *Criteria for Excellence*. Washington, DC: National Science Teachers Association.

Olson, A.E. (2001) The artistry of exemplary educators: building a model of effective teacher practice (doctoral dissertation, Harvard University, 2001), *Dissertation Abstracts International*, 62(04A): 1370.

Penick, J.E. and Yager, R.E. (1983) The search for excellence in science education, *Phi Delta Kappa*, 64(9): 621–3.

Penick, J.E. and Yager, R.E. (1986) Trends in science education: some observations of exemplary programs in the United States, *European Journal of Science Education*, 8: 1–8.

Peters, T.J. and Waterman, R.H. (1984) *In Search of Excellence: Lessons from America's Best Run Companies*. New York: Warner Books.

Roth, W.-M. (1998) Teaching and learning as everyday activity, in B.J. Fraser and K.G. Tobins (eds) *International Handbook of Science Education*. Dordrecht, The Netherlands: Kluwer, pp. 169–81.

Roulet, R.G. (1998) Exemplary mathematics teachers: subject conceptions and instructional practices (doctoral dissertation, University of Toronto, 1998), *Dissertation Abstracts International* 59(12A): 4387.

Tobin, K. and Fraser, B.J. (eds) (1987) *Exemplary Practice in Science and Mathematics Education*. Perth: Curtin University of Technology.

Tobin, K. and Fraser, B.J. (1990) What does it mean to be an exemplary teacher? *Journal of Research in Science Teaching*, 27(1): 13–25.

Tobin, K. and Garnett, P. (1988) Exemplary practice in science classrooms, *Science Education*, 72(2): 197–208.

Acknowledgements

It is a pleasure to acknowledge all those involved in the generation and writing of this book. First and foremost, we would like to thank all the teachers and students who kindly responded to our call for examples of exemplary practice. Their dedication, innovation and openness act as role model for us all. We would also like to thank the scholars for their readiness to engage in the unorthodox process of multi-perspective analysis and the eagerness with which they took up the challenge of writing with a series of cross referenced comments. We have learned much from your work which has extended our thinking and writing. Thank you Bill for your feedback and supportive comments in the Foreword.

A very special thank you goes to Barbara Soren and Ashifa Jiwani for their patience and invaluable editorial expertise. The multi-layered format would not have been possible without their enthusiastic support. We would also like to thank our Open University Press editorial team (Fiona, Melanie, Malie, Jenni and Maureen) who have been nurturing beyond the call of duty.

Our personal thanks go to all our colleagues at York University, The University of Surrey Roehampton and Ontario Institute for Studies in Education, University of Toronto. Thank you for all the conversations, provocative ideas and practical advice over the years. A very special thank you goes to a dear friend and mentor, John Hewitt. Last but definitely not least, we dedicate this book to our families for their continuing support, inspiration, love and care.

INTRODUCTION
Creating possibilities

Steve Alsop, Erminia Pedretti and Larry Bencze

As teachers we all have our favourite lessons. Lessons that we cherish and start with heightened expectations and desires; lessons that we feel self-assured showcasing to evaluators; lessons that we readily describe, perhaps even dramatize, and share with colleagues and friends. This is a collection of such lessons: the following pages contain teachers' descriptions of special experiences. They feature here to introduce readers to a series of teaching approaches and how these might be analysed. The descriptions of practice are all set within science and technology classrooms although we feel they are also of value to teachers of other subjects.

Our text comprises chapters with a common goal: to define features of high-quality teaching and learning in the sciences. Through analysis of accounts of teaching and learning we aim to combine discussion of practice with theory. Part 1 houses narratives of teaching experiences written by well-respected and innovative science educators in the United Kingdom, Canada and Australia. Part 2, written by scholars of international standing, explores, discusses and analyses the accounts with a particular focus (a theoretical lens). Discussion of teaching and analysis is cross-referenced by a series of annotated comments. In the concluding part, the final two chapters explore implications for classroom practice and future research.

In broader terms our text describes a research project that we hope will serve to engage you in an ongoing dialogue about effective teaching and professional development. As teachers, the quest for better practice drives our personal and professional growth. It is simply not sufficient for things to stay as they are, perhaps even stagnate. Teaching is a dynamic, evolving enterprise and as such necessitates 'a quest for a better state of things for those we teach and the world we share' (Greene 1995: 1). Our professional development is a continual journey, with a multiplicity of paths and a host of external and internal influences. But without the desire to grow, a willingness to experiment and openness to learn, our practice would arguably be reduced to the level of instructional automation and functionality.

The term *exemplary practice* appears regularly in the language of teacher evaluation, pre-service education, curriculum policy and educational reform. Globally it seems, teachers, advisers, policy makers and researchers have become unusually unified in the quest for exemplariness. Paradoxically, our text both builds on the widespread use of this term but also questions its very existence. What might it mean? Should it exist? Is it a useful concept to explore? What role might it play in teacher professional development? We raise the issues here and return to discuss them in more detail in the concluding chapters.

Our journey starts with a deceptively straightforward question:

Could you describe an aspect of your practice that you consider exemplary?

Groups of teachers and students in three continents were posed this reflective task. The teachers are recognized as leaders in their field (science coordinators, head teachers, senior teachers and department heads in middle and secondary schools). The students were attending secondary schools in Toronto and London. Accounts of their exemplary practice follow in Part 1. It was our hope that the teachers' and students' willingness to enter into a dialogue, to share their actions and experiences with us, would provide a mechanism to showcase their extraordinary expertise.

In education today – too often it seems – discussion of teaching has become bound to a series of external measurements and evaluations. The language of accountability in the form of 'competencies', 'rubrics' and 'look-fors' shape contemporary educational policy. Most western countries have a series of external accountability measures for teachers – benchmarks which commonly focus on the gateway to the profession, the pre-service and newly qualified teaching stages. Successful teaching, it seems, has become eminently quantifiable, dusted down and tidied up into a series of discrete themes which might be practised in private and tried out in classrooms.

In contrast, for Schön (1987) the very essence of successful teaching resides, not in external, but in internal processes of self reflection both *in* practice and *on* practice. Survival in what he describes as 'the intermediate swampy zones of practice' (1987: 3) necessitates expertise grounded within the practicalities and pragmatics of daily life in schools and science classrooms. Teachers inhabit the complexities and intricacies of their classrooms: every day they balance the priorities, expectations and aspirations of pupils with the requirements of the curriculum, the pragmatics of the institution of schooling and their desire to get things done. The following discussions draw from the richness of teachers' writing about their experiences (personalized reflections *on* practice). The resulting narrative embodies complexity and pragmatism; a very different representation of effective practice than an atomized list of teacher competences.

Teachers' accounts of successful practice

The book grew out of a conversation in a café in Quebec City. At a very early stage we wanted to develop a text showcasing science and technology teaching. There are many excellent method texts available that offer advice and guidance on effective ways to teach. They often explore particular themes: planning for teaching, equity, computers in classrooms, materials for science teaching, teaching and writing, role play and so on (see for instance, Bentley and Watts 1989, Trowbridge and Bybee 1996 and Alsop and Hicks 2001). Their approach is to present a synthesis of research in an accessible and generalized form that the practitioner can then look to use to shape their practice.

In contrast, we wanted to base our discussion, not on a synthesis of research per se, but on retold experiences through personal narrative. Bruner (1986) describes narrative as a *paradigmatic* mode of knowing; it is sensitive to the uniqueness of experience and ideally suited to explore the messiness of social events. Our choice of content was selected with pre-service teachers and in-service teachers in mind as well as others involved in science education policy and reform.

The use of the case study has a long and established history in medicine and business dating back to the middle of the nineteenth century (Taylor and Whittaker 2003). Most MBA programmes and medical degrees now incorporate case studies. Harvard's MBA programme, for instance, is based on a case method learning model, indeed its publicity proudly boasts that '80% of all cases sold in the world are written by Harvard Business School Faculty' (HBS 2004). Although early examples do exist, the proliferation of case method learning in teacher education is much more modest, and is largely a product of the past decade.

In science education the choice of case can vary quite dramatically depending on the field, context, subject and emphasis. Cases come in various forms and styles including: critical instances (Nott and Wellington 1995), anecdotes (Bell and Gilbert 1996), stories (Wallace and Louden 2000) and dilemmas (Wallace and Louden 2002).

There is much to admire, for instance, in Wallace and Louden's

(2002) and Koballa and Tippin's (2002) case collections, which provide the basis for insightful reflections on problems and dilemmas in practice. Our agenda, however, is different. Rather than exploring discrepant events, teaching dilemmas or problems, we purposefully sought to understand success. We wanted to base our text on efficacy. You can clearly learn from the problematic, but you can also learn much from reflecting on accomplishment, understanding aspects of teaching that went well, perhaps even better than expected. We refer to our cases as *accounts* (not stories, anecdotes or instances) in part, to underscore our emphasis on the positive. We wanted to bring attention to particular practices which experienced practitioners classified as exemplary: teaching they feel is extraordinary, meritorious, ideal and praiseworthy in some way. When reflecting on performance there is always a tendency, we feel, to fixate on weakness.

In compiling the text we adopted a very interactive style which among case collections is rare. We sought to create a theoretical framework which facilitated layered reflections. In the first instance teachers were encouraged to share their reflections *on* practice (Part 1). This was followed by analysis: a reflection on the teachers' accounts by academics (Part 2). Finally, we leave the last word to the practitioners: we sent a copy of the manuscript to the teachers and asked them to reflect on all the cases and analyses. Their concluding comments are housed in Part 3. This three-way iteration afforded us, as coordinators, the opportunity of analysing in some depth the interactions of theory and practice (see Part 3).

In search of exemplary practice

Our choice of the term exemplary is not without considerable thought and some trepidation. It immediately raised a concern: might a unitary vision of teaching (termed exemplary) usefully exist? While there might be some shared understanding of aspects of effective practice, we adamantly reject the very notion of an educational blueprint, a definitive guidebook for teaching success. So why have we taken the bold, some might say foolhardy, position of collecting a group of writers and teachers together under the auspices of uncovering what might be considered the educational equivalence of the Holy Grail? As one might imagine, charting the pristine waters of exemplary practice has been tried in the past and these attempts have too often run aground.

We use the term partly because it has global educational currency. Educational jargon steers perceptions both positively and negatively in policy and reform. The very existence of the term, for us, serves to raise important debate about exemplification, standardization, functionality and hierarchy. At a time when school boards, local educational authorities and governments are aiming to raise standards by developing highly structured guidelines for teachers, it is important to question how this 'willingness to help', 'to offer exemplars' might be inadvertently serving to undermine teacher autonomy and creativity. In this regard the dual meaning of exemplary is perhaps revealing. The Oxford English Dictionary (OED) defines exemplary as 'fit for imitation' 'representative, typical' and this is its common usage. But the OED also lists another meaning, 'serving as a warning', 'an admonitory'. We feel the juxtaposition of these two definitions is edifying: while exemplary practice is admirable and commendable, its very existence serves to raise concerns about the dangers of regimented, mass-produced practice.

The term also serves a pragmatic function. It provides a convenient mechanism to isolate the particular; a means to select an instance from a spectrum of experience. In the editing process, we found it fascinating to reflect on our teachers' selections, the different manifestations of exemplary wrapped up and embodied within their accounts. The criteria for 'exemplariness', it seems, is far from homogenous. For some, it associates with innovation, uniqueness and the extraordinary. Contained within the accounts there are certainly lessons which are unusual alternatives to the common diet of science teaching. For others, exemplary is coupled with the tried-and-tested – familiar lessons which are guaranteed to yield a satisfactory outcome at any time in the school day. Our collection contains lessons which will be well known to those working in the field. In most of the accounts, a sense of predictability is evident; the ability to plan, structure and create learning environments that yield predictable outcomes is a generic feature. Perhaps Susan Yoon's lesson (Account 7) stands alone as an example of a teacher, reflecting in practice, responding to the unexpected and changing direction mid-stream.

Our question specifically focuses on teaching, but it is rarely desirable to separate teaching and learning. In this regard, exemplary teaching might usefully be equated with exemplary learning – presumably increased quality and quantity of learning. There are a number of incidents of learning transformation documented – difficult concepts made easier and subjects made interesting. At this early point, you might wish to put yourself in the shoes of one of our participants and think about a teaching event that you would share. Why did you pick this one? What informs your pedagogy of exemplary?

Accounts of teaching science and technology

We compiled the book by approaching a large number of teachers and students. Our tact was guided by our experience; we wanted to invite teachers and mentors who continue to be highly influential in the school system. Our choice of location, classrooms in Ontario,

London and Perth, was largely opportunistic. Collectively the editorial team had recent experience of working with teachers and researchers in these settings.

In the first instance, we requested a short overview of a lesson (or a series of lessons). At an editorial meeting we selected ten of these and asked the participants to develop them in more detail. Our selection was made primarily on the basis of perspective and breadth of coverage. We wanted to include the perspectives of both teachers and students (ten teachers and three students feature in the final selection). The students were asked to comment on their experiences of exemplary practice. At the time of writing Josie Ellis had just completed her post-16 Advanced level courses, Vivien Tzau was an undergraduate student and Desmond Ngai was a high school student. Further detail about all the participants can be found in the List of Contributors.

Breadth of coverage was also an important consideration. To guide our selection here we used a framework from one of our authors. Derek Hodson (1993) suggests that school science should comprise three elements:

- *Learning science*: learning the products of science and technology, including laws, theories and inventions;
- *Learning about science*: learning the properties of science and technology, including the characteristic of these fields and their interactions with each other and with society and the environment and, as well, characteristics of people working in these fields, including the existence of bias and the possibility of human error;
- *Learning to do science*: learning the proficiencies of science and technology, including cognitive and psychomotor skills needed to construct scientific investigation and design products.

In the UK, Canada and Australia it is possible to identify Hodson's elements in the science curricula. They are demonstrably evident in our case selection (see Table 1).

We were also eager to include a diversity of teaching approaches and subject areas. Our final collection includes biology, physics and chemistry lessons with pupils from ages 7 to 18. It also displays a variety of pedagogical methods, including computer-enhanced learning, role play, dissection, demonstrations, investigations, drama, problem solving and design and make. Most of the descriptions focus on a lesson or a series of lessons in a particular classroom. An overview of the ten accounts follows at the start of Part 1. As editors we have carried out some minor editing to the accounts, but felt it best to preserve and honour the teachers' and students' voices.

Table 1 Breadth of coverage of teachers' accounts

Emphasis	Account	Account title
Learning science	1	Kidney function and dysfunction: enhancing an understanding of science and the impact on society *Keith Hicks*
	2	Episodes in physics *George Alex Przywolnik*
	3	Recollections of organic chemistry *Josie Ellis*
	4	The science class of tomorrow? *Richard Rennie and Kim Edwards*
Learning about science	5	Science with a human touch: historical vignettes in the teaching and learning of science *Karen Kettle*
	6	Exploring the nature of science: reinterpreting Burgess Shale fossils *Katherine Bellomo*
	7	Motivating the unmotivated: relevance and empowerment through a town hall debate *Susan A. Yoon*
Learning to do science	8	Mentoring students towards independent scientific inquiry *Alex Corry*
	9	Learning to *do* science *Gabriel Ayyavoo, Vivien Tzau and Desmond Ngai*
	10	Practice drives theory: an integrated approach in technological education *James Johnston*

In search of a common place: analysing accounts of exemplary practice

Part 2 documents analysis. Here, authors tackle the teachers' accounts with a particular perspective in mind – a theoretical lens. We found Joseph Schwab's (1973) idea of a common place useful in guiding our selection of lenses. For Schwab, the basis of all educational thought is embodied within the intersection of four common places: the learner, the teacher, the milieu and the subject matter. 'None of these', he writes (1973: 509), 'can be omitted without omitting a vital factor in educational thought and practice'.

The ten analysis chapters start with subject matter. Derek Hodson, in the opening chapter, operates from a philosophical perspective. His argument is one of (mis)representation – in the past school science has offered a distorted and confused view of science. Drawing from the history and philosophy of science he promotes an authentic image of science embodied within the teachers' accounts. In the second analysis, Sibel Erduran and Jonathan Osborne continue discussion of knowledge. Building on their acclaimed research, they draw attention away from detailing the what-we-know of science towards a consideration of how-we-know. Their particular focus is argumentation, 'the coordination of evidence and theory to support or refute an explanatory conclusion' (see page 106). In the chapter they underscore the argumentation strategies contained with the accounts. Erminia Pedretti concludes discussion of subject matter with a chapter on science, technology, society, environment (STSE) education. STSE, as she notes, is a loosely defined amalgam of different approaches and theoretical perspectives. She brings our attention to four seminal principles emerging from the case accounts: values and mindfulness, epistemology and community discourse, informed decision making and personalization and empowerment. In concluding, Erminia asserts that the exemplary vision of education offered by the cases is both 'post-positivist' and 'progressive'.

Keith Taber initiates discussion of the learner. He draws from an assortment of theoretical perspectives – cognitive science, developmental psychology and conceptual change learning – to explore learning with a particular focus on conceptual development. In concluding Keith uses the discussion of learning to generalize about teaching. 'Teaching for conceptual development', he writes, 'requires teachers to start where the students are, and to present new information in appropriate learning quanta' (p. 128).

Learning in the form of problem solving is under the microscope in Analysis 5. Here, Ann Marie Hill and Howard Smith comment from the perspective of problem-based learning (PBL) and learning in context. These authors both have a distinguished background in technology education and draw from this perspective to highlight instances of *doing* as opposed to abstract de-contextualized, disembodied knowing. There is much to learn from their conceptually-grounded analysis.

Discussions move in Analysis 6 to the teacher. Steve Alsop kicks things off with the role of emotion in education. The work of Paul Pintrich and colleagues at the University of Michigan offer the lens of analysis. Steve mines the accounts for teaching approaches which serve to increase motivation in the form of task value and task expectancy. There is much to be gained in science education, he concludes, by a closer investigation of intellectual and personal identity. It is often contended that technology has the potential to revolutionize schooling. In Analysis 7, Jim briefly rehearses some of these bold claims and then looks to extract instances in the accounts which serve to illuminate efficacious use of technology. His analysis has three themes, exploring the extent to which technology serves to: (i) make abstract concepts concrete; (ii) create tools to analyse scientific processes; and (iii) support connections between people. John Wallace's chapter, Analysis 8, has a distinctive style. Building on his internationally acclaimed case study work, John looks to represent central themes in the teachers' accounts. The eight themes emerging offer alliteration as well as insight – the tenacity of teaching, the

immediacy of input, the centrality of context, the plurality of pedagogy, the expedience of epistemology, the legacy of the laboratory,
the disguise of dilemma and the motive of morality.

Schwab (1973) uses the concept of 'Milieu', to represent the
internal and external socializing aspects of education. In Analysis 9,
Léonie Rennie glimpses at the internal milieu, the classroom, through
the lens of equity and the inclusive curriculum. Her analysis is shaped
by two questions: What does inclusion mean? How can I be sure all
students feel included in the curriculum? Building on Katherine
Bellomo's definition of inclusivity (see Account 6, p. 46), Léonie
seeks to identify ways in which the accounts describe inclusive
practices. The final analysis is left to one of the editors, Larry Bencze,
to pose some provocative questions: Is school science serving to
promote consumerism? Does science education act as social engineering? Might our system function primarily generate compliant
workers and enthusiastic purchasers of products of business and
industry? How might we subvert the discriminatory practices of
elitism? Larry presses the teachers' cases for a vision of science
education routed in social justice, democracy and civic responsibility.

So in Schwab's language, we move from the curriculum to the
learner, to the teacher and finally to the milieu. Our exploration, of
course, has boundaries – there are many prominent aspects of science
education which we simply are unable explore. We might, for
instance, have considered assessment, classroom management, differentiation and language. In the end, we opted for a balance of
perspectives: contemporary perspectives in science education which
we felt map onto the four common places and lend themselves to the
methodology we deployed, the analysis of teachers' narratives.

Contradictory realities: linking theory with practice

Probably the oldest maxim in education is that theory has nothing to
offer classroom practice. The chasm between research and teaching
has plagued educators for decades. Schwab (1973), for instance,
writes of education being 'inveterately theoretic' and as a consequence is 'moribund'. Millar et al. (2000: 1) more recently, have
sought to explore why the impact of research on practice is apparently
so slight.

In designing the text we were always conscious of the
quintessential difference between practical expertise (know-how
embedded and enacted upon within specific complex real-time social
settings) and research (generalized, decontextualized, detemporalized
theories-of-practice). Our choice of approach is rooted in this difference. We deliberately selected *accounts* because we felt – with
support from the literature – that teacher-narrative would offer a
richly detailed portrait of a particular social phenomenon. Teachers'

written reflections about their practice are readily accessible and serve multiple audiences. They give readers a particular window into science education – albeit with a frosted glass (see Part 3). The accounts, above all, are about specific occasions, which only the teachers (and pupils) will ever experience. Such is the contextualized nature of experience. But while we know that you will not encounter the specific events documented, we are confident that you can take away things that can influence your teaching.

In comparison, the analysis chapters have a more academic feel. Assertions are supported with reference to the literature and the arguments seek to extract some general trends. As Robson (1993) notes, in case analysis it is the investigator's role to provide theoretical generalizations about process. It is not their role to offer generalizations about content. The analyses in Part 2 serve not to determine if the accounts of teaching are typical or atypical, but to bring to attention facets of the cases which the researcher feels (and literature suggests) are significant. Through this process, the frenzied, dazzling complexity of the classroom is slowed down to elicit hidden meanings and signpost future possibilities. This is another way to understand teaching; we are confident that the analyses afford you with an opportunity to further reflect on your teaching.

So our discussion of theory and practice is structurally and linguistically different, serving, we hope, to display experience and expertise in different ways. But in editorial meetings we wanted to push things a little further and try to bring conversations together, to isolate some common themes spanning the theory–practice divide. Connecting theory and practice is often difficult because a single classroom reflection is so complex that it can spawn a labyrinth of connections between theory and practice. Although our accounts and analyses are essentially rooted in the same phenomena – ten classroom experiences – the basis of their inclusivity is so multifarious and insuperably complex that it can easily escape reconciliation.

Using annotated comments to link theory and practice

In the text we link theory and practice with a series of cross-referenced, annotated comments. These take the form of summary statements located in the outside margin. Each account of teaching, as one might imagine, generates a multiplicity of comments that link with analyses. Each analysis chapter, in the same way, points to a succession of aspects of practice. A distinctive feature of our text is the use of these hypertextual statements giving the book a web-like character.

Hypertext is, of course, more commonly associated with the Internet – we have little doubt that readers will be familiar with Hypertext Markup Language (HTML) and Uniform Resource

Locators (URLs). In print, however, it is relatively rare. We turn to it here as a way of acknowledging and representing the complexities inherent in bringing together theory and practice. It offers us a way of extending the two-dimensional textual structure (paragraphs, chapters and parts) into a kind of three-dimensional representation in which *links* hold an axiomatic function. As a leading academic in the hypertext field notes: 'Hypertext is an information technology in which a new element, the link, plays the defining role, for all the chief practical, cultural and educational characteristics of this medium derive from the fact that linking creates new kinds of connectivity and reader choice' (Landow 1996: 154).

For us it facilitated nonlinearity, enabling readers to start at any point in the text and be transported to a different section by using the cross-referencing supplied. Moreover it created a sense of empirical transparency; the reader is able to juxtapose discussions of theory with practice and vice-versa. We required analysis authors to embed comments within their writing (located in the right hand margin) that cross-reference to specific passages/instances in the teachers' and students' accounts. In this way, their actual analysis (in educational research terms referred to as coding) becomes apparent, serving as a textual navigation form. As you might imagine, cross-referencing hundreds of hypertextual comments adds considerable complexity to the authoring process. But more significantly, we feel, it offers both diversity and richness. In editing the final piece, we became increasingly intrigued by the way in which particular sections of the accounts and analysis coalesced. Landow's (1996) notion of 'Velcro-text' became alive, as different segments of text began attaching themselves – stretching out and reaching over the theory–practice divide.

Navigating the text

As previously mentioned, annotated comments in the outside margins link content in Parts 1 and 2. For a specific example, take the first right-hand marginal comment in Account 1 (p.15), which reads as follows:

> Knowledge cannot simply be transferred
> from teacher to student
> (*see Analysis [4.2], p. 128*).

These comments have a common code. The number in the square brackets, [4.2], refers to Analysis 4, statement 2. Analysis 4, entitled 'Conceptual development', starts on page 127 and the marginal comments are chronological in this section – i.e. statement 2 is the second statement in Analysis 4 on page 128. Turning to page 128, you will also note that an identical statement appears in the margin and this cross-references to the Account by page number (p.15). In this way, Keith Hicks's pedagogical discussion about kidney function and dysfunction (Account 1) is linked to Keith Taber's discussion of conceptual development (Analysis 4).

Using this code you can navigate between Part 1 and Part 2. Reference to the links (in the above example [4.2]) also appear in the main body of the text in both parts, enabling the reader to identify the exact piece of text associated with the comment.

Getting started

We designed this book with middle school and secondary school science educators in mind, and feel the discussions can hold court in pre-service, graduate and non-degree professional courses. The text is not designed to be read in a single sitting and we leave it up to you to decide how to sequence sections. We urge you to try to utilize the cross-referencing supplied, but fully acknowledge that this might not suit all readers, in which case the text can be navigated in more conventional ways. At different points in your teaching you are likely to identify with some accounts and analyses more than others. We have not sought to order the discussions in any developmental way, although the final section (Part 3) is probably best explored once you have some familiarity with the preceding sections.

We hope the juxtaposition of teaching accounts and analyses serves to offer constructive ways of looking at teaching and learning, and the annotated comments bring these discussions together. As you shuffle between accounts and analyses look to actively reflect *on* your teaching. Hopefully, the book offers insight into practice, educational theory and research methods. But above all else try to use the sense of freedom that the hypertextual structure provides to shape the discussion to meet your needs. Critically and creatively reflect on how the evolving dialogue might offer future possibilities for your practice.

PART 1

Accounts of exemplary practice

Our first four Accounts have a conceptual focus. In Hodson's terms (1993) they are about *learning* the products of science. In Account 1, Keith Hicks details a series of lessons for post-compulsory learners that seek to develop understanding of the kidney. In his experience the structure and function of the kidney is often poorly comprehended. His goal is to make the subject meaningful. The eight lessons described include dissection, modelling and presentations. George Alex Przywolnik, in Account 2, writes about a series of activities for different age groups in the areas of astronomy, vibrations and waves, collisions and motion. There is much to marvel at in the creative way in which he makes potentially remote, abstract concepts appear real. In the third account, the student Josie Ellis reflects on her experience of chemistry teaching. She points to active learning as well as the significance of 'enthusiasm for the subject' as features of exemplary teaching. The science classroom of tomorrow occupies Richard Rennie and Kim Edwards's thoughts in Account 4. They advocate the use of technology in science education and recount their experiences of moving a grade 9 (age 14–15) chemistry course online. This pilot seems to be an overwhelming success and the use of computer enhanced learning has spread throughout their school.

In Account 5 the conversations skip into learning *about* science, Hodson's second element. Karen Kettle eloquently portrays her experiences of teaching about scientists. She describes a science in society course which incorporates drama and role play to challenge stereotypical images of 'white males in lab coats'. There is much to admire in her account, which peppers a description of pedagogy with autobiographical details. Katherine Bellomo (Account 6) continues the discussion of the nature of science with the story of Burgess Shale. Based on Stephen Jay Gould's famous book, she documents her use of explanatory story to stimulate debate about the social construction of knowledge. Mitchell, a charismatic student with a robust past, is the subject of Susan Yoon's account (Account 7). In the setting of the school laboratory and a field trip centre she reflects on her teaching of environmental education and how it served to transform Mitchell's attitude to study. As previously mentioned, this account has a sense of adaptation; Susan changes her teaching in response to the class's reaction.

The final three accounts explore Hodson's third element. Alex Corry reports on an apprenticeship teaching approach in which he mentors students in inquiry skill development (Account 8). Gabriel Ayyavoo joins with two of his ex-students, Vivien Tzau and Desmond Ngai to reflect on science fairs (Account 9) and James Johnston challenges pupils to design and build a model car powered by a mousetrap (Account 10). These accounts seek to scaffold pupil investigations, helping pupils to *do* science. Teaching, in this case, is about nurturing independence, creativity and problem solving.

Account 1

Kidney function and dysfunction: enhancing understanding of the science and the impact on society

Keith Hicks

An area of weakness

The structure and function of the kidney is an area of biology that features in compulsory (pre-16) and post-compulsory schooling in the UK. It is also an area, in my experience, where students have great difficulty in recalling details about the functioning of the kidney beyond a basic ability to name some of the components of the nephron. Too few students, it seems, are able to explain how the nephron contributes to maintaining osmotic and water balance in the body. Despite lessons of careful explanation, few students are able to adequately describe or explain the role of anti-diuretic hormone (ADH) on the kidney.

What is the problem?

Learning is dependent upon teaching. The consistent failure of students to be able to demonstrate the required levels of understanding led me to review the way I taught the topic. Clearly, if learning was to be improved then the teaching of the topic also needed to be improved. In order to get behind the reasons for students' failure to grasp the concepts involved in this area, I sat down with a small group of 15-year-old students to ask them what they could recall of the lessons on the kidney, and to give me their reasons why they had done poorly in answering questions on this topic in the examinations. One of the clearest messages to come out from this meeting was that the topic was difficult to grasp, as it was presented in a rather abstract way [4.2]. A nephron was not something they could see or touch and explanations were largely dependent on the use of diagrams in books.

Knowledge cannot simply be transferred from teacher to student *(see Analysis [4.2], p.128).*

These had been photocopied and then annotated through class discussion, led by the teacher working quite didactically from the front of the class.

One part of these lessons that the students *had* appreciated was the use of a video programme about the treatment of a boy, about their own age, who was undergoing dialysis and another young man who had had a kidney transplant [3.4]. The video contained a brief animated section on how the nephron worked in comparison to the dialysis machine. However, even when this section of the video was replayed, it did not seem to have a great role in enhancing the students' understandings. An additional problem with the video was that the programme was made in excess of twenty years previously, and technology of the dialysis machine had made huge advances in the intervening period. One of the first decisions I made in reviewing the teaching of this topic was that this video now deserved an honourable retirement, but its positive contribution to teaching about the treatment of kidney disease would need to be presented in some new way in the work scheme.

Real life issues create powerful opportunities for organizing the curriculum (see Analysis [3.4], p.119).

Setting about creating a solution

It seemed clear that part of the problem was that the students were not taking an active part in their learning and were expected to 'soak up' knowledge presented in class through some sort of absorption process. The new lessons would encourage students to be more active in their learning and require them to take on some responsibility for it. The students needed concrete models they could handle, and the opportunity to articulate their understandings through discussion in order to structure their knowledge [2.7; 2.8].

In researching different strategies for dealing with this topic, I looked back through some old resources gathering dust in the science department for some helpful ideas. Looking back through old texts, the most striking feature was the almost uniform approach taken by both old and new textbooks in delivering this material. This was the same 'failed' approach I had used in my teaching for years. One feature that did impress me was the move away from actual photographs of nephrons and kidneys, embedded in dense small font text, to highly schematic and colourful diagrams in modern textbooks, set within the context of the ubiquitous double page spread.

The diagrams in the text, which are similar in nearly all modern books, struck me as very abstract compared to the photographs. This had also been pointed out to me by students. However, the diagrams were very colourful and the textbooks looked much more inviting than the old black and white tomes of the past. But what did the diagrams mean to students who had never seen a real kidney (except perhaps in a steak and kidney pie), or seen the magnified photographs

Group discussions encourage argumentation and active learning. They enable structuring of knowledge and understanding (see Analysis [2.7], p.112).

Peer interaction promotes learning (see Analysis [2.8], p.113).

of nephrons? In other words, without a frame of reference the diagrams were meaningless to the students. I therefore took the decision that it was time to reintroduce dissection into the classroom. I wanted to ensure that all students actually saw a real kidney, and that a teacher (but preferably one of the students) teased out a nephron or part of a nephron from the kidney prior to viewing any schematic diagram [5.10].

All learning is embodied (see Analysis [5.10], p.143).

The new scheme of work [8.1; 8.4]

The tenacity of teaching (see Analysis [8.1], p.172).

I decided that this topic would need to be taught through eight lessons of 50 minutes each, basically consisting of:

The plurality of pedagogy (see Analysis [8.4], p.175).

• introducing the kidney: a kidney dissection;

• explaining the function of the kidney: how a nephron works;

• building a nephron: students in small groups make models of nephrons and prepare presentations to the class on their models;

• showing what happens when ADH is present through presentations;

• turning models into wall displays and posters;

• reviewing and answering examination questions on the kidney.

Introducing the kidney: a kidney dissection

The issue of dissection in school science has been contentious for some time, and has largely disappeared from even the Advanced Biology syllabus. While acknowledging that some students find the idea distressing, many find it highly motivating. However, it does need a teacher with good skills in order to use it successfully to promote learning. From the start of the lesson, the following objectives of dissection, as an introduction to the kidney, were made very clear to the students:

1   To be able to experience the feel of the kidney;

2   To identify and isolate the three main connections into the kidney (the urethra, renal artery and renal vein);

3   To examine the internal structure of the kidney;

4   To appreciate that the functional unit of the kidney is the nephron, which is very small, and its function cannot be determined by a simple dissection.

The kidneys for students to dissect are easily obtained from any supermarket, where they are often to be found in packs of eight in the frozen food section. However, there is a problem with these kidneys

Avoid induction; promote deduction *(see Analysis [10.1], p.195).*

PBL (problem-based learning) uses real-world problems to engage student learning in the problem-solving process and in the acquisition of disciplinary knowledge and skills *(see Analysis [5.2], p.139).*

Scientific observation has to be taught *(see Analysis [1.1], p. 98).*

Making learning 'concrete' will help many learners to relate to science concepts *(see Analysis [4.3], p. 128).*

in that very little remains of the ureter or renal vein and artery. For students, unused to carrying out dissection, it was necessary to first demonstrate the procedure they were to follow [10.1]. This was done with a larger kidney that I was able to purchase from a local butcher. The kidney had the advantage of having clear remains of the ureter and blood vessels still attached [5.2]. During discussions with the students, these attachments were isolated and identified in the demonstration dissection, before the kidney was split to reveal the cortex, medulla and pyramid regions of the organ.

Students were then given their kidneys and asked to try to identify the three points of attachment of the ureter and the blood vessels [5.2]. This was much harder to do with the smaller, prepared-for-cooking frozen kidneys. Nonetheless, by going from group to group, and using the opportunity to revise the difference in structure between arteries and veins, all students were able to identify the remains of these features. Not all students were required to carry out the dissection – I made it clear that it was a personal decision. If they felt squeamish or uncomfortable about doing it they did not need to do so. A few students (two or three in each class) did opt out of actually carrying out the dissection itself, but they all took an active part in discussions with class mates about the dissection as it proceeded.

Following the dissection, students completed standard diagrams of the kidney, labelling the different features that had been discussed. As students were carrying out their dissections, I took a number of photographs of them at work, and of their dissected kidneys, using a digital camera. I planned to use them in a wall display at the end of the unit.

Students were brought back to the demonstration bench and there followed a discussion on what we could deduce, from our observations, about the way the kidney functioned [1.1]. I still had the larger kidney on the front bench and we were able to make reference to it as the discussion proceeded. A general consensus was established that, other than the fact that the kidney had a very good blood supply and that the urine drained to the bladder via the ureter, little could be concluded on how it functioned. At this point, I used a pair of seekers to gently tease apart a piece of the kidney to reveal its thread-like structure [4.3]. This is best done if a section of the kidney is placed in a petri-dish of water. I explained to the class that these 'threads' were the individual functional units of the kidney known as nephrons, and that each kidney consists of at least a million nephrons. What is usually separated from the kidney are clumps of nephrons, but students readily appreciate the microscopic nature of the nephron and the fact that it is impossible to establish how these nephrons work with the naked eye alone.

Explaining the function of the kidney: how a nephron works

The next lesson started with a recall of the key learning objectives from the previous lesson. Students were easily able to recall the gross features of kidney function, and the idea that the nephron is the basic functional unit of the kidney, and is microscopic. From this point, the structure and function of the nephron were taught in the 'traditional' way, using diagrams from textbooks and going through all the different aspects of nephron function. However, the difference here was that the students had 'seen' a nephron teased out from the kidney in the previous lesson. Hence, the diagrams in the textbooks could be directly related to what they had experienced at first hand.

The process of ultrafiltration in the glomerulus and Bowman's capsule was additionally illustrated by attaching a rubber hose pierced with a number of holes to a tap. By gently squeezing the end of the tube so that the pressure was increased, the water could be made to come out of the holes with some force [7.3]. This demonstration is a good excuse for making yourself very wet and injecting some humour into what can be a rather dry lesson! This simple demonstration also helped to establish differences between the size of the afferent and efferent capillaries entering the glomerulus. With skilful handling, most of the water entering the rubber hose can be made to leave via the holes in the tube. This can lead to a useful discussion about why most of the liquid leaving the glomerulus and entering the Bowman's capsule has to be re-absorbed into the blood to prevent the body rapidly dehydrating.

Connecting real-life objects to representations (see Analysis [7.3], p. 163).

Previously, having taught how the nephron works through the process of ultrafiltration and re-absorption of useful substances back into the blood, I would have moved onto the role of ADH. However, I was determined to reinforce the structure and function of the nephron in the following lesson. This would be done to ensure a better recall of these key concepts in terminal examinations [4.8].

Learning is likely to be incomplete and fragile until reinforced (see Analysis [4.8], p. 129).

Building a nephron [5.10]

All learning is embodied (see Analysis [5.10], p. 143).

A brief question-and-answer session on the previous lesson clearly established that students were already beginning to struggle with recalling details of the structure and function of the nephron. Since this was what I had expected, I set students the task of building a model nephron and preparing a presentation of their model for the class in the next lesson [10.5].

As well as their notes and diagrams of the nephron produced in the previous lesson, I provided the students with the following materials:

Promote proactive perspectives on knowledge development (see Analysis [10.5], p. 197).

- a piece of stiff card (A3 size) for the base on which they were to build their models
- lengths of woollen yarn (red and blue)
- pieces of netting
- pipe cleaners
- straws
- clear plastic tubing
- rubber tubing
- scissors and sticky tape
- sticky labels for annotating and labelling their models.

Learning through collaboration *(see Analysis [7.4], p. 163).*

Group work to increase participation and mix skills *(see Analysis [9.6], p. 188).*

In the most effective learning episodes, students experience an intense state of flow where the activity is rewarding in itself *(see Analysis [4.16], p. 134).*

Scientists use models *(see Analysis [1.9], p. 101).*

PBL engages students in learning through practical activity, where they use both head and hand to solve authentic tasks *(see Analysis [5.4], p. 140).*

Students were expected to work in teams of three or four to produce a preliminary drawing of their proposed model within 10 minutes. They were then given 30 minutes to make their model, and 10 minutes to prepare a short presentation to explain their model nephron to the class during the following lesson [7.4; 9.6]. As an additional incentive, I announced that there would be prizes for the best model, the most inventive model, the best teamwork, etc.

What followed can best be described as a period of educational chaos, with great fun, creativity and intense learning [4.16]. I was amazed at how well the students responded to the challenge of this task, and at the level of comprehension shown in the conversations within their groups, as they set about explaining their ideas and conceptual understanding of the nephron to each other. The models they produced were actually very good and in many ways an improvement on the two-dimensional diagrams found in the text-books [1.9]. The use of the woollen yarn to show the close association between the blood capillary and the nephron was especially effective [5.4].

The timing for this lesson proved to be just about perfect, as it ensured students were engaged at a good pace and were able to complete the task. As I went around the groups, contributing to their discussions, I was able to earmark three groups whose models were distinctive and were prepared to give presentations. I wanted to avoid having seven or eight presentations in the next lesson that were going to be predictably similar.

Showing what happens when ADH is present through presentations

The next lesson commenced with three groups giving their presentations, using their models to explain how the nephron functions. One group, which had previous experience of giving presentations in science and other areas of the curriculum, came equipped with a PowerPoint presentation they had prepared using the school library. This was an indication of the students' commitment to the work and the PowerPoint presentation showed that they had done additional research on the topic. The presenters attempted to explain in detail how re-absorption occurred through the loop of Henle. After these three presentations, I awarded small prizes to the groups as outlined in the previous lesson. While it may seem strange to have only three presentations out of a class that had eight models, this strategy ensured students were not subjected to essentially the same material over and over again. It also took into account that some groups were less organized in preparing presentations due to the time they spent preparing their models in the previous lesson.

At this point, I introduced the class to the role of ADH – its effects on the kidney function and control of the blood's water content. I did this simply by using the standard Biology textbook and discussing the need for control of the blood's water content with the class. Having previously studied the control of temperature and blood glucose, the idea of having some mechanism for homeostatic control was not new to the class [4.10]. Following this, I instructed the students to add materials and/or annotations to their nephron models to explain the action of ADH. Some groups suggested making a second model to show the presence of ADH and another to illustrate the absence of ADH. However, time constraints prevented students from doing this.

Meaningful learning is only possible when the learner finds material relevant to previous learning (see Analysis [4.10], p. 130).

Turning models into wall displays and posters

In a brief plenary at the end of the lesson, I called upon groups who had not made presentations earlier in the lesson to use their model nephrons to explain the role and actions of ADH to the class [4.17; 10.3]. I collected all models and mounted them in a display on the wall, including photographs taken during the kidney dissection. The three-dimensional nature of this display proved very attractive to other students using the classroom. The students interacted well with it and the display was a very useful starting point when I began teaching the kidney to the Advanced Biology group later in the term.

Language is a key mediator in learning and the means by which learners can explain new ideas (see Analysis [4.17], p. 134).

Accommodate for difference (see Analysis [10.3], p. 196).

Reviewing and answering examination questions on the kidney

For the final lesson in this sequence, I simply selected a number of questions on the kidney taken from a range of summative assessment examinations and set over recent years. I told students that they were now judged to be experts in this field of the syllabus. I asked them to go through the questions in pairs, and using their notes and the wall display, to write answers that would construe a 'mark scheme' for an examiner to use. We spent the last part of the lesson discussing this and coming to a consensus about what was an acceptable answer for each question.

Conclusions

The success of this approach to teaching this difficult subject can be judged in two main ways. First, I assessed performance in summative examination questions about the kidney at the end of the course. As the final examination papers of candidates are rarely returned to the school, the performance of students with internal examinations was the only data I had to go on. Using the rest of the year's group as a control, including a parallel group of similar ability who had been taught this topic in the more traditional way, it was clear that students could demonstrate more thorough and accurate recall of this topic in the examination. In particular, the students showed a much sounder understanding of the structure and functioning of the nephron in their answers – exactly that area of the syllabus described by examiners as 'an area of weakness'.

Second, and perhaps equally important in judging the success of this approach, is the students' attitude to the material in class. The students responded very well to this approach. They seemed to enjoy the lessons and be more involved in the content. Certainly there was a lot more 'talk' in these lessons and a lot less 'chalk' than is usually the case. Also, the fact that some of the discussions initiated in the classroom continued over lunch indicated a high level of student involvement [4.16]. Steak and kidney pie will never be quite the same again for these students!

In the most effective learning episodes, students experience an intense state of flow, where the activity is rewarding in itself *(see Analysis [4.16], p. 134).*

Account 2
Episodes in physics

George Alex Przywolnik

A philosophy of teaching and learning

In my view, the content I teach and the techniques I use are vehicles by which students may accumulate and practise skills that will help them to succeed in our society [8.8]. These skills include effective communication, modelling, decision making and collaborative and individual problem solving [9.2]. I want to expose students to as wide a range of experiences as possible, so that students with 'non-standard' learning modes can learn effectively. But this is harder than it sounds.

The motive of morality *(see Analysis [8.8], p. 180)*.

Making science personal and real-world *(see Analysis [9.2], p. 187)*.

In my experience, most, perhaps all, teachers operate from a comfort zone that includes a range or repertoire of tried and tested teaching behaviours. We're unlikely to use a new technique or a new technology effectively until we include it in our repertoire. However, such inclusion only happens after we use it repeatedly [8.1]. My repertoire includes using role play to help students visualize abstract or invisible processes and involving students in large scale data collecting or simulation exercises.

The tenacity of teaching *(see Analysis [8.1], p. 172)*.

Astronomy

I've found that the role-playing technique is particularly effective in teaching some aspects of astronomy [2.6]. The vastness of astronomical distance is very difficult to get across to students brought up with images of quick and simple space travel in science fiction films and television programmes. I get the class to calculate the spacing they will need to form the scale model on the school oval, with the Sun on one edge and Pluto at the opposite edge. Then students, who have volunteered to represent the Sun and the planets, pace out the relative distances and set up a model solar system. On this scale, the Earth and Moon are closer together than the students' centres of mass can comfortably be, and Alpha Centauri is tens of kilometres

Role play promotes an understanding of different arguments and positions *(see Analysis [2.6], p. 112)*.

away. Most students are astounded that the greatest distance travelled by humans is from the Earth to the Moon, a distance too short to show up on this scale, and that the trip to Mars is likely to take many months [6.6]. For many students, the subsequent discussions about interstellar travel and the existence of alien visitors often lead to new understandings about the difficulty, danger and sheer expense of space travel, and about the likely nature of UFOs. Interestingly, a small but consistent minority of students refuse to accept the new ideas, preferring to retain a 'science fiction' view [4.11].

Many beginning astronomy students – variously Years 8 to 10 (13- to 15-year-olds) – have great difficulty in altering their viewpoint from the Earth's surface to a hypothetical observation platform somewhere in space. These students find it very hard to comprehend the off-Earth view that we use to illustrate the Moon going around the Earth. They literally cannot see how the Moon can undergo one rotation on its axis for every revolution around the Earth [1.3]. If the Moon always presents one side to us, how can it possibly rotate on its axis [1.6]? When this comes up, I choose two students, preferably ones who have demonstrated some understanding of the concept, to role-play the Earth and the Moon while others watch. It's most effective to have the volunteers on the ground floor as the rest of the class observes from a balcony above. Then I have the Moon move in quarter-circle segments, turning toward the Earth all the time. It's quite easy to establish the fact that the Moon does indeed rotate. I've tried this with model globes of the Earth and Moon, but student responses and the resulting learning were nowhere near as satisfying.

Vibrations and waves

I like to use students as props whenever I can. A good example with senior classes (Year 12, mostly 17-year-olds), involves role-playing particles to develop the ideas of longitudinal and transverse waves and their dependence on the properties of the medium. A few instructions on how molecules behave, some comments about what is appropriate student behaviour, and we're off [10.1]. While students become the waves, I video them and we later view and discuss the patterns they see. Only then do we move to more abstract demonstrations (wave machines, slinkies), and to graphs in the text [4.8]. It's very important to discuss both the accuracies and the inaccuracies in the model, and I prefer to set this as a writing exercise followed by discussion.

The digital camera I've used to record the waves has low resolution and records video and sound in 15-second segments, but the general idea comes across quite well even if the picture is not especially clear. While this technique lends itself well to introducing the topic and assisting students to visualize abstractions, it occurred to

---

Margin notes:

Relating science to people *(see Analysis [6.6], p. 153).*

Ideas students bring to teaching may prove very tenacious *(see Analysis [4.11], p. 131).*

Observation is theory laden *(see Analysis [1.3], p. 98).*

Experimental data has to be interpreted *(see Analysis [1.6], p. 100).*

Avoid induction; promote deduction *(see Analysis [10.1], p. 195).*

Learning is likely to be incomplete and fragile until reinforced *(see Analysis [4.8], p. 129).*

me, belatedly, that it would also work well as an informal diagnostic assessment – are students able to make the model work on their own after a period of instruction on the properties of waves? That will have to wait until next year.

It's often frustrating that so much of what I do is so episodic. Useful reflection on the things I do, or that I get students to do, usually can't be followed up while it's all fresh in my mind. If I don't write it down straight away, the idea is likely to evaporate by this time next year.

Collisions [5.10]

All learning is embodied (see Analysis [5.10], p. 143).

This particular activity is a personal favourite but has a definite downside. Adolescents tend to show little restraint when modelling collisions between molecules, and classes can get a bit boisterous. I once contributed this as a show-and-tell at a science teachers' conference and one (adult) participant was knocked over by an enthusiastic (adult) neighbouring molecule. The lesson here, for me, was that activities like this need a lot of room in order to work safely.

The senior students' responses to role-playing molecules were very positive, so I adopted variations (without video) for Year 11 chemistry and physics classes learning about molecular motion and Kinetic theory. In this way, we cover states of matter, changes of state and diffusion. The students are usually quite good at picking some of the deviations of the atomic model from their own experience, such as speed, spacing and the essentially two-dimensional universe their molecules would inhabit. Other departures of the model from their experience are not so obvious to beginners, even after some discussion. The intermolecular interactions, both attractions and repulsions, that determine much molecular behaviour are a good example. The notion that molecules attract at some distances, repel at others and have essentially no effect at still others is not easy to model.

Encouraged by a recent session on Kinetic theory, I suggested to a student teacher that a teaching practice was an ideal, low-risk opportunity to try some alternative curriculum delivery modes such as role play. After some discussion, we agreed that he would try this with a Year 9 (14-year-olds) chemistry class who were being introduced to reactions between ions in solution. First, the student teacher demonstrated the actual reaction between solutions of potassium carbonate and barium chloride. Then, some students were given stick-on signs identifying them as barium or potassium cations, or chloride or carbonate anions. We marked out an area of lab floor that would be the beaker in which the reagents would be mixed. Students were asked to predict how the reagents would exist before being dissolved (say, two potassium ions for every carbonate), and the reagent ions assembled. Then we 'dissolved' them.

Other students were asked to use a set of solubility rules to predict the outcome of a meeting between particular ions in solution, and so direct the precipitation part of the role play. We were both very impressed with the students' enthusiastic participation and the speed with which they picked up the central concepts. The enthusiasm level was so high that we felt obliged to repeat the exercise, using different starting combinations of reagents, until every student who wanted to had the chance to participate as an ion in solution.

Measuring sound

Probably my first large-scale outdoor experiment, as opposed to a role-playing exercise, involved taking a Year 10 physics class out into a nearby public park with a starting pistol, measuring tape and stop watches. The experiment was to measure the speed of sound in air by timing the echo of the bang when the pistol was fired.

The results were never particularly precise as the uncertainties in measurement are large, but the data allowed fruitful discussions of accuracy, precision and reaction time [10.8]. For example, students often pointed out that there was little point in compensating for the distance error incurred when the team with the measuring tape went up a short, steep bank between the oval and the buildings. However, they rarely carried the analysis through to massive uncertainties in time measurement.

Promote realistic conceptions of the nature of science(s) and relationships among sciences, technologies, societies and environment (see Analysis [10.8], p. 199).

Students seem to have almost infinite faith in the precision of stopwatches calibrated in hundredths of a second, and have little or no appreciation of the contribution of reaction time and anticipation to measurement errors. We no longer do this experiment, as an intensive building programme at the school changed the configuration of reflecting walls and spaces to the point where the returning echoes are complex and difficult to interpret.

I now prefer to explore the concept of sound intensity level and, in particular, the logarithmic decibel scale using an outdoor experience. In the lab, students use the sound level meter to measure the decibel level of a television set, and become familiar with the meter's selectable scales (0–70 dB and 70–120 dB). Then we go to a remote corner of the school grounds and the class shouts or screams as loudly as they can, one at a time as others measure the sound intensity level attained. One individual screaming typically scores about 85–90 dB at a distance of a metre or so.

Observation is theory laden (see Analysis [1.3], p. 98).

Despite having worked simple calculations involving decibels, students can rarely predict the level attained by two screamers at the same distance [1.3]. Usually, they predict that two 85 dB screamers will register 170 dB and send the meter off scale. They are similarly baffled by the decibel level for three simultaneous screamers. For these students, the logarithmic decibel scale is counterintuitive and the experiment becomes a cognitive conflict situation [4.15]. Students who participate in this exercise remember the unexpected result, and are much more likely to appreciate the way the scale works. They also have a healthy respect for the occasional screamer who can attain 91 or 92 dB on their own [7.5; 7.12].

Measuring motion [7.6, 7.13]

Another favourite outdoor experience takes a Year 11 physics class out to a long, straight section of access road. All students have a stopwatch, a pencil and a notebook to record data, and a small team also has a long tape measure. They mark out eight 10-metre intervals along the road, and one or preferably two students take up positions at these marks. Then I drive my car at a slow and (as far as I can achieve it) constant speed along the road, and the watch-bearers record the time taken for my car to reach their position [5.2]. We repeat the constant speed run a couple of times. Then I accelerate from rest along the road once, and we pack up and return to the lab. Here, students pool their times and start discussing the patterns (or sometimes lack of pattern) in the data. Usually, we see the effects of poor timing and the students begin to understand why a data graph, such as a displacement-time, velocity-time or acceleration-time curve, should not be treated as a 'join the dots' exercise. One year, the timing became so precise that the velocity-time curve for the final, accelerating run clearly showed where I had changed gear twice. I was impressed.

The first year I tried this I became so enthused by the results and the students' obvious enjoyment of the exercise that I expanded the data-gathering to include students on bicycles on the same track, and a student on roller blades going down a short stretch of inclined pavement. It didn't work. The students reached a kind of saturation point early on in the bicycle exercise, and were quite offhand by the roller blade exercise. I had forgotten that what excites a teacher does not necessarily have the same effect on students, and had neglected to vary my approach enough to keep their interest. I use both these extensions more sparingly now, and insert other types of activity between them to keep the approach fresh, or at least less stale. The first time always generates the strongest student response.

Rocket science

One such alternative activity involves low-tech rockets. We make them out of two-litre soft drink bottles, and a rubber bung with a bicycle valve inserted in it. Students mount the 'rocket' on a tripod, as used to heat matter over a Bunsen burner, and use a bicycle pump to increase the pressure inside the bottle until friction can no longer

Sometimes teachers bring about change by challenging students' expectations (see Analysis [4.15], p. 113).

Using sound meters (see Analysis [7.5], p. 164 and [7.12], p. 167).

Tracking motion with stopwatches (see Analysis [7.6], p. 164 and [7.13], p. 167).

PBL uses real-world problems to engage student learning in the problem-solving process and in the acquisition of disciplinary knowledge and skills (see Analysis [5.2], p. 139).

keep the bung in. The sudden release of air lifts the bottle a short distance. Other students measure the angular elevation reached at a measured distance, using crude inclinometers made of large protractors each with a plumb line attached. The first attempts are really just calibration runs, and few exceed half a metre or so above the launch platform. Once they start to get more or less consistent results [1.6], I pose the question: What is the optimum amount of water, to be ejected from the bottle, to get the rocket to its maximum height? The result is a fairly wet bunch of rocket scientists who have learnt a lot about experimental technique, control and minimizing errors and uncertainties. I rarely have to tell students much about the details – they tell each other, often quite loudly. This is definitely a fair weather, outdoor activity. The launch team always ends up covered with water, as the propellant is ejected from the rocket in the first few centimetres of its flight.

This may be 'rocket science' but the imprecision inherent in the technology obscures much useful information [1.7]. I thought that the video technique would work well here, as long as the rocket launches were against a regular background, i.e. a high, featureless brick wall at one end of the gym. Record a launch, stop the motion and measure, frame by frame, how far up the wall the rocket has travelled. It sounded simple but the detail defeated me when we tried it out recently. The school has acquired a digital video camera that is a delight to use, but to get the most out of it I'll have to master some video-editing software [7.7; 7.11]. I love this job. There's always a challenge and I have the chance to do things slightly or very differently every time.

Experimental data has to be interpreted (see Analysis [1.6], p. 100).

Experiments are set in a particular theoretical framework (see Analysis [1.7], p. 100).

Tracking rocket flight (see Analysis [7.7], p. 164 and [7.11], p. 167).

Account 3
Recollections of organic chemistry

Josie Ellis

Organic chemistry

As a secondary school student, organic chemistry was something I used to dread. I suspect that this was because of the difficulties I came across in trying to understand it. The subject was so abstract that the numerous reactions I had to learn seemed merely words on paper. I could not imagine how or why all these reactions were taking place [4.1] and consequently, I considered organic chemistry to be both abstract and dull. However, by the time I had finished my A level course, organic chemistry became my strongest and most favoured part. The fundamental reason behind this transformation, I believe, was teaching. Due to exemplary teaching, I was able to understand and relate to topics that I was finding very challenging, and so my confidence in my abilities increased.

Learning is facilitated once students can see patterns in the science content *(see Analysis [4.1], p. 127).*

I preferred organic to the inorganic and physical topics, because by learning reaction mechanisms I gained an overview of the subject area. In comparison, some of the inorganic or physical topics specified that we should recall some but not all explanations, so my understanding was in many instances frustratingly incomplete. Another reason why I enjoyed organic chemistry more, was the way there was an overlap with biology, e.g. lipids or changing structures to alter retention time. Biology is what I am passionate about and therefore, the more my chemistry related to biology, the more I enjoyed it [6.2].

Learners often co-exhibit task mastery and performance orientation goals *(see Analysis [6.2], p. 151).*

The order in which we were taught the various topics was important – we were taught about isomers first. One of the activities we did while studying isomerism was constructing models of the compounds using molecular model sets [1.9]. All of the class found this very helpful, as working out how the different elements fitted together with certain types of bonds made the various types of

Scientist use models *(see Analysis [1.9], p. 101).*

Models help comprehension (see Analysis [7.1], p. 161).

isomerism easier to understand and recall [7.1]. A key example is when I constructed a molecule with a single bond and then another with a double bond. The fact that I could rotate elements in molecules with single bonds but not those in the double bond molecules, helped me remember that double bonds restrict rotation. Three-dimensional models make learning easier and more enjoyable than two-dimensional pictures [4.3; 4.7].

Making learning 'concrete' helps many learners relate to science concepts (see Analysis [4.3], p. 128).

We then went on to learning mechanisms, which for me was the key to understanding all of the reactions I would have to learn in the course. Once I knew the mechanism of a reaction, I could understand why a particular transformation had occurred [4.5]. I also found myself visualizing the steps and patterns involved, and this enabled the prediction of other reactions. For example, once I knew the nucleophilic substitution mechanisms, the reactions of the halo-alkanes with a range of nucleophiles suddenly became a lot simpler. To start with, we were helped to understand a certain mechanism, but as we became more confident we were encouraged to come up with the mechanisms ourselves when provided with the reaction.

Physical manipulation of apparatus can provide an additional way of learning and recalling information (see Analysis [4.7], p. 129).

The perceived complexity of new learning depends upon the way existing learning can be used to organize new knowledge (see Analysis [4.5], p. 129).

Although mechanisms were constantly revisited in our lessons, once they were behind us, we moved on to the reactions stated in each topic. It seemed a vast number of reactions to learn, and the fact that we also had to know conditions and reagents added pressure. All of the class found that practical work helped because setting up the equipment and using the various reagents and conditions made these details easier to remember [5.10]. I really enjoyed the practical work in organic chemistry because as I observed each reaction I would think about the mechanism taking place [4.12]. In addition, understanding exactly why the changes were occurring was satisfying.

All learning is embodied (see Analysis [5.10], p. 143).

Teaching materials often act as 'scaffolds' for student learning, helping to structure the learning process (see Analysis [4.12], p. 132).

Student participation was key in our lessons [2.8]. There were many instances when a student would explain something to the rest of the class, or be asked to draw something out on the board. This increased our individual confidence and developed the class's ability to help one another, which we continued outside of the classroom. I got into the habit of working with a fellow chemistry student, going over each other's problems. One of us would ask a question and the other would try to explain the answer. This was a good indication of how well we understood what we were explaining, and helped determine whether we should seek a teacher's explanation if there was something we were finding particularly difficult [2.8].

Peer interaction promotes learning (see Analysis [2.8], p. 113).

Effective teaching is available to students with different learning styles (see Analysis [4.6], p. 129).

Another aspect of our lessons that made comprehension easier was the fact that we were encouraged to write up all notes (even photocopied sheets) in our own handwriting. This was not hugely popular with all the students, but personally I found it very useful because I needed to put things in my own words to understand them [4.6]. My notes were incredibly detailed. An example that interested me was how Nylon 6,6 got its name from being discovered at the same time in New York and London. Since I found this interesting, I could recall it easily and then the structure of Nylon 6,6 would also come into my head.

I had to persistently revisit organic chemistry to ensure I did not forget all the reactions and mechanisms I had learnt. Here, I found using CD-ROMs designed for students at my level useful, as they provided a different type of learning environment including images of compounds that could be rotated and practice questions to probe my comprehension.

The revision for examinations that we did in class was very useful. A folder divided into the topics of our specification was provided to all students. In each section there were numerous past exam questions with answers from the exam board. I found using past exam questions to be an extremely useful technique for revision, and having the answers was especially helpful for seeing exactly what the examiner was looking for. I would revise a certain topic, for example carbonyl compounds, then try some questions to see how much I'd understood and taken in. This was far more enjoyable than just rote learning [6.2], as it was more varied and good exam practice. We were also provided with complete tests, so that when it came to doing the real exam we would feel at ease with the layout and style of the questions. When the class went on study leave, the chance to photocopy these resources was given to all of us, allowing us to continue using the practice questions at home.

Learners often co-exhibit task mastery and performance orientation goals *(see Analysis [6.2], p. 151)*.

By the time I reached the exam I was obviously very nervous but I felt confident in my knowledge of organic chemistry. I'd had a year that was intense, mainly through the sheer vastness of material to learn, and the revision period had been even more so. However, the year had also been in my opinion a time of positive development, mainly in understanding, but also in confidence.

To pick out the qualities that I feel contribute to exemplary science teaching, I draw upon my experiences of being taught organic chemistry. A combination of factors made the teaching so effective. An enthusiasm for the subject was transfused onto the students and, as a result, lessons were interesting [6.1]. The range of resources and practical experiences made the topics real, and the way in which we were encouraged to put things into our own words encouraged reflection. The way that lessons were varied, with a mixture of making models, taking notes, class discussions and practicals, definitely increased my interest [8.4]. In addition, the reassurance that I could get help almost anytime of the day was very supportive [8.8].

Teachers' relationship with their subject infuses their practice *(see Analysis [6.1], p. 150)*.

The plurality of pedagogy *(see analysis [8.4], p. 175)*.

When I started the course I had a great deal of self-doubt about my abilities. However, the encouragement I experienced was very significant in developing my confidence. This was an important year for me. I am so lucky that I had the opportunity to experience such quality teaching, and I am looking forward to studying science at university.

The motive of morality *(see Analysis [8.8], p. 180)*.

Account 4
The science classroom of tomorrow?

Richard Rennie and Kim Edwards

Introduction

A technology rich environment provides a very different 'science' experience for high school students. Our case study is set in an 'Apple Distinguished School', with all students in Years 5 to 10 (ages 11–16) having their own **iBook**™ laptop computer. The laptop program was started in 1993 and has grown steadily each year. The school's computers are 'wireless networked', which means that students and staff have access to email, printers, server and the Internet from anywhere on the campus, 24 hours a day. The wireless network has a fibre optic backbone and runs a gigabit ethernet. Every student has their own email address that they can use freely and responsibly. This case study describes the evolution of our technology mediated learning experiences.

The SCOT project: background and teaching philosophy

A number of science teachers in the school were keen to explore the potential of e-learning and, with this agenda in mind, we formulated the Science Class of Tomorrow (SCOT) project. Initially established for Year 9 students (aged 13–14 years), it eventually included other grades as the project developed.

There are a number of fundamental premises underlying the SCOT project, including that all students can learn and all students must take increased responsibility for their own learning [6.3]. These caused us to shift the focus of our curriculum from the teacher to the learner [5.1]. More importantly, we felt that the 'one size fits all' approach to teaching and the curriculum was inappropriate. We began to view computers and associated technologies as tools, which could address our concerns by providing the power and flexibility needed to individualize the science programme, and allow students to

Promoting learning autonomy promotes mastery orientation *(see Analysis [6.3], p. 152)*.

PBL is grounded in constructivism *(see Analysis [5.1], p. 138)*.

advance at their own pace [9.3]. We hoped that the SCOT project would give students autonomy and control over their learning.

Individualizing the curriculum *(see Analysis [9.3], p. 187)*.

Structure, preparation and distribution of materials

In the SCOT project, our aim is to put *students* online, not just curriculum materials. We decided to make full use of all the inter-active and audio-visual capabilities of the computers, and push the laptops to their limits [5.9]. To achieve this, we created a totally digital Year 9 science curriculum. The course was embedded in students' laptop computers, with the curriculum materials linking students to various interactive software packages, CD-ROM, World Wide Web, and other digital materials. For example, at a relevant point in the chemistry unit, we linked students to a number of online Periodic Tables. These provided a wealth of information, which was not available in students' textbooks, and allowed students to move at their own pace.

Learning is mediated by tools of the culture *(see Analysis [5.9], p. 143)*.

As a team, we began preparing materials several months in advance. Our collaboration helped us to produce quality materials; this we hoped would enhance student motivation to learn science. We started with a set of basic outcomes, and then developed the curri-culum materials to support the achievement of these outcomes. Our approach [5.1] was to work with existing modules. For example, starting with the Year 9 chemistry course we:

PBL is grounded in constructivism *(see Analysis [5.1], p. 138)*.

- restructured the course into a core of about eight electives, and broke it up into a sequence of small chunks which we referred to as activities;
- transformed what was previously a paper-based course into a digital course, creating animations, movies, sounds and digital photos, inserting appropriate www links where needed; and
- produced support material, such as lists of outcomes, level of achievement indicators, assessment criteria, research guides, investigation guides and revision packages.

We structured materials so that students entered the unit through a main menu, providing them with an overview of the whole course. We distributed most of the curriculum materials to the students by CD-ROM. Also, since all students have their own email address, we used this as an efficient means of providing students with other information, for example, solutions to assignments and tests, test results, information about summer schools and camps, and infor-mation about competitions, etc. Email also allowed students to communicate directly with each other, assist each other and

Using email to share information *(see Analysis [7.9], p. 165).*

communicate directly with us on a personal basis [7.9]. Indeed, email became a very useful educational tool in the SCOT project. As a back-up, we also placed curriculum materials on the student server.

Catering for a range of learning styles

Effective teaching is available to students with different learning styles *(see Analysis [4.6], p. 129).*

Learning science and doing science are not identical activities *(see Analysis [1.5], p. 99).*

A therapeutic practitioner is skilled at promoting benefits and reducing the costs of learning *(see Analysis [6.11], p. 156).*

The digital science curriculum materials we produced made extensive use of digital multimedia. We deliberately presented the work in a variety of ways so that students could use their preferred learning styles [4.6]. Some students may prefer to learn by reading or listening or watching demonstrations, while others may find participating in practical hands-on laboratory activities to be most useful [1.5]. In the Year 9 chemistry unit, for example, we inserted audio buttons alongside key definitions and instructions. Students who had difficulty with reading could click on these buttons and hear a sound byte of information read to them by the computer. For some students, this proved to be very helpful [6.11].

In addition, and where appropriate, we added specialized software (often freeware) to the curriculum materials. For example, a digital oscilloscope was embedded in the sound and music topic, so that every student could analyse the wave patterns of their sounds on their own computer. Sound recording software was also given to students so they could create their own audio material.

Computer animation illustrates movement *(see Analysis [7.2], p. 162 and [7.11], p. 167).*

To help those students who required visual information and interpretation, we used the power of computer animation and 3D graphics for many topics [7.2; 7.11]. For example, in the chemistry, unit, 3D graphics were used to illustrate the shapes of molecules. The students could manipulate these 3D molecules on their laptop screen. In the electricity unit, we used computer animation to illustrate the movement of electrons around an electric circuit. Movie clips were also inserted into the curriculum materials at relevant points. Students could view these movies at school or at home, when and as frequently as they wanted. The movies often demonstrated new laboratory techniques, such as how to measure blood pressure and how to connect up an ammeter. We also created movie clips of us at the whiteboard explaining difficult concepts, for example, the formation of ions, balancing chemical equations and describing electron shells [8.3]. Students (and parents) now had the opportunity and choice to view and review the teacher's explanation of these concepts.

The centrality of content *(see Analysis [8.3], p. 174).*

Differentiation of the curriculum

The computer and related technologies enabled us to provide a truly differentiated curriculum. This allowed students to work at their own pace. The more able students could get on with the course without waiting for the teacher or being held back by the rest of the class, while the less able students could also work at a pace that best suited them.

In most cases, we provided each student with a whole unit of work (about 10 weeks) at the start of the term. We gave students various deadlines and checkpoints to serve as guides. However, it was always made clear that we did not expect everyone to complete the whole course. We would assist each student in mapping out and working through their own science course. As one student put it: 'I have enjoyed science in Year 9 because we got to do our own work, and not have the teacher talking up at the front all the time.'

Sections of the course were set at different levels of difficulty. Students could choose those sections that best suited their ability. We then assessed the students on what outcomes they had achieved, and the levels to which they had achieved them. We specifically designed the units to allow for flexibility, which meant that students studied the course that they had structured from the materials and resources we provided. Since the students always had access to the assessment criteria, they knew what they needed to do to achieve the outcomes. The laptop computers provided the infrastructure necessary to achieve this flexibility and transparency.

Team teaching

We did a number of things to support our collaborative philosophy. Two Year 9 science classes ran at the same time in two adjacent laboratories, with both of us using a team teaching approach. The students were not streamed, so each class was of mixed ability. However, we could regroup the students within those two classes according to their needs or their choice of activities. This flexible approach assisted with the differentiation of classroom instruction.

Mostly, the students worked at their own pace within their own small group. Not surprisingly, students of similar ability often chose to team up. However, at times we would restructure the classes [2.9]. For example, by combining both classes in one laboratory, one of us ran a demonstration or gave an expository presentation, while the other observed students' academic and social behaviour. This also provided us with valuable information for the pastoral care of individual students.

Restructuring of groups can help achieve different teaching goals and learning outcomes (see Analysis [2.9], p. 113).

Sometimes one of us took a small group of students into one laboratory to give instruction on a particular concept they were struggling to understand. The other teacher would then work with the rest of the group in the other laboratory. For example, in chemistry, one of us supervised those students who were coping well, while the other ran small, informal and intimate tutorials for those who found balancing chemical equations difficult [9.4].

As students moved freely between the laboratories, and had choice within the curriculum, they could opt to be in the classroom

Group work and valuing diversity (see Analysis [9.4], p. 188).

that matched their particular elective. For example, in the chemistry unit, some students needed to complete an elective called 'catch-up chemistry'. We ran 'catching up' in one laboratory so we could provide the concentrated assistance needed. On the other hand, students who were ready for learning more advanced chemistry concepts moved to the laboratory that best supported their course needs. From our perspective, the short-term re-grouping of students according to their needs, enabled us to more efficiently direct our teaching efforts, and certainly lowered our stress levels!

Collaboration between staff was one of the critical elements in the success of the SCOT project. Through a team teaching approach, we shared the responsibility for planning and delivering the curriculum. Our relationship is based on mutual trust, commitment and flexibility. We are happy to work in each other's laboratory and observe each other's teaching. This has made all the difference in our work, and in the experience of students [6.1].

Teachers' relationship with their subject infuses their practice *(see Analysis [6.1], p. 150).*

Evaluation survey

The SCOT project provides a very different experience for students, as well as teachers. Therefore, we were curious to know how they felt about their Year 9 science classes. During the first year of the SCOT project, we carried out a review with all 130 students. Table 2 shows some of the data collected. The spread of results, shown in the last question in the table, perhaps indicates the range of learning styles within a class, and we suggest supporting the need for a multimedia approach to the digital curriculum [4.6]. We also collected written responses. These raised a series of issues related to, for example, teachers' roles and pupil readiness. These issues informed our termly reviews.

Effective teaching is available to students with different learning styles *(see Analysis [4.6], p. 129).*

In conclusion, we are delighted to announce that the digital curriculum and the use of laptop computers has now spread throughout our school, such that computers are becoming an integral part of normal everyday school life. Interestingly, the computer is looked upon by the girls as just a tool. Yet it is a powerful and flexible tool, well suited to providing a differentiated curriculum to prepare pupils for the digital online world.

Table 2   The SCOT project: summary of student survey

Question	Answer	Percentage
Should some students be able to work ahead of the class if they understand the work?	All students should be made to work at the same speed.	1
	Some students could work ahead of the class some of the time.	11
	Students could work ahead when they understand the material.	33
	Students should be able to work at whatever speed they can cope with.	55
Should some students be able to slow down if they have trouble understanding the work?	Students should be made to keep up with everyone else.	4
	Students could slow down a little if they do not understand.	19
	Students could slow down when they do not understand.	24
	Students could work at any speed that helps them understand.	53
What do you think should be the role of the teacher?	The teacher should always teach the class from the front.	4
	The teacher should teach from the front most of the time.	28
	The teacher should only interrupt the class when necessary.	54
	I would prefer the teacher to let me get on with the work.	14
Did the sound bytes on the computer help you understand the chemistry topic?	The sounds were a great help to me.	16
	The sounds were of some help to me.	34
	The sounds helped me a little.	25
	The sounds were of no help to me.	25

Account 5

Science with a human touch: historical vignettes in the teaching and learning of science

Karen Kettle

Lights, camera, action! [5.12]

Learning is situated *(see Analysis [5.12], p.144)*.

The stage is set. The curtain is about to go up and I can hear the rustling anticipation in the audience out front. The scientists and inventors are almost ready. Thomas Edison is checking his light bulb equipment, Darwin is mulling through his Beagle Diary, and Jane Goodall is fussing with her slides of chimpanzees. It's almost time to step out into the spotlight and take the audience back in time to meet our honoured guests. A quick look around. Lights – check! Actors – check! Props – check! Sound – check! Audience – ready! Wait a minute, I'm a science teacher ... How did I end up here?

Early influences

Teachers' relationship with their subject infuses their practice *(see Analysis [6.1], p. 150)*.

The use of historical perspectives gives science a human face *(see Analysis [3.1], p. 118)*.

Relating science to people *(see Analysis [6.6], p. 153)*.

Making science human *(see Analysis [9.8], p. 189)*.

I enjoyed science as a student, especially the natural sciences, and any excuse to go outdoors [6.1]. I also had an insatiable desire to read, and was often found curled up with a book hiding from large family gatherings. But somehow I managed to get all the way through a biology degree, several years teaching high school science and into my Master's degree in gifted education before I got hooked on biographies of scientists. They opened a door for me to understand science in a totally different way [3.1; 6.6; 9.8].

All of a sudden the science was not separated from people who created it. I could follow their lives from their childhood interests, discover the experiences that crystallized their desire to lead a scientific life, explore the role mentors may have played in the development of their talent, and get to know them as people. The science came alive. It was no longer a logical sequential march towards 'truth'. There was tedious laboratory work to be sure, but there were also daring field studies, brilliant flashes of inspiration, serendipitous discoveries, false leads, creative collaborations, cut-throat competitions, political pressures and long lasting feuds. Science was much more personal and socially embedded than I'd ever realized [10.8]. I'd discovered a world that would intrigue my students.

The play's the thing

I stumbled across the idea of dramatizing the lives of eminent individuals in a creativity course and decided to give it a try. I was teaching a Grade 9 (age 15) gifted interdisciplinary studies class and it was the perfect place to start. The curriculum was open ended, so students could follow their interests as they selected creative producers to study in fields that sparked their curiosity [10.9]. Also, the course was unfettered by a tradition of how it 'should' be taught. Therefore, it was easy to convince the young people that this was a logical way to learn about creative productivity [10.10].

Students researched the lives of eminent people, wrote essays and selected a dramatic moment or turning point in the person's life [8.4]. They then created a 3- or 4-minute script, planned costumes, and prepared to answer questions from the audience in first person [3.5; 8.4]. Parents, teachers and friends were invited to be our audience, and travelled back through time with us to experience these memorable moments. We also dug into different disciplines, studied the nature of creativity as an interaction between individuals' thoughts and their socio-cultural context, and discovered how eminent people actively transformed their passions into creative contributions through a process of self-construction. We developed an appreciation for the courage and commitment it took to live a creative life.

Dramatic insights

I learned a lot. First of all, anyone can do this but you need to ask for help with the skills you don't have. I found a very supportive drama teacher who was willing to do a little theatrical work with my students, and also showed them how to operate the lights and sound. The technical aspect of theatre fascinates some teenagers, so the knowledge was handed down from student to student and I never had to learn it.

Second, something magical happened when a student stepped into another person's life. They got comfortable in the new shoes and stretched to understand the individual's experience, in a holistic and personal manner. This was very different from merely learning about what the person accomplished. You had to 'be' the eminent person to talk about 'your' life and answer questions in first person [3.2].

Promote realistic conceptions of the nature of science(s) and relationships among sciences, technologies, societies and environments *(see Analysis [10.8], p. 199)*

Promote naturalistic (as well as rationalistic) curricula and instruction *(see Analysis [10.9], p. 200)*.

Rationalize curriculum expectations, thus leaving time for increased quality of learning *(see Analysis [10.10], p. 200)*.

Students engage in the consideration of multiple viewpoints and critical analysis through role play in order to better understand various stakeholder positions and controversy *(see Analysis [3.5], p. 120)*.

The plurality of pedagogy *(see Analysis [8.4], p. 175)*.

Drama and role play can challenge traditional images of science while addressing cultural, social and political contexts *(see Analysis [3.2], p. 118)*.

Third, videotape is powerful. Showing students the previous year's performance guaranteed that they would outperform their predecessors. And fourth, it was fun. All sorts of people graced the stage – Catherine the Great, Mahatma Gandhi, Leonardo da Vinci, Diane Fossey, Anne Frank, Johnny Carson, The Wright Brothers, Mozart, Thomas Edison and many more. Chip and Dale even talked and sang about the life of their creator – Walt Disney.

Spotlight on science in society

A few years later, I implemented a new senior science course called 'Science and society'. This focused on the interactions of science, technology, society and the environment. It seemed like a perfect opportunity to bring together my growing collection of scientific biographies and the experience I'd banked running 'Celebration of creative producers'. The unit was easily adapted to the tighter curriculum and time restrictions of a senior science course. The theatrical performance was refocused into a news conference format that could take place in class, in an evening show, or as individual presentations at local elementary schools, depending on the interests of my class.

Countering the stereotype of a scientist *(see Analysis [1.12], p. 104)*.

Sometimes teachers bring about conceptual change by challenging students' expectations *(see Analysis [4.15], p. 133)*.

Refuting stereotypical images of scientists *(see Analysis [6.12], p. 157)*.

We started by exploring cultural stereotypes of scientists. Students drew large pictures of 'a scientist at work'. These images often included a slightly mad-looking, able-bodied, white male scientist dressed in a lab coat and working alone in a laboratory, either mixing explosive chemicals or experimenting on animals [1.12]! As we discussed their artwork, students identified the cultural stereotypes of scientists that appeared in their pictures [4.15]. We identified sources that inspired their artwork, determined the validity of images, sought out exceptions, discussed influences of the media, and considered the impact on groups who were disenfranchised by the stereotypes [6.12].

Students were then provided with enough background information to make informed decisions as they decided who to research. It amazes me that many students get stuck naming scientists after they get beyond Einstein, Newton and Curie. While scientists appear in textbooks and lend their names to theories, laws and laboratory equipment, they seem to disappear before they become fully human or truly memorable. Students needed a sincere interest in order to read an adult length biography or to undertake the extensive hunt to find information on lesser-known individuals. Their curiosities were piqued with a variety of short articles, videos and children's books. For fun, I created a 'who am I?' game where students matched one-page descriptions of early experiences to the lives of eminent scientists. Biographical videos served as a springboard to discuss both content and process.

We analysed why some scientists are considered renowned, the characteristics and choices that helped them to succeed, their research methodology and the impact of cultural expectations on their work. We also discussed how the scriptwriters researched the scientist's life, how they decided which anecdotes to include to illustrate the scientists personality and accomplishments, how the actors prepared for their roles and how decisions were made regarding props and costumes. This introduced students to the complex roles of researcher, historical interpreter, writer, actor and producer – roles into which they soon stepped [2.6], [3.9].

Role play promotes an understanding of different arguments and positions (see Analysis [2.6], p. 112).

Engaging in thoughtful decision-making requires consideration of multiple viewpoints, gathering of information and critical analyses (see Analysis [3.9], p. 123).

Now playing: 'Scientists' Lives'

In recent years, biographies of an increasingly diverse group of scientists have been published, and I've enjoyed reading them. This allowed me to guide students towards stories that were of high scientific and/or human interest. I also made sure that the length and complexity of materials matched reading levels of my students. Our school librarian purchased a couple of biographies or collections of profiles every year because they were well used. There were stories to catch the interest of every student. Science involves extensive fieldwork (Eugenie Clark, Mary Leakey, Jane Goodall), as well as work in the laboratory (Louis Pasteur, Chien-Shiung Wu). Some scientists combine their talents to become important authors and to confront established institutions (Rachel Carson, Galileo Galilei), while others must invent the technology required to further their investigations (Jacques Cousteau). Certain lives illustrate the importance of collaboration and the divisions that occur because of politics and war (Lise Meitner and Otto Hahn) [10.4]. Minority groups (George Washington Carver, Granville Woods), women (Barbara McClintock, Rita Levi-Montalcini) and physically challenged individuals (Stephen Hawking, Geerat Vermeij) have overcome many obstacles to pursue their passions. Dramatic tensions arise if students present scientists from opposite sides of a controversy (Donald Johanson and Richard Leakey), mentors and their protégés (Lewis Leakey and Dian Fossey), husband and wife teams (Carl and Gerty Cori), competitors who are disputing priority for a discovery (Isaac Newton and Gottfried Leibniz), or scientists who are involved in a technological race (Sergei Korolov and Werner von Braun). We used these fascinating lives to explore underlying themes, such as career pathways, ethics, environmental protection, gender and ethnocultural equity, human potential, politics and technocracy [1.13].

Problematize science (see Analysis [10.4], p. 196).

Science can be humanized (see Analysis [1.13], p. 104).

I provided students with a set of questions to guide their research.

Teaching materials often act as 'scaffolds' for student learning, helping to structure the learning process *(see Analysis [4.12], p. 132).*

Careful scaffolding assists students in developing their own arguments *(see Analysis [3.6], p. 121).*

Science can be humanized *(see Analysis [1.13], p. 104).*

[4.12, 3.6]. The questions encouraged them to break away from a sterile chronology of dates and delve into personal anecdotes that explored the humanity of their scientist, as well as the processes involved in creative productivity [1.13]:

- What events early in the scientist's life might indicate, or have sparked, an interest in science and technology?
- What role did mentors play in developing the interests and talents of the scientist?
- What was the state of knowledge that existed in the area of study when the scientist entered the field?
- How did the major cultural, economic and political situations of the time impact on the person's work?
- What were the major accomplishments of the scientist, the methodologies used and the principles of science that were upheld?
- What key opportunities provided turning points in the individual's life?
- What personal choices did the scientist make to construct his/her success?
- What personal anecdotes best illustrate the characteristics of the individual necessary for his/her success?
- What hardships or roadblocks did the individual overcome?
- What were the individual's limitations as a scientist or as a person [10.6]?

Provide students with an apprenticeship for the development of expertise for knowledge creation in science and technology *(see Analysis [10.6], p. 198).*

The questions focused students' attention, while material was selected for their biographical essays and provided a basis for peer editing and identifying patterns. Students were expected to read a biography, supplemented by anecdotes from documentaries and shorter works. Children's books provided a rich source of stories about young scientists and illustrations that made costuming easier.

The essays were anything but dry. Childhood stories flourished. Eugenie Clark's romance with sharks began during her long vigils at the New York aquarium while she waited for her mother to finish work. Richard Feynman walked in the woods with his father, who taught him to notice things, to wonder, to ask penetrating questions and to translate scientific information into real world applications.

Science is a culturally located activity *(see Analysis [1.15], p. 105).*

Other stories illustrated the connections between science and society of the times [1.15]. Barbara McClintock showed infinite patience as she waited 20 years for the rest of the scientific community to catch up and accept her work on jumping genes. The Second World War impacted on the development of nuclear science.

It also created political divisions that forced scientists with a Jewish heritage, like Lise Meitner, to leave colleagues and experiments behind and flee Nazi Germany. Rachel Carson wrote about the growing danger of pesticides and so gave birth to the environmental movement.

There were also stories of overcoming great obstacles. George Washington Carver was born as a slave in Missouri. He was 30 before he saved enough money to enter college, and yet his botanical knowledge of peanuts and sweet potatoes greatly influenced agricultural patterns. Geerat Vermeij became an eminent evolutionary biologist despite his blindness. Stephen Hawking continues to unravel cosmological mysteries, while coping with ALS, a degenerative and physically debilitating nerve disorder. Hence, biographies have the power to inspire – to become 'mentors in print' for students with scientific curiosity.

With their essays complete, students selected information and anecdotes to create a 3- to 4-minute, first-person script. A critical moment in the scientist's life served as a focus. For example, the announcement of a major discovery, reflections on a major setback, a letter to a colleague regarding a decision, or the acceptance of an award. The scripts only reflected knowledge up to a critical point since the scientist could not see into the future. Autobiographies and collections of letters were extremely useful, as they provided anecdotes in the scientist's own words. Peer editing of essays and scripts was also beneficial. Using the guiding questions as a foundation, students helped each other select critical moments and thought-provoking anecdotes [10.7]. They brainstormed potential questions that might be asked during the news conference and practised answers [3.7; 5.11].

I acted as a creative consultant. Some students needed encouragement to take risks and include scientific demonstrations in their presentations, while those uncomfortable performing on stage were encouraged to choose situations where there was a reason to have their script with them [10.3; 9.10]. For example, Charles Darwin reviewed his letter to his mentor (Dr Henslow), from aboard the HMS Beagle as he toured the Galapagos Islands.

Having a script on stage provided a safety net that prevented performance anxiety, associated with memorized speeches. Classes enjoyed watching video clips from previous news conferences. These models set a high standard and provided hints for staging and costuming. Individuals with stage fright found the video clips reassuring as they watched people, just like themselves, performing and living to tell about it.

We practised as much as we could within the time restrictions of the curriculum. This ensured success, and modelled the ongoing quest for excellence that is often overlooked in everyday assignments.

Promote social learning and assessment *(see Analysis [10.7], p. 199).*

Talk can mediate student learning, allowing for shared perspectives and articulations *(see Analysis [3.7], p. 121).*

Learning is distributed across groups and situations *(see Analysis [5.11], p. 144).*

Accommodate for difference *(see Analysis [10.3], p. 196).*

Building students' confidence *(see Analysis [9.10], p. 190).*

Students used their peers as prompters and drama coaches. When everyone was working at the same time activity level was high and students were not self-conscious. Students presenting in pairs, such as Banting and Best, required more rehearsals to work out their timing, and to decide how to continue if someone forgot a line or developed the giggles. This happened frequently in practice but rarely on stage. After students were comfortable with their scripts they turned their attention and energy to their performances [10.5].

The last part of the news conference was a question and answer period. Students used the lists of practice questions to prepare potential answers ahead of time. Key questions were planted with friends so that everyone got off to a good start. Students practised how to skilfully avoid inquiries they didn't wish to answer without appearing flustered. For many, the question and answer period was initially worrisome, but became the most enjoyable and spontaneous part of the presentation, especially when they presented to elementary school audiences.

Anyone involved in a drama production has experienced how the pressure and adrenaline rush of opening night escalates preparation and the quality of the performance. Some semesters students designed programmes and invited their teachers, parents and friends for an entertaining evening. At other times, they presented in class or took their show to a local elementary school. Having an audience other than their classmates increased the quality of their performances.

They designed simple costumes, found appropriate props, planned make-up, and created lighting effects. Strong presentations were selected for the start and finish, and a variety were provided to change the pace throughout. Nervous students were placed close to the beginning so that their part was over quickly [6.11]. A full dress rehearsal was required the day before to make sure that the lights, staging and costumes didn't present problems. This provided an opportunity for the camera person to practise.

The audience was always a key part of the show. I provided a prologue to the action, explaining that we were travelling back in time to interview eminent scientists, and that they would have an opportunity to ask questions of their famous guests.

The day after the news conference we usually ate popcorn and watched the videotape of the performance. This was a celebration of the cast's success and an opportunity to reflect. Students described what went well, what they would have changed and gave me words of wisdom to share with students performing the following year. With the emotion of the performance behind us, we returned to an analysis of the scientific content [9.9]. By this time students were extremely familiar with the lives of the eminent scientists they had studied.

As a class, we compiled a list of characteristics that aided the

Promote proactive perspectives on knowledge development *(see Analysis [10.5], p. 197).*

A therapeutic practitioner is skilled at promoting benefits and reducing the costs of learning *(see Analysis [6.11], p. 156).*

Reflection and discussion *(see Analysis [9.9], p. 189).*

scientists in the self-construction of successful careers, discussed the interactions between the development of talent and cultural expectations, identified barriers to success, debated social responsibilities and compared scientific methodology. Students drew pictures to illustrate their scientists' careers. We compared this artwork to the original pictures they drew of 'a scientist at work' [9.9].

Sometimes I extended the unit by having students create an interview protocol to investigate the work of contemporary scientists. The biography study provided students with the background [4.9] they needed to create intelligent and interesting questions about early interests, education, mentors, personal qualities, professional choices and scientific methodology [6.7]. Individuals with scientific careers were easy to find in our neighbouring communities. Email and Internet chat lines opened long distance avenues for communication. Interview transcripts provided rich sources of data for students to begin exploring qualitative methods of research. Writing biographical profiles provided closure by bringing the independent study full circle. Students planning for careers in science found this particularly useful.

Prior experience acts as a substrate for new learning-for making sense of new ideas *(see Analysis [4.9], p. 130).*

Making science more interesting and relevant *(see Analysis [6.7], p. 154).*

To [re-]live is to know

Back to that rising curtain – as it goes up the magic takes over. As my students perform on stage, I can watch them think, feel and respond from the perspective of an eminent scientist [3.10]. Their answers shatter the myth that talent is an innate gift, and the diversity of characters illustrates the narrowness of stereotypes of scientists that appear in popular culture. The audience gains an appreciation of different creative lifelines and the wide variety of forms scientific research can take. They also appreciate that individuals control many of the choices concerning purpose, prolonged work and repeated encounters with tasks that allow them to become productive. Should we put science and theatre together? Why not? It comes alive. Everyone learns!

Through excitement and engagement in a topic, students become motivated to learn and feel empowered *(see Analysis [3.10], p. 124).*

Account 6

Exploring the nature of science: reinterpreting the Burgess Shale fossils

Katherine Bellomo

Background

Evaluation of evidence in contrasting arguments is a significant aspect of the nature of science *(see Analysis [2.2], p. 110).*

Science can be biased *(see Analysis [1.14], p. 104).*

Sometimes conceptual change requires restructuring of existing knowledge *(see Analysis [4.14], p. 133).*

The use of anomaly can be an effective strategy for promoting argumentation *(see Analysis [2.3], p. 111).*

Many years ago I read the book *Wonderful Life – The Burgess Shale and the Nature of History* by Stephen Jay Gould (1989). It's a wonderful book and I knew then that I had chanced upon a treasure. The book tells the story of the reinterpretation of the fossils from the Burgess Shale (British Columbia, Canada) [2.2]. These are fossils collected by Charles Walcott between 1909 and 1913. He examined them briefly and wrote about them. The fossils are of soft-bodied organisms from the Cambrian Period, which were covered in mud (probably from a landslide) and preserved.

Walcott interpreted the fossils applying the view he held of evolution and diversification of organisms. Sixty years later, a different group of scientists re-examined these same fossils, interpreted them in a different way and drew a dramatically different conclusion [1.14, 4.14]. The reinterpretations give us a new iconography of the so-called 'tree of life', so often depicted in biology textbooks, and suggests that most diversity was in existence at the beginning of the emergence of invertebrate life. Since then, variation has occurred within the few surviving taxa.

The story of the Burgess Shale fossils is a wonderful story for me as a biology teacher. It has many layers and holds deep significance as an example of the culture of science. The interesting thing for me was that when I read this book, I knew that it was the best example I had seen for showing science as a dynamic, changing and culturally determined practice [2.3].

The story had a clear and compelling 'message' that needed to be explored in my classroom. I knew that this story could be used to demystify scientific practice and explore, with my students, questions such as: what is science? What research was done to arrive at this knowledge? What questions were not asked? Is science about finding the truth or about constructing knowledge [3.3]?

I first offered the following lesson to a senior science class in a multicultural, large urban high school. I have also shared it with pre-service science students. In teaching this lesson, I hoped to address some of the broader issues that I felt my students and I face. We are often unaware or not fully aware of these issues, I would argue, but they impact upon our curriculum choices and delivery.

Inclusion of the nature of science perspectives allows for the exploration of complex epistemological questions (see Analysis [3.3], p. 119).

I wanted to move towards a more inclusive science curriculum but needed to ask myself: How do I understand inclusion, and how do I include all students? Do all students see themselves in the curriculum so that individuals do not feel marginalized? Is school science honest in how it portrays the nature of science, and the philosophical underpinnings of the process of knowledge construction? Could I show science to be – as I believe it to be – biased, human and idiosyncratic [1.14]? Could I address issues of race, class and gender, that block some students from entering into the culture of science – or at the high school level into the subculture of the science classroom?

Science can be biased (see Analysis [1.14], p. 104).

The lesson: what do I do? [8.1]

The tenacity of teaching (see Analysis [8.1], p. 172).

I begin the lesson by asking my students to complete the sentence: 'Science is about_____.' They respond with a number of answers such as: 'Science is about nature, understanding the world, experimentation, collecting and analysing data, money and getting funding for your research, politics, ideas, and asking a question' [3.6].

Careful scaffolding assists students in developing their own arguments (see Analysis [3.6], p. 121).

The story of the Burgess Shale is an ideal tool for addressing many of the above aspects as well as the nature and history of science. In particular, the story helps students explore 'ignored history', by which I mean history that does not enter the realm of textbooks or other curriculum materials [3.1]. Students, I believe, think it is fun to complete the sentence: 'Science is about_____.' But some do wonder what the correct answer is! I then proceed to tell the story of the Burgess Shale. I give a condensed version, and tell them of course that for the fuller and more compelling version they will need to read Gould's book. Here is the story I tell them. As a written account it seems a bit dry, but when told as a 'story', it comes to life!

The use of historical perspectives gives science a human face (see Analysis [3.1], p. 118).

In 1909, Charles Walcott (the secretary, which means 'boss' of the Smithsonian Institute), was on vacation in British Columbia in an area known as the Burgess Shale. There, and for several summers after, he found and collected specimens of fossilized soft-bodied organisms. He crated up and shipped these thousands of specimens back to Washington. Over the subsequent years, he proceeded to identify and classify some of these into what he believed to be the

Status plays a key role in theory acceptance *(see Analysis [1.4], p. 99)*.

correct taxonomic groupings. He was a well-respected, competent scientist – and a very busy guy [1.4].

At the time of Walcott's death, only a fraction of the fossils had been closely examined. This might have been, in part, because of his time-consuming duties as an administrator. It's hard to know how Walcott reasoned through his classifications, but he clearly held the view that the Burgess organisms could be classified within established modern phyla. He assumed that the found fossils were ancestral to present/modern forms. Gould describes Walcott as a man with a conventional outlook, which resulted in a conventional interpretation. So you can well imagine Walcott's approach: if an organism looked as if it could be ancestral to an arthropod, that is how it was classified.

The fossils remained in drawers at the Smithsonian for decades. Sixty years later, three scientists from the UK got permission to further examine the fossils. Harry Wittington, Derek Briggs and Simon Conway Morris tell of their amazement as they opened drawers at the Smithsonian. The scientists could not believe their eyes as they took in the spectacle of hundreds and hundreds of well preserved soft-bodied animals in fossil form.

Relating science to people *(see Analysis [6.6], p. 153)*.

In the process of describing, drawing and classifying these fossils, a fascinating thing happened. Whittington, Briggs and Conway Morris came to an interesting conclusion [6.6]. Many of these fossils were not ancestral to present day forms. Some were of course, but many others, for reasons we cannot know, were evolutionary dead ends. They were not survivors through time and today leave no ancestors. This conclusion dramatically changes a diagram of the 'tree of life' so often depicted in biology. I will return to the iconography of the 'tree' later. But for now, I suggest Walcott shoe-horned the fossils into existing taxa and the later examiners had a moment of insight (perhaps a eureka moment) where they said something like: 'Wait a moment, the branching tree version of natural history is not supported by these fossils! We need a new tree with most of the branching at its base and only some limbs surviving to the present.' No one can explain how these moments of insight happen, but when they do happen we have a major shift in how we understand some aspect of science [1.3].

Observation is theory laden *(see Analysis [1.3], p. 98)*.

I have now recounted this story many times in a variety of classes. The students are always, without fail, engaged and interested. It's a good story and they know it. Also, it's not unusual for students to inform me, weeks later, that they have begun to read Gould's book for themselves. I follow up the story telling with some overhead transparencies of a few of the drawings of Burgess Shale fossils. We pretend we are Walcott and try to consider what each fossil might be ancestral to in present day forms [5.12]. This is a game of sorts. We examine body structure and make predictions. In examining the fossil

Learning is situated *(see Analysis [5.12], p. 144)*.

drawings we can, as a class, conclude to what extent a particular fossil might be ancestral. For example, students have suggested that these fossils that I show them might be ancestral to a sow bug, a shrimp or a flatworm (planaria).

Students know that Walcott and, later, Wittington, Briggs and Conway Morris had more information at their disposal, but that in some ways we are simulating a process similar to theirs [1.7]. Using diagrams, and not the real fossil, we speculate on the possible classification of these unusual organisms. The students seem to enjoy the, albeit contrived, guessing/predicting game. I always end with the diagram of Hallucigenia. It is an odd, weird specimen. I use it to show how difficult the process of classification is, and also to show the conclusion that this specimen might be a dead end is logical. Finally, I show them diagrams of the 'tree of life' iconography: the traditional tree (or cone of increasing diversity) and then the reinterpreted tree (or decimation and diversification). These two diagrams invariably lead to student questions, as they sometimes struggle to put all of these ideas together [9.12]. As a class, we discuss what it means for the fossils (that most are dead ends) and then compare this notion with what we know about body structure among modern taxa of the animal kingdom (for example, many, many organisms are arthropods).

Experiments are set in a particular theoretical framework (see Analysis [1.7], p. 100).

Students think about the construction of scientific knowledge (see Analysis [9.12], p. 190).

Once it seems that all students are clear about how the fossils have been reinterpreted, then we consider why this shift in interpretation took place [3.8]. This is fun for students and even though it is totally speculative, it demonstrates how many perspectives we have within our class. Some will say that the UK team of scientists were smarter, more careful, more open to a new ideas. Others will say it's all luck. Yet others will ask how we know that this newer interpretation is correct after all [3.10] or if there is some even better answer waiting ahead for us. This last point, and it usually arises, is my perfect lead-in to share with them that the story does indeed continue to change (for example, Hallucigenia has been re-described recently).

Students are learning not only to talk science but also epistemology (see Analysis [3.8], p. 122).

Through excitement of engagment in a topic, students became motivated to learn and feel empowered (see Analysis [3.10], p. 124).

Eventually we turn to their textbook to see what is written there. Without fail, their textbook contains very little of this rich story. There is usually a mention of the importance of this fossil find and sometimes a drawing of Hallucigenia (odd since it is not a representative Burgess fossil), but little else. Some texts even continue to portray the tree of life iconography as some form of a cone of increasing diversity. I use this opportunity as a example to point out my bias that the textbook, as valuable as it can be, is limited. As a class, we sometimes critique the issue of data collection in the practice of science. How is science affected by the process of designing an experiment and collecting data versus data 'finds' or data that is 'out there', such as fossils [1.14]?

Science can be biased (see Analysis [1.14], p. 104).

In bringing the lesson to a close, I raise two final questions for the class to ponder. First, I ask them to consider what this story tells us about the nature of science. As a class, we sometimes brainstorm what insights this example provides into the practice of science. This part of the lesson is unpredictable and depends on the particular mix of students within the group. Some students will be engaged in exploring the question, what makes an endeavour science? While others are persistent in the notion that science, if done 'properly', will yield 'good' results [4.11]. They are resistant to the idea that it is not a simple algorithm to be carefully followed.

The ideas students bring to teaching may prove very tenacious *(see Analysis [4.11], p. 131).*

Finally, I ask the class to consider what makes a good scientist and what we have learned about who can be a scientist. At this point, we can make a list of what characteristics and qualities the scientists in this story have. There is huge variety among what students say and perhaps some projection of their own beliefs. In the end, the student-generated list of characteristics usually includes: scientists are hard working, persistent, open to new ideas, careful and lucky! I take the opportunity to point out to them that scientists are not unlike themselves.

Student reactions

Scientific knowledge is negotiated *(see Analysis [1.8], p. 101).*

Overall, student reactions are mixed, and I suppose in some ways predictable. Students sometimes embrace this story. It seems to confirm what they knew or suspected – that science is not definitive. Some understand my message that scientific knowledge outcomes are affected by scientists and that the results are not static [1.8]. Results change with new evidence but also depend on who the scientist is. Interpretation of data is in some ways a personal reaction. Another individual asking a different question might react to the same data in a different way. Some students reject the message. They feel that if a part of scientific knowledge is changed, reinterpreted or modified then it was not done 'properly' or thoroughly in the first place. For them, the story of the Burgess Shale tells them that Walcott was a sloppy scientist, and those that followed him were more careful, less rushed in their thinking and so more accurate in their conclusions. I cannot expect all my students to have 'nature of science epiphanies' from one example, but this is a wonderful story and, without fail, it gets them thinking [8.7].

The disguise of dilemma *(see Analysis [8.7], p. 179).*

Over the years some students have taken my suggestions and read Gould's whole book. Some have done other research to find out the current status of the classification of Burgess Shale fossils, since some continue to be re-examined and re-classified. I think that the students see that science does, in some ways, begin with a question and who gets to ask questions, and that how those questions are researched is never neutral. I believe that students begin to see that it *does* matter who does the asking. I also believe that they begin to see science as socially constructed and culturally determined [1.15].

Different people will 'do' science in different ways, and therefore contribute in a variety of ways. My intent is also for students to see the possibilities within science, rather than only the barriers they face or the personal limitations they perceive [6.8]. I want students to see that science is done by people, and that scientists are not so much exact and perfect as persevering [8.5; 10.4]. I cannot say that the story of the Burgess Shale is the important penny that drops for my students. However, I suggest that many of these sorts of examples show students they too are able to have questions that could be pursued, and can also potentially do science, become scientists and, therefore, generate knowledge themselves [3.11; 6.8; 6.7].

Learning from the past

My goal for this lesson is to address the nature of science and how I, as a teacher, might portray it [10.8]. What is the image of science in student-accessed resources? How is the nature of science examined and taken up for discussion within classrooms? How is it understood by my students regardless of their age, background or future aspirations? I want all of my students to see themselves as having the capability of entering into the culture of science.

Why do some students love biology (or science) and some hate it? Why docs 'scientist' become a career choice for so few? For many students, the experience of school science is foreign and difficult. It involves memorization and little of the interpretative features of science practice [4.2]. Students see science as a foreign culture, which is perhaps a little like travelling to a foreign country where a tourist does not speak the language and cannot read the road maps. Students feel lost and alienated. Most don't see scientists as real people, and they don't see scientists as 'like themselves' [9.1]. Many students see themselves as 'not smart enough' or 'not good at memory work', and so not fit to be scientists.

Science class, too often, leaves out the stories of the practitioners of science. The science that students learn (often from a textbook) seems to have been born in the text, not in the mind, work, sweat, tears, frustrations and pleasures of the working scientist [6.13]. I want all students to see themselves as potentially able to enter science in spite of barriers they face from race, class and gender.

However, I do not want to address these issues by parading by minority groups or women scientists in what I would call a weak attempt to be inclusive. I want to find examples illustrating that who you are will influence the work you do, the questions you ask, and the lens you look through as you collect and analyse data. Since people

Science is a culturally located activity (see Analysis [1.15], p. 105).

Developing a positive relationship with knowledge is axiomatic in learning (see Analysis [6.8], p. 154).

The expedience of epistemology (see Analysis [8.5], p. 176).

Problematize science (see Analysis [10.4], p. 196).

Students participate in developing solutions for issues/problems that are relevant and thoughtful (see Analysis [3.11], p. 125).

Making science more interesting and relevant (see Analysis [6.7], p. 154).

Promote realistic conceptions of the nature of science and its relationships among sciences, technologies, societies and environments (see Analysis [10.8], p. 199).

Knowledge cannot be simply transferred from teacher to student (see Analysis [4.2], p. 128).

Scientists are real people (see Analysis [9.1], p. 186).

Science is more than an emotion-free objectification of the world (see Analysis [6.13], p. 158).

Socio-cultural
construction of science
*(see Analysis [9.11], p.
190)*.

do science, it matters who those people are [9.11]. Many types of people should enter the field, because only then will we have multiple and diverse perspectives, and I would argue, better science in the future. As I construct my curriculum, I strive to include an honest view of science as a practice.

Account 7
Motivating the unmotivated: relevance and empowerment through a town hall debate

Susan A. Yoon

Encounters of an accidental kind

I used to see Mitchell sitting on the floor outside of the science room every other day, with no books in hand and looking solemn. I would stop and tease him a little about being kicked out of class again. I often quipped about making sure he was one of my students next year, so that he could make up for all the learning opportunities he had missed. There was typically no response, just an embarrassed smile and a cowered head. Our interactions were a far cry from the descriptions of outrageous behaviour his teacher would regularly speak of during our department meetings.

Mitchell was a popular, athletic and good-looking boy with average intelligence. He had a loud, articulate voice and often held off-topic, disruptive discussions with students around him; a compensatory strategy he likely developed to mask the learning barriers he experienced in reading and writing. He was not alone in facing these challenges.

When the teaching assignments were announced in early August of the following school year, I found out that I would be teaching 9B science. One-third of the students in the class were designated with moderate to serious forms of cognitive and social difficulties. Another third were low or underachievers, a few of whom were waiting for special education assessments. The last third were among the highest achieving in grade 9 (age 15), placed specifically in this class to be role models, and because they were especially good-natured and patient students. I also found out that this would be the first year that a special education resource teacher would *not* be assigned to this class. There were many more variables to consider, not the least of which was the fact that I had no formal special education training.

Fortunately, I was also 9B's staff adviser (form tutor), which meant that I was involved in working with the students on guidance-related issues such as improving organizational, study and social skills. In the staff adviser programme, I drew on a number of cooperative learning and community-building approaches such as shared problem solving using 'think aloud', role play, simulations and collaborative group discussions [6.4].

A collaborative environment helps promote mastery orientations *(see Analysis [6.4], p. 152).*

As is usually the case, we were given a number of extra time-tabled periods during the first weeks of September to focus on staff adviser goals. This time proved to be absolutely invaluable that year, as I was able to acquire a sound understanding of each student's character early on. As a class, we reviewed collaborative discussion techniques such as listening without interrupting, turn-taking and using affirmative language.

Once these skills were sufficiently practised, I found that there was little variation between students regarding analytical reasoning skills, motivation to participate and conceptual understanding of guidance topics. For example, in small group discussions concerning an issue on drugs and peer pressure, a heated debate ensued over a situation that had occurred with one of the students. Everyone had an opinion and everyone felt they were able to contribute. Mitchell was always especially vocal during these sessions, and he was very rarely off task.

I believe the success of the staff adviser (form tutor) programme was largely due to the fact that each of the topics resonated with an aspect of the students' lives. They were using familiar vocabulary, exchanging and negotiating ideas from their experiential knowledge and making decisions based on a range of diverse beliefs and real-world evidence. In addition, I believe that allowing students to participate in alternative forms of learning opened avenues for some students to actively construct and display their knowledge. For students like Mitchell, who had a greater oral capacity relative to other language modes, talking through concepts enabled him to relate both to his peers and with the content [6.10; 8.7].

Developing learners' opinions of themselves as learners *(see Analysis [6.10], p. 156).*

The disguise of dilemma *(see Analysis [8.7], p. 179).*

There were, however, some major differences between the students with special educational needs and the other students. Where the latter had adopted strategies for regulating their own learning, such as planning strategically when studying for evaluations and monitoring their own progress, the students with special educational needs seemed to lag behind in this area of development. Furthermore, when more difficult concepts arose with unfamiliar terms and vocabulary, the students with special educational needs had a higher tendency towards demonstrating low self-efficacy characteristics, such as giving up more readily and feeling helpless. I believe this lack of metacognitive awareness played a pivotal role in the students' achieving success. However, I also understood that all students when faced with new learning challenges, whatever they may be, need to be provided with appropriate and timely scaffolds to bridge the gap between experience and new levels of competencies. This latter notion was, and still remains, a core belief in teaching for me.

In order to fully comprehend what new levels of competencies entail, a focus needs to be placed on highlighting avenues for investigating a broad range of influences and perspectives. During that first month, I came to understand that, although students in 9B were working through their own specific learning challenges, with the right scaffolds they all had the potential to achieve success.

The outdoor education centre

In late October of that year, I was given an opportunity to take one of my classes to our local outdoor education centre. It was the perfect chance to combine some of the insights gained in 9B's staff adviser programme with our focus in science, which was at the time, understanding the nature of science; that it is, among other things, a socially constructed enterprise, where decisions are based on critical evaluation of multiple points of view and influences in society.

Before our visit, I met with one of the outdoor education staff members to discuss what the day would look like. Among the usual list of choices, such as team-building, environmental clean-up and orienteering activities, she mentioned that a family of beavers had moved into the area and that the centre was considering whether or not to relocate them. Their presence was creating some environmental changes in the forest ecosystem. This inspired me to ask if she would consider running a special event for my class [3.4].

Real-life issues create powerful opportunities for organizing science curriculum (see Analysis [3.4], p. 119).

Getting into role

We constructed a role-play activity in which students would act as representatives from six special interest groups (SIGs) [10.6; 2.6; 3.2; 5.10; 10.8]. These had specific concerns about the beaver issue. Two students were assigned to a SIG and provided with the following role information:

Role play promotes an understanding of different arguments and positions (see Analysis [2.6], p. 112).

Provide students with an apprenticeship for development of expertise for knowledge creation in science and technology (see Analysis [10.6], p. 198).

Drama and role play can challenge traditional images of science while addressing cultural, political

- *Science Teachers' Alliance:* you have interests in teaching about ecology, animal rights and preservation of species. You are concerned that students will not have an opportunity to see how movement of beaver populations can effect ecosystems. Outdoor education centres have an important place in the curriculum. You feel that altering the natural circumstances of the land will diminish the value of educational experiences.

- *Federation of Local Naturalists:* you believe that everything in and social contexts *(see Analysis [3.2], p. 118)*.

All learning is embodied *(see Analysis [5.10], p. 143)*.

Promote realistic conceptions of the nature of science(s) and relationships among sciences, technologies, societies and environments *(see Analysis [10.8], p. 199)*.

nature is beautiful and serves a purpose and humans have encroached on land originally belonging to animals and not the other way around. You consider the beaver's life to be of equal value to a human's. Forest ecosystems should not be tampered with. The natural course of succession should be allowed to take place.

- *Parks and Recreation Municipality*: you are interested in keeping the parks in pristine shape. Beavers entering the system could mean spending money to clean up the potential mess. Trees would be in danger if a flood was created by a beaver dam, and people will not be able to enjoy the parks in their usual way.

- *United Farm Owners*: if a dam is erected by the beavers, your farmland could be flooded. You are a struggling farm owner. This is how you make a living and put your kids through school. The beavers erecting a dam would mean that a good portion of your land will be under water rendering your land useless for farming.

- *Local residents:* you are concerned about your homes and gardens being destroyed by a flood and your children playing near deep water. You have attended many meetings to discuss this issue and feel that your sentiments represent the majority of the people who live in your community. A beaver dam could have grave consequences, ranging from safety issues with your children to economic problems if your homes and gardens become flooded.

- *News reporter:* you have been following this issue in the news and are being asked to do a cover story. You need always to consider your viewers and what they may be thinking about the issue. After all, you want them to tune in not tune out. You must make some decisions about whether the beavers have a right to stay or not.

Three students were also assigned to be Town Hall Council Members and were given this description:

- *Town hall council members*: you have no opinion on the matter before you listen to the various special interest groups. Your job is to travel through the site inspection with the other people and jot down some ideas. You are not to listen to the pleas of any special interest groups along the way. You will listen only during the town hall meeting and make a decision about whether the beaver stays or goes.

On previous occasions when I used the strategy of role play, I normally allowed students to research which groups in society had a vested interest in the specific issue. I asked them to determine, on their own, which side of the issue they advocated. However, in this case, given the exceptional circumstances of the class, and the fact that this was the first role-play activity we had attempted that year, I felt it necessary to provide them with some minimal guidelines. In effect, assigning the roles and outlining their positions were strategies for scaffolding used to facilitate conceptual organization. It should be noted however, that in subsequent role-play and simulation activities, students were given full control of these decision-making processes with the resulting learning outcomes being highly successful [5.3].

Students were told that, as members of the SIGs and Town Council, they would be travelling to the beaver's habitat to survey the surrounding environment. Here, they would assess the risks and benefits to both the environment and society, and gather evidence to be used later in a town hall meeting. In order to organize their observations, the following worksheet was provided as an additional support [3.6; 2.10]:

Community-based projects lead naturally to problem solving in real-life contexts *(see Analysis [5.3], p. 140)*.

Name of Special Interest Group:
Group members:

You will need to take notes about the beaver issue. You might find the headings below helpful in forming your argument. Your argument needs to be presented at the town hall meeting, back at school. Remember to analyse the issue critically, you need to understand all the various perspectives and put forward convincing evidence to back up your arguments.

What is the issue?
What are the risks to the environment?
What are the benefits to the environment?
What are the risks to society?
What are the benefits to society?

Careful scaffolding assists students in developing their arguments *(see Analysis [3.6], p. 121)*.

Writing frames scaffold students' generation and evaluation of arguments *(see Analysis [2.10], p. 113)*.

On the morning of our site visit, the staff at the outdoor education centre greeted the students as if they were in their special interest group roles and ushered them into a conference room where refreshments, name tags and handouts were waiting. For the first hour and a half, the staff presented information about the history of the outdoor education centre using historical documents and a short film. The topography and climate patterns of the region were presented through maps and charts. Statistical information about the growth in population of the area over time, and density of urban residents was also given. Finally, information about the flora and fauna, unique environmental characteristics such as erosion patterns and type of forest ecosystem was discussed.

Sitting in their SIGs, students were given time to collaborate, record the information and ask questions. Observing their interactions, I noticed that each and every student took their role seriously. Also, during group discussions, several of the SIGs with mutual interests in the issue came together to help each other form arguments. One local resident approached the Parks and Recreation Municipality to say that the construction of the storm drain at the bottom of the valley originally cost the city a great deal of money, and if the beaver dam disrupted the flow of water into the drain during a storm, more money would need to be spent to prevent a flood.

Elsewhere, a member of the Science Teachers' Alliance group talked to the Federation of Local Naturalists to figure out what the term 'succession' meant. Both groups decided that this might be a key concept to understand in order to construct their argument, and promptly enlisted the aid of one of the outdoor education staff. The Discovery Channel reporters decided to split up and visit with members of the various SIG groups to listen and contribute to their discussions [3.9]. All of this occurred without prompting from me.

After lunch, equipped with pens and clipboards, we walked through the outdoor education grounds. Our guide pointed out various signs that revealed the variety of animals inhabiting this forest ecosystem. Students took note of deer, racoon and fox tracks, listened to calls from black-capped chickadees and the sound of woodpeckers tapping the trees for insects. They watched as the leader dissected some scat that exposed remnants of undigested mouse bone and fur. Each time we came across a new species of tree (predominantly black oak, birch, cedar and maple) the leader stopped and had the students observe the differences in root formation, trunk cover and leaf structure [1.1; 1.3; 3.9; 4.3; 10.2].

As we moved closer to the beaver 'catchment' area, we saw how various parts of the ecosystem changed. The water level of the large stream that ran into the river was visibly deeper. Several small trees had fallen and many showed signs of beaver teeth markings. Where the dam was being constructed, much of the terrain was submerged under water, including the hiking trail that normally led to the other side of the river. Students took some time to survey the territory and discuss the risks and benefits to the environment.

On our walk back, the leader showed us spots where the flood, resulting from Hurricane Hazel in 1954, had eroded the land. Nearing the end of the hike, she also made us aware of the number and location of residential houses encompassing the region. Students were given time to assess the beaver issue in terms of the risks and benefits to society.

Engaging in thoughtful decision making requires consideration of multiple viewpoints, gathering of information and critical analysis *(see Analysis [3.9], p. 123)*.

Observation is theory laden *(see Analysis [1.3], p. 98)*.

Scientific observation has to be taught *(see Analysis [1.1], p. 98)*.

Making learning 'concrete' will help many learners to relate to science concepts *(see Analysis [4.3], p. 128)*.

Make the abstract concrete and, where appropriate, contextualize it *(see Analysis [10.2], p. 195)*.

The town hall meeting [6.5]

Back at the school, the students took a few days to consolidate their positions and do further research [4.8]. It is important to note that apart from the initial structure offered to the students prior to the site visit, I had no further substantial input into the learning events that followed. During the lunch hour of the day of the town hall meeting, several of the special interest groups came into the science classroom early to discuss last minute additions and deletions to their arguments. They drew maps and charts on the chalkboard and changed into role attire. The three members on the town council, including Mitchell, used a sheet they had designed to record notes. This listed all of the special interest groups and their potential positions [3.5].

In the role of town council chair, Sumeet welcomed the special interest groups to the town hall meeting: 'We have gathered today to discuss an issue of great concern to the various constituents of our local outdoor education community', he began. 'Each special interest group will have three minutes to state their respective positions which will be followed by three minutes of questions and answers from other groups, and then two minutes of clarification and discussion led by town council members.' The representatives from the Parks and Recreation Municipality spoke first. In their argument, they discussed the economic costs to the city if a large storm hit the area, and flooding of the river was to occur due to the blocking of drainage pipes from the beaver dam. In their additional research, they also found statistics that tracked the urbanization patterns in the city. They stated that in 1950, roughly 15 per cent of the area was urbanized. In 1994 the number had jumped to 80 per cent, with a projected rate in the year 2021 at 91 per cent based on an estimated population of 6.7 million. They noted that given the closeness of residential houses to the outdoor education centre and the growth in urbanization, the risks to society would be great if the beaver family was allowed to remain.

The Federation of Local Naturalists asked what they planned to do with the beavers once they were moved. The parks and recreation group replied that they would find a more suitable place for them to live. Tara, the third member on the town council, pointed out that the beaver family was living in its natural habitat and moving it would be like forcing it to leave its home. Sumeet added that vacating the beavers was a serious issue and asked what would happen if they could not adapt to their new surroundings. One of the local residents voiced the opinion that if the beavers were able to adapt to the environment of the outdoor education centre, they would be able to adapt in many other areas. He added that many local areas contain spaces with similar environmental and geographic characteristics, such as fresh water lakes and rivers and large forested areas. Mitchell

Mastery orientation goal encourages higher order reasoning skills *(see Analysis [6.5], p. 152).*

Learning is likely to be incomplete and fragile unless reinforced *(see Analysis [4.8], p. 129).*

Students engage in the consideration of multiple viewpoints and critical analysis through role play in order to better understand various stakeholder positions and controversy *(see Analysis [3.5], p. 120).*

brought up the fact that if the decision was made to move the beavers, finding a new place for them to live, gathering them up, shipping them off and then monitoring their ability to adapt would cost a lot of money and would likely raise taxes.

The United Farm Owners spoke next. Using a map they had drawn on the front chalkboard, which showed the location of several farms around the periphery of the outdoor education centre grounds, they argued that the beavers should be relocated. This was due to the potential risks and costs involved if valuable farmland was flooded. They reasoned that many of the crops grown on their farms, such as pumpkin and corn, were sold in local markets. If a disaster struck, prices would increase astronomically.

To alleviate some financial strains on the general public, the United Farm Owners suggested the special interest groups that had a vested interest in seeing the beavers relocate should pool their resources. Sumeet asked whether the farmers had considered moving their farms to different plots of land. One parks and recreation representative rebuked, if the beavers had difficulties adapting to a new environment, surely the farmers would have an equally, if not a much more difficult, time adapting to a new piece of farm land. Sumeet responded that the farmers were different from the beavers. The farmers could utilize farming aids such as fertilizers to improve the success of their crops. However, the beavers' abilities to survive was dependent on the availability of natural resources.

After carefully considering many of the arguments, one news channel reporter offered a solution: 'Moving the beaver isn't just for the benefit of the residents around them,' she began, 'it's also for the benefit of the beaver. Instead of leaving them in an area where they are around homes and people, put them in their natural environment and natural habitat where they will be around other beavers. Also, if you take a better look at it, it costs more to relocate the farmers than to take the time to research where to find an appropriate place for the beavers to live. We're not saying move them overnight. We're saying take the time to move the beavers where they can be happy and where everyone will benefit in the long run.'

The reporter's solution seemed to summarize all the arguments presented so far in the meeting. There were, however, a few more special interest groups to come. Both the Federation of Local Naturalists and the Science Teachers' Alliance groups put forward convincing arguments for keeping the beavers at the outdoor education site. They suggested that rather than reading about ecological changes in textbooks, students would be able to visualize first hand how small perturbations in one part of the ecosystem could lead to large and unpredictable effects in other parts. They further stated, because humans held a powerful position within the broader ecological framework, it was incumbent on them to be stewards of the Earth.

Humans should therefore make prudent decisions based on the needs of all living organisms, and not simply around their own needs [1.16]. Many of the students agreed with these statements.

Science can be redirected (see Analysis [1.16], p. 105).

The class discussion seemed to pause for a brief moment while they pondered the complexity of the issue. Mitchell finally broke the silence by saying, 'I have a little question for you. You say that students will not be able to visualize them first hand ... but we also have zoos around here ... there [a zoo] is first hand for you.' This comment again triggered a whole slew of reactions [3.7]. The representatives from the Science Teachers' Alliance became visibly agitated. They challenged this statement by saying that animals placed in cages could in no way mirror the reality of animals observed in their natural habitats. The Science Teachers' Alliance also mentioned that students in urban areas were already deprived of valuable outdoor experiences and that putting further limits on their ability to learn was only making the situation worse. Moreover, they reasoned, people were not placed on Earth to dominate the whole of nature. All living beings had an equal right to exist in their chosen space. Sumeet then asked, if all living beings had an equal right to existence, where did the rights of the trees factor into all of this? A local resident added, 'and we also need trees. As you very well know, trees play a huge part in purifying the air, taking out the carbon dioxide and other impurities. We need to consider this aspect as well [3.10].'

Talk can mediate student learning allowing for shared perspective and orientation (see Analysis [3.7], p. 121).

The last group to speak was the local residents. Their main argument stemmed from concerns for the safety of their children, who normally spent recreational time in a section of the outdoor education grounds. They believed that moving the beavers was a small price to pay for securing a feeling of comfort in the neighbourhood. 'But ensuring that your children are safe is the responsibility of parents,' one of the science teachers responded. 'You have to make sure that you are keeping an eye on your kids as they play in your backyard and other places around.'

Through excitement and engagement in a topic students become motivated to learn and feel empowered (see Analysis [3.10], p. 124).

This fruitful and heated discussion continued for several more minutes. I filmed the entire interaction during the town hall meeting to capture the incredible motivation and excitement that had been generated from this activity. I believe, however, that students already understood the level of excitement in the classroom.

While the town councillors were out of the room trying to reach consensus, students continued to discuss the pros and cons of the issue. When the town council was ready to announce their decision, the first moments of silence in 50 minutes of debating fell over the class. Mitchell started to speak: 'After considering all of the perspectives heard here today, we have come to the conclusion that allowing the beavers to stay in their present area at the outdoor education centre poses greater risks than benefits to both the environment and society.' Tara added, 'We understand and agree that the welfare of the beavers is of utmost importance and we are prepared to devote substantial funding towards seeking out the best possible alternative for the beavers' new home.' Sumeet concluded, 'We thank you all for your input and look forward to seeing you at our next town council meeting [3.11].'

Students participate in developing solutions for issues/problems that are relevant and meaningful *(see Analysis [3.11], p. 125)*.

I am not overestimating when I say the atmosphere in class was one of sheer jubilance [4.16]. I heard students laughing and talking about the meeting on their way out of the door and through the hallways. When I walked into the locker area, I saw one of the brightest students in 9B pat Mitchell on the back and say, 'Great job!' Mitchell's former science teacher, whose classroom was next door to mine, poked her head in the door after school and asked what the excitement was all about. We sat together for ten minutes and watched the video. She was truly amazed at Mitchell's level of engagement. Science turned out to be one of the most successful academic subjects for Mitchell, and for a number of students in the class [9.5].

·Different abilities and perspectives are highlighted in group work *(see Analysis [9.5], p. 188)*.

Two years later, the beaver issue and town hall meeting activity is now the outdoor education centre's most popular programme. The beavers have remained in the area and have now built two dams. Several human-made and environmental structural changes have occurred to accommodate them, and for the most part, everyone seems to be content.

Account 8
Mentoring students towards independent scientific inquiry

Alex Corry

A teacher transformed

Early in my career, the breadth of scientific knowledge fascinated me. This inspired me to want to infuse the desire for knowledge in my students. It soon became clear to me that not all if not most students shared my passion. Yes, they wanted to learn, but of greater importance was the achievement of a credit. I became dismayed, and had to rethink what I wanted students to really be able to do, and how they were to demonstrate their knowledge [8.8].

Motive of morality *(see Analysis [8.8], p. 180)*.

I now believe it's not what the students know, but rather how they *use* their knowledge that is most important [6.9]. Therefore, I structure lessons around what students currently know and want to know and then piggyback the 'curriculum' on exploring their beliefs. To help them with exploring their beliefs, I provide several lessons and activities that are meant to improve their abilities to carry out inquiry projects similar to those conducted by scientists.

Utility value is an articulated feature of this pedagogy *(see Analysis [6.9], p. 154)*.

An apprenticeship for scientific inquirers

Before grade 9 (age 15) students begin to learn about particular scientific concepts, such as structure and behaviour of atoms and molecules, they learn several scientific skills, including: question and hypothesis development, measurement, graphing, data analysis and reporting [1.10; 8.5]. At the same time it is important that they learn such skills in relation to particular topics. So I start their course with an inquiry unit that gets them to focus on biological, physical, chemical, and earth science concepts related to the general theme of water.

Learning through apprenticeship is important *(see Analysis [1.10], p. 101)*.

The expedience of epistemology *(see Analysis [8.5], p. 176)*.

In getting them to learn some skills through their interactions with water in different contexts, I first point out to them that any observations they make about phenomena, such as water, will be

We need to teach students about observation *(see Analysis [1.2], p. 98)*.

theory laden [1.2]. For this, we use a variety of optical illusions and then discuss issues relating to validity, reliability and certainty. For example, using the image below, students are asked 'which line is longer?'

Having hopefully convinced the students that observing something tells them more about what's in their minds than what is 'true', I get them to make as many observations as possible about some objects and events that we set up around the room. Most, if not all, stations will contain objects from their common everyday experiences. These include various brands of sealed carbonated drinks, cans floating (or not) in an aquarium, eggs immersed in salt water, oils of various viscosities, pond life, limp and turgid celery sticks and tea bags in hot and cold water [4.15, 8.6].

Sometimes teachers bring about conceptual change by challenging student expectations *(see Analysis [4.15], p. 133)*.

The legacy of the laboratory *(see Analysis [8.6], p.178)*.

Developing scientific inquiry skills *(see Analysis [7.8], p. 165)*.

The stations are interactive and students are challenged to observe certain events with the use of cue cards. The cards provide some guidance by asking questions such as: 'What do you see?' 'What changes occur?' 'How could you measure these changes, and what do you think causes each change/event? [7.8]' This strategy is then adapted to future units, courses and grades, using objects and events at stations that relate to key concepts from each unit.

After students have built up a rich stock of observations about water-related phenomena, we then use these to suggest strategies for developing questions that they might want to try to answer through their own inquiries. For example, a template is used (see below) that guides students to write their observations in the central box, variables they believe may result from each observation in the right-hand box and possible causes of their observations in the left-hand box [8.2]:

The immediacy of input *(see Analysis [8.2], p. 173)*.

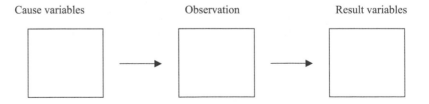

After the students have brainstormed sufficiently large lists of possible cause (independent) and result (dependent) variables, relating to their observations, they are asked to develop 'cause-result questions', using the following textual template: 'What is the effect of increasing (or decreasing) _____ on _____?' In the first blank, students place the cause variable that they believe to be the most likely to influence the event. The event itself is inserted into the second blank. If time permits, the students are asked to generate these types of questions for all the stations. A minimum of three questions is required by the conclusion of this lesson. I then ask the students to choose the one question that is most personally appealing. I inform them that the selected question will eventually be used by them to generate a hypothesis and self-directed inquiry. The idea that they will be allowed to perform their own investigation has great appeal to the students, and some may revise their question when they find out they will test their own ideas.

Anticipating carrying out their own inquiry projects also motivates students to think in terms of possible answers to their questions. This gives me a perfect opportunity to help students with how they might develop hypotheses and predictions. I try to do this in a number of ways [2.10; 4.17]:

- I present another template for the students to help them develop their own hypotheses (including predictions):

  If/As _____(cause variable)_____ is increased/decreased, then the _____(result variables)_____ will _____, because _____(the student's theory)_____ .

- The students are then asked to formulate their hypothesis based upon each of the questions they had previously generated. The hypothesis template, displayed on an overhead transparency, can be used to randomly add different cause and result variables, challenging the students to generate different hypotheses. This has been done as a mock game show – complete with teams, timers and awards.

- As a class, we share and develop a hypothesis. An event from the observation activity that students did not choose is used to collectively brainstorm cause and result variables.

- Students are given lists of cause and result variables and asked to suggest how combinations of them might relate and then to develop theoretical explanations for relationships between variables.

- Graphs are examined and the students explain correlations in the graphs and suggest potential hypotheses.

Writing frames scaffold students' generation and evaluation of arguments *(see Analysis [2.10], p. 113)*.

Language is a key mediator of learning, and the means by which learners explore new ideas *(see Analysis [4.17], p. 134)*.

- Scientific work reported in the popular media is used to generate or infer hypotheses.

- I sometimes read a short murder mystery to the students and asked them 'Who dunnit?' (and, 'How do you know?'), i.e. 'What are your hypotheses?'

- As a class, we make rubrics and checklists to assess their hypotheses. The students apply the assessment tools to their own and peers' hypotheses. A collection of sample hypotheses is distributed and we play 'you be the teacher', which means that the students evaluate the hypotheses with the assessment tools.

Eventually, the students become quite proficient at developing hypotheses and are able to generate them with excellent results. This is beneficial for future units, when we expect them to develop hypotheses without assistance. For example, I recently asked my grade 11 (age 16–17) biology students, 'What makes plants grow?' On the left of the chalkboard, I wrote down all the responses. I then asked, 'How do you know a plant is growing?' These responses were tabulated on the far right side of the chalkboard. In the middle, I quickly posted the hypothesis template and asked students to choose one from the left, two from the right, and give me a reason. In no time, the students had developed their hypotheses! At the same time I recognize that, no matter how good they are at developing hypotheses in general, their hypotheses depend on what scientific knowledge they have. Therefore, I make sure that I base my evaluations of their hypotheses on students' familiarity with different subjects in the course. In other words, I take into account that their hypotheses will improve as I cover the topics in each unit.

Referring again to the inquiry unit at the beginning of the course, after students have made observations, developed questions and conceptualized hypotheses, they are eager to develop their own investigations. Since ninth grade students tend to have relatively simplistic ideas about how to develop an experimental investigation, I provide them with another checklist, shown opposite:

Before challenging students to conduct their own scientific inquiries, I help them to use the checklist to set up a reasonable experiment. I do this in several ways, including as follows:

- I work with them on designing an experiment to test a fictitious hypothesis, such as, 'If the amount of sunlight is decreased, then plants will use less water because they do not drink as much to stay cool'.

- I get my students to peer- and self-assess 'experiments' from their science textbook and student work from a variety of sources, to see if these items meet the science criteria. A rubric that identifies

(✓)	Checklist for investigations	My decisions
	Measures the cause variable	
	Increases the cause variable	
	Measures the result variables	
	Repeats the observation	
	Averages results	
	Summarizes and organizes the data (charts and tables)	
	Reports the information	

each criteria and level of development is shared or developed by the class. Also, exemplary reports of different levels of proficiency are posted to use as benchmarks for their own performance.

- One year, the checklist was incorporated into a science T-shirt, awarded for outstanding students at the school recognition assembly.

- In future units, the template is reviewed and the students design without actually running an investigation. This technique allows the students to reflect and plan for inquiry, without actually doing the investigation.

After all of this work on questioning, hypothesizing and experimental design, my students are very comfortable with carrying out student-led scientific inquiries on topics that interest them [6.3; 1.10]. Usually, they have enjoyed them so much that they are eager to share their results, and are curious about their peer's investigations. This is a teachable moment whereby students can appreciate the importance of *reporting* in scientific inquiry. Their enthusiasm and energy is channelled into learning formal reporting procedures and other culturally specific methods of sharing knowledge.

Promoting learning autonomy promotes mastery orientation (see Analysis [6.3], p. 152).

Learning through apprenticeship is important (see Analysis [1.10], p. 101).

Again, I try to provide them with a variety of approaches for scientific tasks. They learn various components of a traditional lab report in a role-playing fashion. I tell the students to think of themselves as a government organization that screens scientific research. I ask them what they would want to know about the research if a group approached the screening body (students) for permission or funding for a scientific investigation. What questions would they ask? Their questions tend to serve as an excellent guide, along with some I inject for how to frame a traditional lab report. These include guidelines for the introduction, materials and methods, results, discussion and bibliography sections [4.4].

Students are also challenged to use alternative reporting methods, such as: drawing cartoons, writing letters, creating stories and myths, developing dance routines and/or generating songs or even

The teacher needs to break the material to be taught into manageable 'learning quanta' (see Analysis [4.4], p. 128).

Alternative assessment *(see Analysis [9.7], p. 189).*

Effective teaching is available to students with different learning styles *(see Analysis [4.6], p. 129).*

pen poetry to illustrate what they have learned in their investigation [9.7; 4.6]. It can be a teachable opportunity for students to learn how knowledge from other cultures was/is recorded in such a fashion. To solidify this understanding, I actively seek stories to read to the class from indigenous peoples, supporting the life or earth sciences portion of the curriculum. My students have said such an opportunity to express learning is 'way better than what we did before'.

I am happy to say that, after all of this focus on particular skills for developing scientific inquiries, students need much less guidance in carrying out investigations in future units. An example of this relates to students' studies of chemical reaction rates (one of my favourite investigations) in their chemistry unit. After students have been introduced to concepts such as molecules, bonding, chemical change and chemical reactions [10.1], they are asked to observe a demonstration. Here, an Alka Seltzer® tablet and water are added to a film canister and sealed with the canister's lid. After a period of time, when some may believe it is yet another failed Mr C demonstration, the pressure builds and the lid forcefully pops off! The students are then asked questions such as:

Avoid induction; promote deduction *(see Analysis [10.1], p. 195).*

- What happened?
- Why did it happen?
- How could you make a bigger pop?
- How could you test your ideas?
- Can you share your findings with the class?

As they struggle through each question and answer, I prompt them with queries such as:

- What are the cause and result variables?
- How do you think increasing one variable will affect the other?
- What could be a potential hypothesis?
- How will you accurately test your ideas?

The variety of answers the class generates is astounding. They choose variables such as temperature, amount of reactants, types of reactants, size of canisters and numerous others. The students then rush to test their ideas. They have to be restrained to ensure all parts of the design/questions are answered prior to the testing date. The exuberance in the room is palpable as the students design tests of their own ideas!

Reflections on taking this route

Teaching a scientific inquiry unit in this fashion can cause some difficulty with students, as well as new staff, who may not believe they are actively learning science in this unit. To alleviate their spoken or unspoken concerns, lessons have agendas highlighting the intended learning matched to the government prescribed curriculum. Further, I initiate and close a lesson by stating, 'We are learning about scientific inquiry', and point out how the lesson has supported this end. I say, 'Today we will learn about ... observations ... We need this skill and will use such knowledge to allow us to ...'.

Teaching these concepts takes time and can be frustrating. If the time is invested initially, the remainder of the course and future courses taken by students, can reinforce and further develop the skills. By the time the students have taken two courses, they are usually able and expected to develop and run their own investigations without teacher intervention. A challenge is what to do with students that join our programme later in their high school career who do not share these prior learnings. The students and teachers are forced to make up for lost time by completing a self-directed 'catch up' study unit. This is not a great beginning to a new school and programme. To tackle this issue, we are currently exploring the use of student mentors to assist and guide such new students.

There are trials and tribulations to enacting a student driven programme. The students may feel a sense of unease when they are called upon to develop their own ideas. In the past, they may have been spoon-fed laboratory activities for which they copied and reproduced 'recipe/cookbook'-type laboratory tasks. When challenged to develop their own investigations they may become apprehensive as they wish to do the 'right' investigation and get the 'correct' answers. They have not gained the intellectual independence to plan and act on their own. There is always a student who can't believe there isn't a right answer!

Similarly, other students might say, 'I need to know the right answer. I'm trying to go to university'. With patience and time, even the most strident objector can be won over and students often say, 'this is neat, can I really do anything I want?' The answer is usually, 'yes,' after their investigations have been closely scrutinized and approved in regards to safety and equipment logistic.

Another challenge when instituting this type of unit is that students may formulate beliefs that scientific investigations and reasoning follow a linear pattern from observation and question development to testing and reporting. As the teacher, we have to gauge when they 'get it', and balance this against providing learning opportunities that refute this linear progression [1.11]. I often find the introduction of innovation and technology, or correlational

Timing of intervention is crucial *(see Analysis [1.11], p. 102).*

studies as venues, to illustrate how ideas may come after products (how they work), or data that indicates a potential hypothesis after the fact. I share with the students classic examples of the steam engine, or relationships such as smoking and lung cancer that were understood prior to the 'scientific' evidence or knowledge. It is beneficial to wait until later units before this piece is added. Also, once correlational and innovation investigations are later introduced, the same apprehensions will arise.

I am committed to this programme since students experience success, become excited about 'doing' science, and even increase their test scores. I hope that this testimony will lend strength to others who are following such a difficult path, or provide food for thought for those who are trying to introduce student-led investigations into their science programme. Good luck!

Account 9
Learning to *do* science

Gabriel Ayyavoo, Vivien Tzau and Desmond Ngai

Introduction

For students to develop expertise, enabling them to conduct scientific investigations and/or invention projects under their control, requires careful support from others along with considerable effort from the students. Support students get from the school system can be limited in cases where students attempt to function at levels approaching that of the 'expert'. In the documentaries provided below, two students (Vivien Tzau and Desmond Ngai) describe ways in which I (their teacher), and experts in various fields of professional science, assisted them in their journeys towards becoming practising scientists.

For over a decade, I have been promoting investigative work among secondary school students. While much of the motivation for students' involvement in science projects can be intrinsic, I also encourage students to become involved in *competitive* 'science fairs', including specialized fairs involving biotechnology. Generally, these are events in which students display, usually on elaborate poster boards, summaries of their science project work, which are then evaluated by a panel of judges.

Students receiving the highest ratings from judges on such categories as: 'scientific merit', 'oral presentation skills' and 'visual appeal' get various awards. These include, for example, certificates, ribbons, medals and trophies. Science fair competitions occur at various 'levels', enabling students to advance from school-level fairs through to regional and national events and, finally, the International Science and Engineering Fair.

Scientific investigations

To prepare students for conducting scientific investigations or invention projects of their design (whether for their own merits or, at students' discretion, for competition in the various levels of science fairs) I provide considerable guidance through a special part of my regular school science programming.

For approximately the first month of my grade 9s (age 15) and 10 (age 16) science courses, I devote about half (between 30 and 40 minutes) of each class period to activities intended to develop students' skills for conducting independent inquiry and/or technological design projects. For this portion of their education, each student records details of their developing investigative capabilities in a separate 'inquiry journal'. In examining these journals, and based on my comments, there are four general ways in which students are mentored in their journeys to becoming independent, scientific and technological investigators. I describe each of these briefly below.

Motivation

Generally, students entering my programme have not previously conducted science or invention projects of their design. Consequently, my first task is to motivate my students to become involved in project work and, if they so desire, competitive science fairs.

One of the strategies that I have successfully used, is to provide students with 'exemplars' of projects previous students in my programme have completed. These include viewing lists of possible project titles, photographs of equipment and supplies used in projects and video recordings of students' presentations regarding their projects. Through this sort of exposure to previous students' successes and difficulties, my students become less stressed and more motivated. Indeed, their level of comfort further increases as students realize that I encourage them to work on projects closely matching their particular interests and levels of conceptual and procedural expertise. I have found that this 'reassures their confidence' [6.7].

Making science more interesting and relevant (see Analysis [6.7] p. 154).

Topic choice

Related to motivation, is a student's ability to settle on a topic or goal for their scientific inquiries or technological design projects. My tack here is to personalize these choices as much as possible. This begins by asking students to brainstorm for homework five possible topics, and rank them from most to least desirable [6.7].

Students often have difficulties arriving at a project goal. So another strategy I use is to ask small groups of students to peruse a variety of magazines, from which they may glean possible areas of interest, for example, *Cosmopolitan*, *Sports Illustrated*, *Men's Health*, *Runners* and *Organic Gardening*. Eventually, and often with considerable prodding, students settle on an initial project topic or goal. While they are often surprised that I allow these to change as their knowledge and perspectives change, they are pleased to find constant and favourable support for modifications that improve their investigations.

Skill development

Having settled on an initial topic or goal, students are then faced with the often daunting task of designing a valid and reliable empirical investigation, which may provide evidence for various scientific or technological claims they might make [2.1]. To lower students' stress level about this, and to motivate them to operate more independently on their own projects, I provide a series of activities intended to help them develop expertise for various aspects of project work. These include: observing, questioning and hypothesizing, design of empirical tests, e.g. experiments, and project reporting [4.4].

To introduce students to questioning and hypothesis development, for example, I frequently use a demonstration involving a Cartesian Diver (see Figure 1) [5.9]. I pretend to move the eyedropper down the plastic lemonade bottle, filled with water, using a plastic pen that I have just rubbed against my shirt, apparently caused by some invisible – possibly static electrical – force. To make this happen, I actually slyly and gently squeeze the bottle, which forces water into the eyedropper, making it more dense and making it sink through the water.

Argument defined as a link between evidence obtained through empirical investigation and theoretical conclusions or claims *(see Analysis [2.1], p. 110)*.

The teacher needs to break the material to be taught into manageable learning quanta *(see Analysis [4.4], p. 128)*.

Learning is mediated by tools of the culture *(see Analysis [5.9], p. 143)*.

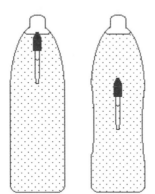

Figure 1   Cartesian diver.

Discussions that follow with students are often quite fruitful in helping them understand, for example, cause–result questioning, predicting outcomes of forced changes (for example, using a wooden pencil, instead of a plastic pen) and control of variables (for example, holding the pen at the same angle along the side of the pop bottle). Students are usually quite excited about being allowed to develop their own questions, hypotheses and prediction, and many find it difficult to believe they are allowed to predict and hypothesize like a scientist.

Beyond this I also conduct interactive lessons, in which students explore, analyse and sometimes critique published investigations in refereed journals, educational magazines and newspapers. To supplement these more teacher-directed lessons, students are invited to design and carry out short-term investigations on topics of their interest.

A typical 'mini project' students might design and conduct is to determine and explain effects of changes of pH on rates of fermentation of yeast, measured as a rate of carbon dioxide production. Mini-projects typically culminate in opportunities for students to report the progress of the projects to their classmates thereby helping students to develop more critical perspectives on their methods and conclusions, oral presentation skills and ideas for future project work. To assist students along these lines, I frequently engage them in analytical discussions relating to science fair projects conducted by other students that I have previously videotaped [2.4].

Reflections on other students' work provides a context for students to evaluate the quality of arguments *(see Analysis [2.4], p. 111).*

Student conferencing

Having been mentored in ways described above, students use ideas, strategies etc. gleaned from these lessons to develop their major course scientific investigations or invention projects [5.8]. This is the point at which my mentoring becomes more enabling than directive. Typically, I pose many more questions than possible answers or solutions for students' projects. For example, I might ask questions such as: 'Are you confident you have repeated your tests enough?'; 'What other factors could account for your results?'; and 'How confident are you about your methods of measurement?' I find that this can be quite time consuming and involve discussions with students over lunch periods, after school and via email in the evenings and weekends. Generally, this sort of conferencing works well with my younger students. One of my students recently said, 'I love discussing the findings with you, because it makes me feel important.'

However, for senior students, whose projects frequently require more 'expert' mentoring, I often encourage them to seek assistance from professional scientists and engineers working in colleges or universities. While only a small fraction of the researchers contacted by students for assistance get involved with projects, these often result in a 3-way link for discussions of students' topics. My continued involvement in these collaborations is essential, since professional mentors must frequently be reminded that the project is the students' own, and that they have the last say in it. Nevertheless, students want teachers and facilitators to be involved with their projects. Academic

In PBL learners negotiate socio-cultural meaning while solving problems in groups *(see Analysis [5.8], p. 142).*

discussions consolidate and reinforce their efforts, and students are thrilled to be involved with researchers, their research laboratories, university associations, numerous financial awards and to be getting peer admiration.

From students' points of view

Overall, because of this kind of support, many students I have taught experienced considerable success in gaining expertise for student-directed science and technology project work. In the following accounts, two of my former students provide some insights into the nature of this support. The first account emphasizes my programmatic mentoring [8.8]. The second elaborates on the support a student can receive from professional scientists and technologists, serving as mentors for advanced level projects conducted by secondary school students.

The motive of morality (see Analysis [8.8], p. 180).

School-based mentoring by *Vivien Tzau*

In my first science lesson during grade 9, I remember quite clearly the discussion of various scientific terms, including: observation, causal question, hypothesis and scientific methods. After that, Mr Ayyavoo, my grade 9 science teacher, assigned each of us to come up with three observations, causal questions and hypotheses.

At first, the task seemed rather tedious. However, with time, I found that this activity was, in fact, very insightful. It encouraged me to observe the world around me, and ponder why things happen the way they do. Last night, I managed to find my grade 9 science notebook. In one entry, I wrote about an observation on helium gas making people's voices awkwardly high-pitched. The causal question for this was: 'What is the effect of the amount of helium gas on the pitch of the voice?' My hypothesis was that the helium affects the voice by shrinking the vocal chords. Other causal questions that I came across in my notebook are based on personal experiences. One dealt with the effect of computer screens on the tiredness of the eye. Another dealt with the effect of the colour of foods on people's incentive to eat them.

I remember that ideas were shared among classmates and possible methods of conducting the experiments were discussed. I found that sharing ideas is extremely important, since it is the main method of scientific development in the real world [1.8]. Class discussions were also especially appropriate in grade 9, since it helped us familiarize with each other.

Scientific knowledge is negotiated (see Analysis [1.8], p. 101).

As I flipped through my notebook, I noticed that a majority of my causal questions centred around chemistry and biology. Little did I know back then that my interests were in this field. In my senior years of high school, my science projects dealt mainly with biotechnology, encompassing aspects from both biology and chemistry. This daily activity did not merely provide me with numerous ideas for potential science fair topics, it also helped me develop skills for forming a causal question and hypothesis, which are important steps in starting any experiment. Most importantly, it helped me discover my own interests within the broad field of science.

Another aspect of doing science involves the ability to make correlations between similar observations. In my grade 9 science notebook, I found a chart listing numerous activities and observations. One of these activities was an experiment about the reaction of calcium with water. I observed that bubbles formed, and rose from the calcium tablet, due to a reaction with water. In addition, I had to suggest other cases where similar observations are seen. So I wrote about the tablets placed in water to clean dentures, and the enzyme tablets used to clean contact lenses [4.3].

Making learning concrete will help learners relate to scientific concepts *(see Analysis [4.3], p. 128).*

When it came to doing my science fair projects, I had to draw correlations from past research done by other scientists, and further apply their findings in another situation. When I started researching for a potential topic on which to build my graduating year biotechnology project, I began with what interested me – food and the body. As I read, I was soon fascinated by the possible efficacy of garlic on eradicating cancer! The topic progressed to incorporate a Fijian plant found to have similar effects. What is it in these plants that makes them so effective on cancer cells?

This inquiry compelled me to investigate the chemical composition of the plants and, to my delight, I found similarities. These similarities in chemistry led to the production of several synthetic compounds, each with a slightly different composition or conformation. These compounds were then tested on various cancer cell lines, to observe whether a specific chemical conformation is needed for eradication of the cancer cells.

However, there is more to a successful science fair project than just causal questions, hypotheses and a student's own interests. Models also are essential. I remember that Mr Ayyavoo would always incorporate models into his lessons. In one particular class Mr Ayyavoo was discussing cytology. He amused us all when he asked for two pencils each from nine students. Creatively wrapping his hand around them, he arranged the two sets of nine pencils at right angles to one another. 'This,' he said while rotating his 3D model, 'is a crude depiction of how centrioles look from the front and side views.' This demonstration was definitely far more effective than if Mr Ayyavoo had just described centrioles as, 'microtubles arranged in a 9+3 pattern'. His model was especially helpful, since the components of a cell are not visible to the naked eye. From this lesson, I learned that models could be creative and effective, yet also economical [10.8; 1.9].

Later applications of Mr Ayyavoo's mentoring

The use of models was later applied in the presentation of my own science fair projects. I knew that many people are visual learners, and so in addition to explaining the molecular basis of my experiment using words, I also used models and flow charts [4.6]. Models of organosulphur compounds used in my graduating year biotechnology project, were made with chemistry model kits to help explain the role of chemical structure in the eradication of cancer cells. A blind test was performed using different compounds, as I wished to show that only compounds with a special disulphide linkage were effective. Furthermore, some models were made to portray the methodology of my experiment. For instance, I attached miniature test tubes made out of overhead projector acetate sheets. These were painted in diminishing shades of colour and increasing volumes to depict the progression of my dilutions.

I also remember my grade 12 year when I had to work on my biotechnology project under a tight budget. I had to come up with an economical way of obtaining fruit flies. Mr Ayyavoo shared with me a story about one of his own experiences with fruit flies and how he noticed their love for bananas. Using this knowledge, I cut up extra ripe bananas and placed them in several jars in the hope of attracting any fruit flies roaming around the school classrooms. I was delighted and filled with excitement [6.7] when I found a total of six fruit flies savouring the banana mush. From there, nature played its role and, after several generations, the number of specimens grew exponentially. This method proved to be affordable and fairly efficient, since the time needed to obtain a population in the range of hundreds took merely a few days.

As my experiments proceeded, I needed to collect data and analyse them. Collecting data is a fairly simple task, but analysing data is more difficult. Throughout my high school years taking science courses, I gradually learned how to be analytical and critical of my work. I remember learning about animal behaviour in the graduating year biology class. Mr Ayyavoo wanted us to get a taste of the strenuous work involved in real scientific work, so we journeyed to the Toronto Zoo in order to observe orang-utans and gorillas.

For hours, we tallied the occurrence of every action performed and made thorough notes on the environment. Mr Ayyavoo made us examine all the possible variables that could have caused the observed results (for example, the role that captivity played in the development of aggressive behaviour and whether aggressive behaviour, observed in captivity, is caused by an insufficient food supply, territorial

Promote realistic conceptions of the nature of science(s) and relationships among sciences, technologies, societies and environments *(see Analysis [10.8], p. 199).*

Scientists use models *(see Analysis [1.9], p.101).*

Effective teaching is available to students with different learning styles *(see Analysis [4.6], p. 129).*

Making science more interesting and relevant *(see Analysis [6.7], p. 154).*

confines, or is it innate behaviour?) Not only was this activity an interactive experience in observing and analysing data as real scientists (or so we would like to have thought), it was surprisingly enjoyable since the animals were so amusing!

The thought process developed after obtaining the data was extremely valuable. When it came to doing my own biotechnology project, I was able to execute the same level of critical thinking, essential in designing any convincing experiment. I say 'convincing' because I knew that any knowledgeable judge would question variables that could affect the outcome of my experiment, and then question whether I knew how to control these variables [1.7].

Experiments are set in a particular theoretical framework *(see Analysis [1.7], p. 100)*.

Positive and negative controls are essential elements of a good experiment. Positive controls assure the feasibility of the assay, and provide the experimenter with a basis to compare and interpret the assay results. Generally, positive controls are needed when the outcome of the assay is unclear. Negative controls test whether results of the experiment can occur by any other means. For example, in order to measure the number of cancer cells destroyed by the organosulphur compounds used in my experiment, an MTassay was performed. The MTassay is based on the fact that the number of cells present in the assay well is inversely proportional to the amount of light that passes through it.

However, to ensure that synthetic organosulphur compounds were the cause of cell death, rather than the procedure of the assay itself, a negative control was included. For instance, if no light is supposed to pass through the well composed of only cells and no compound, then any light that is found to pass through must be accounted for as error. This would serve as a negative control. A positive control would be a test using a cancer cell line that was subject to the same MTassay in other experiments. The result of this particular test is already known, and can be used to ensure the proper function of the assay itself. It can also be used to interpret the results obtained using the organosulphur compounds. Furthermore, duplicate tests were performed to ensure consistency in my results.

These were some of the aspects of critical thinking required of me to conduct a successful experiment with convincing results. Participating in the numerous class activities and lessons from which I learned my scientific skills paid off when I was awarded third place at the Connaught Student Biotechnology Exhibition in 1999. More significantly, I was provided with the foundations necessary for pursuing my career in the field of science.

Mentoring beyond the school by *Desmond Ngai*

My successes in scientific investigations and invention projects stem, to a great extent, from the mentoring I have received from experts

[10.7]. This mentoring extended beyond my school experiences. Through my science fair project, I worked with numerous experts who played a role in helping me to develop my winning projects, as well as extending my thinking as a young scientist. At the same time, Gabriel Ayyavoo was an inspiring educator, and provided much of the foundations for my achievements in independent scientific and technological project work. In all, my teachers, university-based mentors, fellow science fair competitors, parents, judges and my own project-based experiences, have helped me to see there are at least three factors that can contribute to a student's development as an independent investigator in science and technology. These are described below.

Promote social learning and assessment *(see Analysis [10.7], p. 199).*

Motivation to participate

To be able to compete successfully in science fairs, the teacher must show students how interesting science really is [3.10]. In today's education system, there is a substantial percentage of students who think negatively about science. Therefore, the teacher must show students certain experiments to illustrate that science can be very intriguing and is worth exploration. This approach was used by my long-time mentor, Dr Jamie Cuticchia. The first time we met he got me interested in genomics by taking me on a tour of his Bioinformatics Supercomputing Lab. There will be more on Dr Cuticchia later.

Through excitement and engagement with a topic, students become motivated to learn and feel empowered *(see Analysis [3.10], p. 124).*

Also, teachers must be prepared to give incentives to the students. Teachers need to share the successes of previous winners, and indicate the awards that they have received. These strategies enable students to see the potential value of doing a good science fair project, and putting in the time and effort to compete. They would also see the merit of obtaining scholarships and recognition. Moreover, to be successful at a national or an international competition, students must have the drive to work long hours, and be willing to sacrifice some things that might be deemed as necessities.

For me, the motivation for a national title and, eventually, a world title was the publicity and the personal success the 'elite of science fair' received. The motivation was maximized when my former mentor showed me a book about top winners of the 1996 International Science and Engineering Fair. From that moment on, I wanted to compete and win the fair. Six years later, I accomplished my goal.

Expert mentoring

While motivation is one thing, being able to do a successful project is another. Teachers must show their students how to conduct a science fair project. They need to teach students about things such as independent/dependent variables, causal questions, hypotheses, methods, observations, discussions and conclusions. These need to be explored in such a way that students can see and understand the relationships between the different aspects of scientific investigations. This is very important for teachers to do with their students, as it teaches them how to do an experiment in an internationally approved method.

I had to learn about this intricate hierarchy of the various dimensions of science experiments, before I was able to conduct a standard science fair investigation. That is what my teacher, Mr Gabriel Ayyavoo, did with me. As a result of his innovative methods for teaching science, Mr Ayyavoo has generated four national champions and one world champion. However, there is only so much a teacher in school can do once students begin competing at a higher level, such as at a national science fair. In this case, we can get a lot of support from professional scientists and engineers at universities [7.10; 7.16]. Although getting these experts to work with you is not easy.

A common technique used by Canada's top science fair competitors is 'the 2–20–100 rule'. If you write to 100 experts asking for assistance, 20 will respond to you and two will become your mentors. When I did this in the summer of 1998, it worked. Dr Schweighofer in California taught me how to write science fair proposals. In addition, Dr Wolfinbarger in Virginia sent me some materials to assist me with my experiments. These two experts were the stepping stones in my science fair career.

Another expert who supported me was Dr Jamie Cuticchia, former head of the Bioinformatics Supercomputing Lab, at the Hospital for Sick Children. I learned about him through a newspaper story about his research in genetics relating to children. He told me about the possibilities for investigations that could be conducted by a high school student. Dr Cuticchia also taught me some underlying principles of genetics, such as PCR, transcription and gene sequencing. He made those tough concepts extremely interesting and very easy to understand. That is what sparked my interest. His explanations of some highly complicated and intricate biological processes greatly benefited my understanding. Dr Cuticchia agreed to be my mentor and taught me how to use genetics textbooks to help conduct experiments outlined in my proposal [8.3; 1.10].

Dr Cuticchia also introduced me to Brenda Muskat, who taught me how to conduct an investigation in a state-of-the-art genetics laboratory. This was truly an eye-opening experience for me. It opened up a world that I had only seen on television. It was one of the greatest experiences of my life. Ms Muskat was able to break down genetic protocols and explain them to me step by step, along with their role in experiments. I saw science first hand.

Learning with mentors (see Analysis [7.10], p. 166 and [7.16], p. 167).

The centrality of content (see Analysis [8.3], p.174).

Learning through apprenticeship is important (see Analysis [1.10], p. 101).

Although these mentorships were very important to me, the idea for my project still came from my own interests. I told Dr Cuticchia that I was deeply concerned with detecting a person's illness in a fast, yet effective and inexpensive manner. This concern was sparked when I had a sore throat. When I went to a doctor, he said it could be either viral or bacterial infection, but I asked him to give me antibiotics, to be on the safe side [3.4].

Three days later, the doctor called to say that I had a bacterial infection. It was a good thing I took antibiotics, but the three-day waiting period concerned me. I wanted to see whether there was a quicker way to diagnose diseases and characterize disease-causing pathogens. To help me with my search for a topic, Jamie Cuticchia gave me numerous journals to read. He asked me to report to him the following week on what I found interesting and relevant for my science fair project.

Real-life issues create powerful opportunities for organizing science curriculum (see Analysis [3.4], p. 119).

I read a very interesting article on micro-arrays and their unique property of being able to match up genetic sequences. I wondered if in one channel (one column on a micro-array slide), a person's disease sequence could be matched with a section of the same sequence. This section's small size would eliminate the risk of a mutation inhibiting the diagnosis. But there was a problem, there was no method or machine that would generate regions that are unique to a DNA sequence.

Hence, I thought of a computer program. The program was able to quickly go into a DNA sequence and find regions that are unique to it. Those regions would only be found in that one sequence, and not in any other. This information would be inputted into a directory stored on Microsoft Excel™. The data would be used to diagnose diseases more quickly, accurately and less expensively than the current method used by medical professionals [1.9].

I gave my proposal to Jamie and he let me read a publication on bioinformatics, the marriage of computers with genetics. Jamie watched over me as I created the program [1.10], and when it was time to test its feasibility, he introduced me to Dr Jason Goncalves. Jason allowed me to perform my experiments in his micro-array lab at Toronto General Hospital. There I met numerous technicians and scientists. This was quite an experience for me. He gave me the apparatus to conduct my experiments and had James Parris (a technician) show me a demonstration, as this was my first time working with a micro-array.

Scientists use models (see Analysis [1.9], p. 101).

Learning through apprenticeship is important (see Analysis [1.10], p.101).

When thousands of numbers were outputted on the analysis machine that I was using, Jason and James taught me how to analyse them. From the analysis, I was able to understand the results and talk about them in a very non-complicated manner. From this easy method of learning about how to work with micro-arrays and analyse them I was confident that I had carried out a flawless experiment, and was optimistic about my chances at the 2001 Canada Wide Science Fair. This paid off as I took the 'Triple Crown' national title, three first place finishes at the nationals!

My most recent mentor is Dr David Evans, Chair of the Department of Molecular Biology and Genetics at the University of Guelph. He was one of the judges at the 2001 Aventis Biotech Challenge. We debated a variety of issues about diagnostics and primer generation programs. Eventually, I wrote a proposal for the upcoming science fair. I wanted to take a world title, and felt that Dr Evans was the best person to talk to because of his expertise and approachability. He gave me advice based on the proposal and arranged for me to meet with other researchers in the Department of Molecular Biology. That is where Margaret Howes, Manager of the University of Guelph's DNA array facility, came into play.

Margaret Howes assisted me in my investigations and explained the procedures and principles in a manner that I could easily comprehend. Like Jason, she taught me how to analyse my results. From that, I was able to write my analysis in my own words, which is sometimes tough to teach to a high school student, but Margaret did it! She was able to combine humour with science, in an optimum mix. I was able to relate to certain things much more effectively (for example, she once explained the process of separating alcohol and DNA during the removal of DNA from a cell as 'the alcohol has to move out of the DNA's house') [1.10].

Learning through apprenticeship is important *(see Analysis [1.10], p. 101)*.

Learning by doing

Finally, while all this help has been really important, having teachers and mentors let me do things on my own has been essential. Teachers should let students experience, first hand, how to do a science fair experiment. This might spark the interests of certain students who did not know they had an innate interest in science. This is often key in preparing students for success in science fair competitions. In my case, I learned how to follow a set protocol for carrying out an experiment. If a student wants to be successful in science fair, there is no room for error when it comes to carrying out an experiment. The teacher or mentor must assist the student, so that the student masters this process and uses it in any scientific experiment.

Summary and conclusion

My experiences with mentors have been very enriching. They have shown me how to carry out experiments and the intricacies involved in working at the molecular level. For example, my mentors have helped me master concepts underlying the accurate control of variables. This was done by demonstrating the consequences of not controlling variables correctly. In addition, when it came to learning technical skills, my mentors demonstrated time and patience. This was very helpful because students' abilities to conduct experiments efficiently depend on their technical skills. Having these skills can also mean the difference between a successful experiment and a failed experiment. My mentors helped me to build my foundations before I started conducting my science fair experiments. I would learn later that the foundation building was pivotal in my success!

If the three-pronged approach, described above, were used in more schools, I am almost certain that it would generate interest in students who are not normally exposed to science fairs. Science fairs are life-changing events. They have completely changed my life.

Account 10
Practice drives theory: an integrated approach in technological education

James Johnston

Introduction

Most students beginning my integrated technology education course have had few experiences with technological design. I nurture them through a design project that effectively integrates various subjects, and serves as a context for illustrating a technological design process I want to share with students. The project is the challenge of designing and building a model car powered by a mousetrap. It is a project challenge for which there are many resources. A lot of students around the world have taken on this challenge and history shows they tend to enjoy the project [5.5].

Nevertheless, such a project can be daunting for the uninitiated. The guidance teachers provide is extremely important in helping students achieve a point at which they have great comfort in pursuing similar technological design projects in the future.

When problem solving is grounded in real-life, authentic contexts, real-life materials are frequently used to complete prototypes. However, school settings do not always permit this and teachers find alternative situations *(see Analysis [5.5], p. 140)*.

The technological design process

Open-ended problem situations can be frustrating and unpleasant experiences for students if they are not implemented properly. One effective way of guiding students through these events is to organize student activity and arrange for student success by following the technological design process. This is a methodology whereby both process and product are essential components in establishing an end product [5.4]. While there are various models for and ways of describing a design process, the following five 'phases' are typical in meaning and application to most models [8.2]:

PBL engages students in learning through practical activities where they use both head and hand to solve authentic tasks *(see Analysis [5.4], p. 140)*.

The immediacy of input *(see Analysis [8.2], p. 173)*.

1   Identify the problem
2   Develop a framework

3   Choose the best solution

4   Implement a plan

5   Reflect on the process and product.

Introducing students to this process can be done in a manner that challenges their creativity and problem-solving abilities, while at the same time promoting a 'fun' event from which they learn.

The design process in action [5.5]

Phase 1

The first phase of the design process begins with a description of the *problem* for the mousetrap car. The problem statement defines the challenge and establishes minimum criteria to be followed. Briefly, this statement directs students to follow a design process and safely use materials and equipment, to design a vehicle powered by the energy in a mousetrap.

When problem solving is grounded in real-life, authentic contexts, real-life materials are frequently used to complete prototypes. However, school settings do not always permit this and teachers find alternative situations *(see Analysis [5.5], p. 140)*.

The vehicle must travel at least 9 metres to be considered 'successful'. I invite students to work in small teams for this project and, once groups are determined, I discuss logistical information for the challenge. This information is given by way of *criteria* (see Figure 2), designed to provide students with assistance in making critical decisions and judgements about their design [2.5; 10.1].

The use of criteria to evaluate arguments facilitates students' argumentation *(see Analysis [2.5], p. 111)*.

Avoid induction; promote deduction *(see Analysis [10.1], p. 195)*.

Technology project criteria

✓   The design process must be followed and a design report will be due at the end of the unit.

✓   A single mousetrap is provided. If additional trap(s) is/are incorporated, it is the group's responsibility to arrange for this. No rat traps are permitted!

✓   Vehicles must be self-starting.

✓   The minimum distance of 9 metres must be obtained without assistance from the team members (i.e. students may not push or steer the vehicle once it is in motion).

✓   The device may use additional potential or kinetic energy for assistance (i.e. rubber bands).

✓   The teacher will establish the distance trial location.

✓   The time for completion of the mousetrap car project is 14 class periods.

Figure 2   Mousetrap car criteria

After these preliminary arrangements, students begin to develop a focus for the project by conducting some initial information gathering about mousetrap cars. For example, students can:

- access various websites (e.g. www.geocites.comCapeCanaveral/508, www.docfizzix.com and quark.angelo.edu/sps/mouse.htm
- make visits to the library to investigate sources of information
- interview student(s) who had completed the challenge in a previous semester.

Phase 2

Students then develop a *framework* for the project. They brainstorm and use their research list to aid the generation of ideas. For example, students sketch designs of vehicles with three or four wheels, single or multiple trap-powered vehicles, wooden or steel wire frames and methods of gearing. At this point in the process, I introduce a design portfolio. Students insert any research obtained in the portfolio along with rough drafts and hand-drawn sketches of their ideas.

In addition to their own research, they have lots of useful information to incorporate from other school programmes. Science and math units, taught in grades 7 to 9 include: forces, motion, structures, measurement, power and energy, types of machines and mechanical advantage. At the same time, however, students appear to have difficulty applying the concepts learned from these previous theoretical units. To assist students, I teach formal lessons to illustrate everyday applications of topics such as friction, energy, motion, torque, acceleration, accuracy and measurement, and construction and fabrication methods [4.13]. These lessons are designed to be hands-on in nature and usually include various demonstrations [4.7]. However, the lessons are only taught when students need to know something specifically related to their car design and construction topics. That these lessons only occur when necessary is an illustration of the principle 'practice drives theory' [5.7].

Greater conceptual integration should be seen as a key objective for learning science *(see Analysis [4.13], p. 133)*.

Physical manipulation of apparatus can provide an additional way of learning and recalling information *(see Analysis [4.7], p. 129)*.

In problem solving, discipline knowledge and skills are learned as needed to advance the solution *(see Analysis [5.7], p. 142)*.

Phase 3

In the third phase, students choose the *best solution* from among their possible choices. To accomplish this task, students create a project weighting scale with the criteria they establish for a good design. For example, they may choose a scale of 1 (low) to 5 (high). The criteria they establish may include such items as: feasibility of construction, availability of materials, cost and aesthetics.

Students evaluate each possible solution based on the criteria and establish a total score. They choose the 'best' solution and select one idea from those generated that will be their actual technological project. Based on this information, students produce a neat preliminary drawing of their design. They also prepare a list indicating the quantity, size and materials needed to construct their car. The design, drawing and materials list, allow students to visualize the end product. This in turn, will help guide them through the implementation phase.

Phase 4

In this phase, students implement their *most favoured plan*. This is the phase where students' planning and organization, obtained in phases one to three, enable them to begin constructing the product. From their designs, they request materials and supplies needed, and/or arrange to bring objects from home. After their research component, students quickly determine that one of the most significant obstacles to overcome in the challenge is not about speed, but how to get the car to travel the greatest distance.

The first step towards achieving this distance goal in their component construction and assembly, is to accurately measure and assemble a lightweight frame. The majority of cars use a frame made of steel rod – due to its availability, size, weight and strength. However, before assembly can proceed, students must learn some new fabrication skills.

Previously, they learned how to cut and form wood using a variety of processes. Metal fabrication (manufacturing technology), however, requires a different set of tools and skills. Students begin work on the metal by scribing layout marks on their pieces and then use a hacksaw to cut them to length. A metal file is used to remove 'burrs' from the ends of the rod before handling. After the pieces are cut, they attempt a trial assembly of the individual pieces. At this point I provide a demonstration on the safety, operation and proper handling of an oxy-acetylene welding unit.

Most students have never been exposed to any type of welding process or equipment. Discussions and demonstrations are held pertaining to, for example, proper attire, safety equipment and procedures, types of gases used, gauges, hoses, pressures, lighting and extinguishing the flame, flame temperatures, properties of metals and metal expansion and contraction.

In small groups, each student wears protective equipment, and safely lights and operates the torch to perform a sample brazing operation. Following this, students 'weld' pieces of their mousetrap car frame to form an assembled unit. Students receive continuous assistance throughout this sequence of events, either from a peer helper (a senior student assigned to the class) or myself. This is to ensure the safety of all individuals, and to make certain all students have success with their welded project. As an observation, students appear to enjoy the new knowledge and skills acquired when welding. But they generally agree that working with metal and understanding basic metallurgy is a unique and challenging experience.

Once the frame of the car is assembled, wheels and axles are needed. From their research and design, students have chosen the type, number and size of wheels to use on their vehicle. Most students use discarded CDs because they are lightweight and easily obtainable. Students cut a 0.3 cm steel rod to use as their axles. The axles form a friction fit into small plastic wheels that are attached to the CDs using hot glue or an epoxy cement compound. Discussions are held about the safety, advantages and disadvantages, properties and catalytic effect of these bonding and fastening agents (science and construction technology). Once the wheels are assembled, students check the car for alignment (steering geometry), rolling resistance (drag) and friction (maths, science and transportation technology).

When the chassis (frame, wheels, axles) of the vehicle is complete, students modify their mousetrap to incorporate a lever or arm assembly. This is the component part that will transfer the pulling force of the mousetrap spring into energy to drive the wheels. Students try different lengths of arm and traditionally find that a shorter arm allows the vehicle to go faster in speed but shorter in distance. Whereas a longer arm significantly increases distance, but travels much slower. Students permanently attach the arm to the trap by welding it to the trap arm. Before the trap is installed on the frame, students again do research to determine the best location for the mousetrap (Balmer and Harnish 1998 is an excellent resource to use here).

In general, torque and weight distribution problems will arise if the trap is not ideally placed. Groups who utilize more than one trap in their design have the problems compounded. To overcome these difficulties, students experiment with the trap placement to determine if slipping or spinning of the drive wheels occur (i.e. with too much torque and not enough traction, the trap should be relocated away from the drive axle). Conversely, if the trap is located too far from the drive axle, the torque will be insufficient to provide thrust (science, maths, manufacturing and transportation technology). Once the 'ideal' location is found, students attach the trap to a wooden platform (construction technology), using screws to fasten the two objects together. They then attach the platform system to the chassis with hot glue or epoxy cement compound.

Students are now ready to fasten the string from the lever arm to the drive axle. Because the axle is a round, smooth rod, the string is difficult to attach. The easiest solution is to apply tape to the axle which creates a friction surface. However, students use their own creativity and devise an array of methods – ranging from hooks to rubber grommets. When students wrap the string on the axle for the first time, they frequently wind the string in the wrong direction, causing the car to go backwards. Another difficulty students encounter with the string is when it becomes permanently tied to the axle. Also, as it unwinds it comes to the end, thus stopping the car. Another possibility is that the string length is too long/short, which affects the ability of the car to travel the given distance. Trial and error methods are combined with thinking skills to determine the best arrangement [4.3].

Making learning 'concrete' helps many learners to relate to science concepts *(see Analysis [4.3], p. 128)*.

Phase 5

The final phase is a *reflection on the process and product*. Students evaluate the process used and compare the finished product with expectations they established for themselves. In short, the car is tested and the results are recorded. From this evaluation and testing, students frequently modify the production process or their product. Throughout the entire design process, students are continuously testing and modifying their vehicle [5.6]. However, the majority of modifications/changes will occur in this phase. This primarily occurs due to the spirit of competition between students. I have observed these implicit and subtle challenges between groups about which car is 'best' and why. This competitive spirit challenges group members to modify and change their designs in order to build a better mousetrap car. Ultimately, most of their questions focus on design modifications and enhancements, involving utilization of mechanical and scientific principals. Typical problems students inquire about include:

Problem solving used in PBL is an iterative process *(see Analysis [5.6], p. 141)*.

- how to overcome friction (surface and fluid types);
- how to reduce mass without affecting strength (structural properties, cutting and fastening methods, strength of materials);
- how to obtain more traction (types of materials, friction, inertia, force, acceleration);
- how to obtain more propulsion (energy types and sources, inertia, force, acceleration);
- how to increase the distance (transmissions, gearing, momentum, torque, resistance, leverage).

Some of the creative methods students have used to solve these problems include:

- attaching multiple traps, sequentially activated or in unison;
- designing a four-wheel drive system;

- creating a tapered axle, transmission or gearing system to achieve a mechanical advantage;
- modifying the drive system, incorporating a direct, gear or belt system;
- designing a vehicle that has a separate car/trap system that is suspended, and becomes activated upon completion of the initial lever movement;
- Reducing friction by using, for example, straws, lubricants and bearings;
- using vinyl records for rear wheels and removing material from them to assist with weight reduction;
- using elastic bands to supplement the traps' energy potential;
- using balsa wood or other lightweight construction material;
- applying balloons or elastics to the CDs for traction;
- adding a small amount of weight above the axle for traction;
- increasing the aesthetic qualities with accessories, by, for instance, including graphics, wiring in LED lights, and adding plastic figures (passengers).

A race to (the) finish

Having completed their car construction and testing, students participate in a competition or celebration day. Our class for this event is in the hall. I have marked the floor with tape to illustrate the 9 metres minimum distance. Any student group that surpasses the minimum distance will achieve a 5-mark bonus. At this event students present their finished products to the class, describe why they chose their particular design and state what modifications/alterations they made to improve their vehicle. Hence, this activity is useful for promoting communication skills.

The mousetrap car that travelled the greatest distance last semester went 26 metres. In the case of Nick (a grade 9 student), his mousetrap car was a four-wheel drive version and it travelled over 15 metres. Due to an uneven distribution of students in the class, Nick completed this project individually, and without a time extension. This was exceptional because he did not have anyone with whom to share the workload.

During my last semester, all students were successful in obtaining the 9 metres minimum distance. This was partially attributable to having a peer helper, who worked well with the students and provided the needed assistance to keep them on task. At the conclusion of the competition a final design report was due.

Summary

In summary, according to educational research, the concept of open-ended problem solving is considered a key element in students' achieving higher levels of learning. The technological design process approach to learning is a recognized method in technology education, which promotes this open-ended problem solving. It can also be used to plan effectively and organize learning in a structured, consistent and progressive manner, that will serve all students. In the mousetrap car example, the process integrates many subject disciplines. In addition, the knowledge and skills of each area become transferable. Essentially, teaching/learning strategies and integrated activities that are part of the design process characterize effective technological education programmes, and promote the 'practice drives theory' philosophy.

PART 2

Account analyses

Introduction

We now turn our attention to analysis; the process of reflecting on the teaching accounts to bring to the fore influential features. Our aim in what follows is to explore the principles and practices underpinning the teachers' and students' descriptions of education. We aim to expose the theory, if you like, that informs an understanding of Part 1. Such an approach seeks answers to questions such as: what should one look for in these accounts? In what ways are the accounts exemplary? How do these lessons resonate with the recommendations of contemporary research? What features might be extracted to use in other contexts? As you might imagine, such discussions have the potential to be wide ranging and diverse. But here we limit our analysis to areas that we feel are especially significant. The philosopher of science, R. Hanson once famously commented that 'there is more to seeing than meets the eyeball' (see Hodson, Analysis 1). In the following section, our writers' vision is necessarily blinkered; they view and comment on the lessons from the vantage point of ten discrete perspectives, the theoretical lenses as we call them in the subtitle of the text.

An initial analysis of Part 1 gave rise to a series of discrete areas. Discussion and debate among the editors reduced these to the ten perspectives, perspectives that we felt were grounded in the merits of the lessons described. At this point, we contacted writers with specific expertise in these areas. The Analysts are scholars with internationally acclaimed publication records in the area under their scrutiny. They draw on their extraordinary expertise to share with us in a critical celebration of the teachers' and students' work; using their research and knowledge of the literature to shed light on and support key aspects of the documented accounts.

The choice of perspectives, as previously mentioned, was also informed by Schwab's (1973) idea of a commonplace; a venue where content coexists with teaching, learning and context. For Schwab, the basis of success in education (in theorizing and practice) resides in the unification of the curriculum, learner, teacher and milieu. While the following chapters touch on several of these areas (it is almost impossible and rarely desirable to separate these in actuality), each chapter identifies more strongly with a particular perspective. This was planned. We needed a structure in which multiple authors could comment on multiple accounts while avoiding undue duplication and unnecessary repetition.

The first three chapters operate from the vantage point of content; the lens of analyses are the Nature of Science [Analysis 1], Argumentation [Analysis 2] and STSE (Science Technology Society and the Environment) [Analysis 3]. We then turn attention to learning, more specifically, Concept Development [Analysis 4] and Problem-based Learning [Analysis 5]. From the student we move to the teacher and contemplate what the accounts say about teaching? Here, the perspectives of Technology [Analysis 6], Emotions [Analysis 7] and Pedagogy [Analysis 8] guide our visioning. Finally we shift to a broader vista, the social context, or in Schwab's language 'the milieu'. Critical pedagogy – the pedagogy of equity, inclusion and social responsibility – is the spotlight of the two concluding chapters, Analyses 9 and 10.

The authors were set a common task: to immerse themselves in the ten accounts and surface holding a series of defining features to form the basis of recommendations for future practice. From a specific perspective they sought to ascertain what makes the illustrated practice praiseworthy. In social science research jargon, the accounts formed the 'data' and the process of analysis was to 'code' these data into a series of discrete 'categories'. This style of research is extremely popular in education and has its roots within a methodology called Grounded Theory (Glasser and Strauss 1967).

These emerging categories structure the following deliberations. Indeed, they form the basis of the annotated comments; the hypertextual links that cross reference Part 1 with Part 2. The links span the margins and, as discussed in the earlier introduction, contain page references directing readers to and from the accounts. By using this structure, you can shuffle between the accounts (the data) and the analysis (the categories). In many ways, this makes the research process transparent. You are able to see the exact source of the scholars' comments. It enables you to look at the accounts with the benefits of the scholars' accrued wisdom. The merit of this approach is that we hope you see the complex world of the science classroom in new ways and through this process you are positioned to better reflect on your practice and the practice of others. It is often stated that successful teaching is rooted in observation and reflection. Here, we offer the reader different points-of-viewing science education; ten different windows into the classroom. Of course, the authors offer their interpretation of the accounts and in places you might actually disagree with them. Such is the subjective nature of research; what you see is dependent on who you are, what you are looking at but, also, on what you are looking for.

While the following chapters have a more academic feel, the authors whenever possible avoid using excessive jargon. The discussions are modestly referenced but written in a user-friendly style to appeal to a wider audience.

To paraphrase Lewis Carol, we now encourage you to enter the classroom through, in our case, the ten looking glasses.

Analysis 1
Challenging traditional views of the nature of science and scientific inquiry

Derek Hodson

Introduction

Despite two decades of research interest in nature of science issues, many students still leave school with confused or distorted views about science and scientists (Lederman 1992; Griffith and Barman 1995; Solomon et al. 1996; Barman 1997). Among the more persistent and damaging falsehoods is the view that science is distinct from other ways of knowing because it has an all-powerful and universally applicable scientific method. Students are frequently told that this method can be easily and unambiguously described, learned step-by-step, and applied to each and every inquiry.

Too often students are led to believe that scientific observation provides reliable data from which scientists can readily derive authoritative knowledge about the physical world. They are told that when doubt arises, scientists are able to conduct experiments to 'prove' which view is correct. In consequence, the phrase 'shown by experiment' has become verbal shorthand in the world outside school for 'trust me' or 'buy my product'. Furthermore, scientists are frequently portrayed as paragons of humility and disinterest, patiently extending the frontiers of knowledge in an altruistic search for the truth. In reality, science is often messy, uncertain and context specific. Observational data, whether derived from natural or contrived situations (experiments), is sometimes capable of more than one interpretation; scientists are often passionate in their pursuit of a particular idea or theory, whether or not there are data to support it (Hodson 1998a).

While the vast literature of philosophy of science, sociology of science and history of science does not provide a single, universally accepted view of the ways in which scientists conduct the complex business of scientific investigation, and does not provide a simple blueprint for building a science curriculum that teaches students all they need to know *about* science, there are some key points of agreement (McComas et al. 1998: 6–7):

- Scientific knowledge, while durable, has a tentative character.
- Scientific knowledge relies heavily, but not entirely, on observation, experimental evidence, rational arguments and scepticism.
- There is no one way to do science (therefore, there is no universal step-by-step scientific method).
- Science is an attempt to explain natural phenomena.
- Laws and theories serve different roles in science, therefore students should note that theories do not become laws even with additional evidence.
- People from all cultures contribute to science.
- New knowledge must be reported clearly and openly.
- Scientists require accurate record keeping, peer review and replicability.
- Observations are theory laden.
- Scientists are creative.
- The history of science reveals both an evolutionary and revolutionary character.
- Science is part of social and cultural traditions.
- Science and technology impact each other.
- Scientific ideas are affected by their social and historical milieu.

As readers will already have noted, several of these issues arise in the account descriptions, and it is to these particular matters that I now turn.

Making scientific observations

N.R. Hanson (1965) famously remarked that 'there is more to seeing than meets the eyeball'. When different observers look in the same direction, at the same phenomenon or event, they may see different things as a direct consequence of what they know and what they have previously experienced. In other words, people (including scientists) do not see the world as it is; they see it as *they* are. Everything that reaches our consciousness is adjusted, interpreted and schematized in terms of what we already know and how we choose to make sense of the world. Inexperienced children do not see what adults can see, nor do laypersons see what trained scientists can see.

[1.1] Scientific observation has to be taught *(see Account 1, p. 18, and Account 7, p. 58).*

It follows that scientific observation has to be taught [1.1]. Only when students know what to look for, how to look for it and how to recognize the significance of what they see, will they be able to make 'proper' scientific observations. The need to *teach* scientific observation is well illustrated in Account 1 (p. 18), when Keith Hicks instructs students in how to make observations of a pig's kidney:

> I used a pair of seekers to gently tease apart a piece of the kidney to reveal its thread like structure ... I explained to the class that these 'threads' were the individual functional units of the kidney known as nephrons, and that each kidney consists of at least a million nephrons.

[1.2] We need to teach students about observation *(see Account 8, pp. 63–64).*

Good science education also requires that students be taught *about* observation – in particular, that our senses can be mistaken, that observations are theory laden [1.2] and, as a consequence, that all observational evidence has to be critically evaluated. All three of these matters are addressed in the accounts. For example, in Account 8 (p. 64), Alex Corry tells us that one of the first activities in his first year high school science programme involves challenging students' views about observation by means of optical illusions. Students also examine a series of familiar objects, including 'sealed carbonated drinks, cans floating (or not) in an aquarium, eggs immersed in salt water, oils of various viscosities, pond life, limp and turgid celery sticks, and tea bags in hot and cold water'.

Careful, guided observation, enables students to see what they otherwise would not. In Account 7 (p. 58), Susan Yoon tells us that the field trip guide 'pointed out various signs that revealed the variety of animals inhabiting this forest ecosystem ... had the students observe the differences in root formation, trunk cover and leaf structure ... showed us spots where the flood, resulting from Hurricane Hazel in 1954, had eroded the land'. Strongly implied in Susan's description, though not explicitly stated, is that few if any of the students would have made these observations unaided [1.3]. An

[1.3] Observation is theory laden *(see Account 2, p. 24 and p. 26, Account 6, p. 48 and Account 7, p. 58).*

'expert' is needed to teach us how to observe and recognize the significance of what we see.

In Account 6 (p. 48), Katherine Bellomo describes how evidence from examination of the Burgess Shale fossils was interpreted by Wittington, Briggs and Conway Morris, in a way significantly different from Walcott's interpretation 60 years earlier. As she reports, Walcott based his observations on the accepted view that all fossils are 'ancestral to present/modern forms'. However, Wittington and his co-workers were prepared to entertain the idea that many were *not* ancestral to present-day creatures and were, in fact, 'evolutionary dead ends'.

This change of perspective leads to a very different iconography for the 'tree of life'. It neatly illustrates the changing nature of scientific knowledge and theory-dependence of observation. In addition, this example demonstrates how the reputation of a scientist can help to maintain erroneous views [1.4]. (Charles Walcott was Secretary of the Smithsonian Institute.) Tellingly, Katherine points out that many Canadian science textbooks continue to show the 'tree of life' as one of increasing diversity – a warning that students need to be very wary of inaccuracies, inconsistencies and bias in all forms of published material.

[1.4] Status plays a key role in theory acceptance *(see Account 6, p. 48)*.

In Account 2 (p. 24), George Przywolnik describes his use of role play to show Year 12 students how observations or the sense we make of them alter with a change of perspective. Later on, George describes how he leads students to the realization that observational evidence, derived from scientific inquiry, has to be interpreted and evaluated. Sometimes data are accepted as they stand, other times they are rejected, and at times procedures are repeated to obtain data deemed more reliable.

The attendant description of how George teaches about the moon's 'captured rotation' around the Earth is a splendid illustration of how teachers can dispel the myth that observation in science is a simple, straightforward process, particularly for obtaining reliable data on which to base conclusions, generalizations and theories. It also leads directly to my next concern: the myth of the decisive experiment.

Making sense of experiments

The word 'experiment' has an almost talismanic quality in the rhetoric of school science education and the popular public image of science. Science is widely regarded as an entirely experiment-driven activity. Experiments are seen as decisive means of judging the validity of knowledge claims, and all forms of hands-on science learning activities are referred to as 'experiments', by both teachers and students [1.5]. Moreover, in some schools it is assumed that all science learning should be brought about by students 'doing their own experiments' – a view that I emphatically do not share in common with the authors of Account 4 (p. 34): 'Some students may prefer to learn by reading or listening or watching demonstrations, while others may find participating in practical hands-on laboratory activities to be most useful.'

[1.5] Learning science and doing science are not identical activities *(see Account 4, p. 34).*

Since observational data can sometimes be interpreted in ways that are consistent with more than one theory, experiments do not provide a decisive means of judging the validity of theories. In other words, theories are empirically under-determined and there is no compelling reason to accept a theory as 'true' on the basis of experimentally derived data.

In practice, data from experiments are subjected to careful and rigorous scrutiny before they are accepted or rejected. The claim that simple disagreement between theory and observational data leads quickly and decisively to a rejection of the theory – a notion often touted in school science textbooks – is patently false. In practice, data from experiments are often rejected for theoretical reasons, as account studies in the history of science readily illustrate. Schaefer (1986) has pointed out several accounts in which theory-based calculations proved more reliable and valid than experimentally acquired data. Of course, this tendency to back our theoretical judgement in the face of observational evidence can also work to the disadvantage of scientific development. For example, the rejection of William Bray's elegant experimental data because current theory rejected the notion of oscillating chemical reactions, and continued to do so for almost 50 years (Epstein 1987).

Data from experiments are more problematic than data from non-contrived situations. This is because experiments are conceived, designed, conducted and reported within a particular theoretical and procedural frame of reference. Scientists can only seek data they have speculated about and collect observational evidence in ways that correspond to their speculations about the phenomenon being studied [1.6]. It follows that major scientific advances will not usually arise from mere accumulation of data from experiments, as the stereotypical view of scientific inquiry sometimes seems to imply, but from theoretical revision and the significantly different experiments that revision suggests [1.7].

[1.6] Experimental data has to be interpreted *(see Account 2, p. 24 and p. 28)*.

[1.7] Experiments are set in a particular theoretical framework *(see Account 2, p. 28, Account 6, p. 49 and Account 9, p. 78)*.

The passage on 'rocket science' in Account 2 (p. 28) speaks very clearly to students about the complex nature of experimental design and the considerable judgement involved in the interpretation of data. In Account 9 (p. 78), Vivien Tzau, a former student of Gabriel Ayyavoo (the author of Account 9), talks about the importance of critical thinking in designing a convincing experiment: 'I say "convincing" because I knew that any knowledgeable judge would question variables that could affect the outcome of my experiment, and then question whether I knew how to control for these variables.' As Vivien implies, designing an experiment involves decisions about what variables to control and manipulate, and how. That entails extensive theorizing; experimenters can only control the variables they 'know' or have 'speculated' about. Thus, experimental design depends on how the phenomenon under investigation has been conceptualized/theorized. In other words, designing a good experiment is not a just a matter of following a simple, generic algorithm.

A more authentic view is that experiment and theory have an interdependent and interactive/reflexive relationship. Experiments assist theory-building by giving feedback about theoretical speculations. In turn, theory determines the kinds of experiments that can and should be carried out, and determines how experimentally acquired data should be interpreted. Both experiment and theory, then, are *tools for thinking* in the quest for satisfactory and convincing explanations (Hodson 1998b), as well as in the *negotiation* of scientific knowledge within the community of scientists [1.8].

Theories are accepted, rejected or given provisional status as 'interesting and promising ideas' as a consequence of complex interactions among theoretical argument, observational evidence and personal opinion. In Account 9 (p. 75), Vivien Tzau almost casually makes this key point about the significance of argument in theory building when she says: 'I found that sharing ideas is extremely important, since it is the main method of scientific development in the real world.'

We do students a gross disservice when we allow them to believe that experiments are (always) decisive tests of a theory's validity. We also do them a disservice when we lead them to believe that experiments constitute the only methodological tool at a scientist's disposal. In practice, scientists use many other methods of theory building and theory testing, including correlational studies and theoretical modelling [1.9] – especially computer modelling and simulations, as illustrated in Account 9 (p. 81), by Desmond Ngai. Good illustrations of using models to enhance conceptual understanding are located in Account 1 (p. 20), Account 3 (p. 29) and Account 9 (p. 77). Intriguingly, the description of students modelling molecular collisions and other natural phenomena through body kinaesthetic activities in Account 2 (pp. 25–26), is a good example of students *not* behaving like the stereotypical scientist.

[1.8] Scientific knowledge is negotiated *(see Account 6, p. 50 and Account 9, p. 75).*

[1.9] Scientists use models *(see Account 1, p. 20, Account 3, p. 29 and Account 9, p. 77 and p. 81).*

Learning to do science

A prevalent myth of science education is that there is a simple algorithm for conducting each and every scientific inquiry. In practice, scientific investigations are complex, messy, fluid and uncertain. Most importantly, they are context specific – that is, determined by the particular circumstances: the nature of the problem, the phenomenon or event under scrutiny, the theoretical understanding of the inquirer, the scientific 'hardware' and other facilities available to the researchers, and so on. Due to this fluidity, the most effective way of learning to do science is by doing science, alongside a skilled and experienced practitioner who can provide on-the-job support, criticism and advice. It is here that the notion of *apprenticeship* is useful [1.10].

As Jean Lave (1988: 2) says: 'Apprentices learn to think, argue, act, and interact in increasingly knowledgeable ways with people who do something well, by doing it with them as legitimate, peripheral participants.' For Lave, apprenticeship is not just a process of

[1.10] Learning through apprenticeship is important *(see Account 8, pp. 63, 67 and Account 9, pp. 80– 82).*

internalizing knowledge and skills, it is the process of becoming a member of a community of practice. Developing an identity as a member of the community and becoming more knowledgeable and skilful, are part of the same process, where the former is seen as motivating, shaping and giving meaning to the latter.

When they are given opportunities to participate peripherally in activities of the community, newcomers pick up the relevant social language, imitate the behaviour of skilled and knowledgeable members, and gradually start to act in accordance with community norms. The amount and extent of intervention necessary is not easy to judge. Too early and too directive an intervention and students will, thereafter, wait for teachers to tell them how to do it. Too late and too vague an intervention and students are likely to give up in exasperation. This approach and these principles are well illustrated in Accounts 8 and 9. Indeed, Alex Corry (Account 8) even uses the term 'apprenticeship for scientific inquirers' (p. 63) for his programme, where students 'learn several scientific skills, including: question and hypothesis development, measurement, graphing, data analysis and reporting'. Initially, this account presented me with a dilemma. It appeared to conflict with my belief that scientific inquiry is context specific, idiosyncratic and fluid/uncertain by presenting a seemingly algorithmic approach. For example, Alex describes how a '... template is used ... that guides students to write their observations in the central box, variables they believe may result from each observation in right-hand box and possible causes of their observations in the left-hand box' (p. 64). He also provides students with a checklist to help them 'set up a reasonable experiment' (p. 67). This began to look dangerously prescriptive and restrictive until Alex tells us why he adopts this approach (p. 69): 'When challenged to develop their own investigations, they may become apprehensive as they wish to do the "right" investigation and get the "correct" answers.' To help students overcome their apprehension Alex provides what looks like a tried and trusted 'recipe'. Once they have gained confidence, and some experience, they are weaned away from the security of a fixed method, and the expectation that all investigations can and should be approached in the same way. It makes eminently good sense to provide some initial security and then, when confidence is higher, show students that the real world of scientific investigation is not always so simple and straightforward. As Alex reminds us (p. 69), the timing of this shift is crucial to development of intellectual independence [1.11]: 'As the teacher, we have to gauge when they "get it", and balance this against providing learning opportunities that refute this linear progression.'

[1.11] Timing of intervention is critical *(see Account 8, p. 69).*

In Account 9, Gabriel Ayyavoo describes a similar apprenticeship programme comprising four major elements: motivation through presentation of projects completed by students in previous years;

finding an area of particular interest for each student (or group of students); teaching specific procedural skills and laboratory operations (a phase that involves carrying out some small-scale investigations, criticizing the work of others, and receiving criticism); and designing an investigation. The accounts of Gabriel's former students about their experiences are littered with examples of the highly specific, on-the-job nature of good mentorship. The following examples are drawn from Desmond Ngai's account of his experiences: (pp. 80–3):

> Brenda Muskat ... taught me how to conduct an investigation in a state-of-the-art genetics laboratory. ... Ms Muskat was able to break down genetic protocols and explain them to me step by step, along with their role in experiments. I saw science first hand ... Although these mentorships were very important to me, the idea for my project still came from my own interests. ... Jamie watched over me as I created the programme. ... Jason allowed me to perform my experiments in his micro-array lab ... my mentors have helped me master concepts underlying the accurate control of variables ... by demonstrating the consequences of not controlling variables correctly ... My mentors helped me to build my foundations before I started conducting my science fair experiments. I would learn later that the foundation building was pivotal in my success.

Another important aspect of enculturation into the community of scientific practice concerns scientific writing. In Account 8 (p. 67), Alex Corry describes how he exploits students' curiosity about the work of their peers to teach formal scientific reporting, and provides guidance and support for each phase of the report:

> They learn various components of a traditional lab report in a role-playing fashion ... Students also are challenged to use alternative reporting methods, such as: drawing cartoons, writing letters, creating stories and myths, developing dance routines and/or generating songs or even pen poetry to illustrate what they have learned in their investigation.

Alex's reference to other cultural issues is a neat link to the final section of the chapter, dealing with the socio-cultural aspects of scientific practice.

Scientists are people!

Since science is carried out by people, it is subject to the same influences as any other human activity. There is nothing particularly 'special' about scientists, any more than there is something 'special' about accountants, dentists, architects or lawyers. They are just people, like us. This is not the view held by most students at the outset of a science programme [1.12], as Karen Kettle shows in Account 5 (p. 40). In common with other research findings using the Draw-a-Scientist Test (Chambers 1983), a significant number of Karen's students produced images of 'a slightly mad-looking, able-bodied, white male scientist dressed in a lab coat and working alone in a laboratory, either mixing explosive chemicals or experimenting on animals'.

[1.12] Countering the stereotype of a scientist *(see Account 5, p. 40)*.

The view that science is both value free and acultural, and is carried out exclusively in laboratories by dispassionate, objective, disinterested individuals (usually white males), is a widespread, persistent and pernicious notion. Not only is it false, it is unattractive to many students who might otherwise choose science as a career. Significantly, its racist overtones play a key role in dissuading many students of ethnic minority backgrounds from seeking to enter the community of scientists. In Account 5, Karen Kettle provides powerful evidence for the efficacy of history, presented as dramatic vignettes based on a news conference theme, in revealing the human face of famous scientists and the social context of scientific discoveries [1.13]. In the words of Michael Matthews (1994: 52), 'History is a way of putting a face on Boyle's Law, Ohm's Law, Curie's discoveries, Mach bands, Planck's Constant and so on.'

[1.13] Science can be humanized *(see Account 5, p. 41)*.

The work described in Account 5 shows that there are as many kinds of scientist as there are kinds of people, influenced in their endeavours and ambition by the same range of attitudes and emotions as other professionals. It shows that well-chosen biographical material can convey a wide range of messages: science is not confined to laboratories; 'frontier science' is often very controversial; scientists often have to overcome major obstacles (personal, economic, social, religious, political); science and technology are related in complex ways. It would be interesting to take this insight further and use it to shed light on contemporary science and scientists by interviewing practitioners about their current work, why they chose it, and the significance they see it having for society.

Above all else, this kind of historical-biographical work tells us that because science is carried out by people it is a product of its time and place. In the words of Robert Young (1987: 18) 'There is no other science than the science that gets done.' What we do – that is, the questions we ask and the kind of problems we perceive and try to answer – depends on who we are and where we are. Since science is driven by the needs, interests, values and aspirations of the wider society it can exhibit quite pronounced bias [1.14]. This point is beautifully exemplified in Account 6, where Katherine Bellomo shows how, for 60 years, the interpretation of the Burgess Shale

[1.14] Science can be biased *(see Account 6, pp. 46–47 and p. 49)*.

fossils was prejudiced by the status of the scientist and determined by what was currently fashionable. Account 6 also contains an implicit warning against Whiggish interpretations of the history of science – that is, interpreting historical events from the perspective of twenty-first century scientific understanding.

However, as Katherine laments,

> ... some students reject the message. They feel that if a part of scientific knowledge is changed, reinterpreted or modified then it was not done 'properly' or thoroughly in the first place. For them, the story of the Burgess Shale tells them that Walcott was a sloppy scientist, and those that followed him were more careful, less rushed in their thinking and so more accurate in their conclusions.

> (p. 50)

Nevertheless, as Katherine points out, historical studies often succeed – in ways that other methods cannot – in showing students that 'science does, in some ways, begin with a question and who gets to ask questions, and how those questions are researched is never neutral ... it does matter who does the asking ... science [is] socially constructed and culturally determined' (pp. 50–51) [1.15].

[1.15] Science is a culturally located activity *(see Account 5, p. 42, Account 6, pp. 50–51)*.

If it is possible to show students that 'who you are will influence the work you do, the questions you ask, and the lens you look through as you collect and analyse data' (Account 6, p. 51), seeds have been sown that lead to students recognizing that science *could* be different. If people with different values and different priorities were responsible for 'doing science' the trajectory of scientific and technological development would change. If science *could* change, maybe it *should* change [1.16]. This is clearly the subtext of Susan Yoon's town hall debate (Account 7).

[1.16] Science can be redirected *(see Account 7, p. 59–62)*.

By choosing an issue in which it is relatively easy to see how vested interests play a key part in public decision making, Susan is able to impact quite significantly on the values and attitudes of her students. It is enormously gratifying to hear that 'many of the students agreed' with the statement from one of the debaters that 'it was incumbent on them to be stewards of the Earth. Humans should therefore make prudent decisions based on the needs of all living organisms, and not simply around their own needs' (pp. 60–61). Effecting this shift from anthropocentrism to biocentrism is key to solving current environmental crises (Russell and Hodson 2002; Yoon 2002) and should, perhaps, be regarded as the next priority for science education reform (Hodson 2003).

Analysis 2
Developing arguments

Sibel Erduran and Jonathan Osborne

Introduction

In recent years, international policy documents (for example, Department for Education and Employment 1999; National Research Council 2000) have promoted the notion that the teaching of science should accomplish much more than simply detailing what we know in science. Of growing importance in science education is the need to educate students about *how* we know and *why* we believe in certain claims (Driver et al. 1996). The shift from what we know to how we know requires a renewed focus on how science education can promote students' skills in justifying explanations. Put another way, the learning of argumentation (Toulmin 1958) has emerged as a significant educational goal.

The account made is that argumentation, that is, the coordination of evidence and theory to support or refute an explanatory conclusion, model or prediction (Suppe 1998) is a critically important discourse process in science. Situating argumentation as a central element in the learning of sciences has two functions: one is as a heuristic to engage learners in the coordination of conceptual and epistemic goals; and the other is to make students' scientific thinking and reasoning visible to enable formative assessment by teachers. From this perspective, epistemic goals are not additional extraneous aspects of science to be marginalized to single lessons or the periphery of the curriculum. Rather, striving for epistemic goals such as developing, evaluating and revising scientific arguments represent essential elements of any contemporary science education.

In this chapter we will briefly review the literature on argumentation in science education. Here, our purpose is to contextualize the role of argumentation in science learning and teaching as well as to illustrate the potential that argumentation, as a pedagogical strategy, can enhance science learning. Second, we will turn our attention to the study of the teacher accounts presented in this book to highlight their use of argumentation strategies. We will consider issues that deal with the nature of arguments, as well as the pedagogical strategies implicit in the accounts where argumentation is promoted in the classroom. Finally, we will summarize a set of recommendations that would enhance the use of argumentation in the accounts. In the last section, we will conclude with some implications for teacher development in science education.

Argumentation in science education: an overview

Over the past few decades, influential educational projects have laid foundations for the work on argumentation in science lessons. These projects have promoted independent thinking, the importance of discourse in education and the significance of cooperative and collaborative group work (e.g. Cowie and Rudduck 1990; Solomon 1990; Osborne et al. 2001). In addition to these projects, a body of relatively unintegrated research concerning argumentative discourse in science education has begun to emerge (e.g. Boulter and Gilbert 1995; Mason 1996; Means and Voss 1996). Perhaps the most significant contribution to this literature has come from Kuhn (1991), who explored the basic capacity of individuals to use reasoned argument. Kuhn investigated the responses of children and adults to questions concerning problematic social issues. She concluded that many children and adults are very poor at the coordination of evidence (data) and theory (claim) that is essential to a valid argument. More recent work by Hogan and Maglienti (2001), exploring the differences between the reasoning ability of scientists, students and non-scientists found, likewise, that the performance of the latter two groups were significantly problematic.

Koslowski (1996) was less doubtful of young people's ability to reason pointing to the fact that theory and data are interdependent and are both crucial to reasoning. Hence, lack of knowledge of any relevant theory or concepts often constrains young people's ability to reason effectively. While this is an important point, what it suggests is that scientific rationality requires knowledge of scientific theories, a familiarity with their supporting evidence and the opportunity to construct and/or evaluate their interrelationship. Kuhn's research is important, nevertheless, because it highlights the fact that, for the overwhelming majority, the use of valid argument does not come naturally. The implication that we draw from the work of Kuhn and others is that argumentation is a form of discourse that needs to be appropriated by children and *explicitly taught* through suitable instruction, task structuring and modelling. Just giving students scientific or controversial socio-scientific issues to discuss will not prove sufficient to ensure the practice of valid argument, which needs to be fostered by teachers. Similar conclusions were reached by Hogan and Maglienti (2001: 683) who argued that, 'students need to participate over time in explicit discussions in the norms and criteria that underlie scientific work'.

A significant problem confronting the development of argumentation in the science classroom is that it is fundamentally a dialogic event carried out among two or more individuals. Scott (1998), in a review of the nature of classroom discourse, shows how discourse lies on a continuum from 'authoritative', which is associated with closed questioning and IRE (initiation-response-evaluation) dialogue – to 'dialogic', which is associated with extended student contributions and uncertainty.

However, the combination of power relationships that exists between the science teacher and student, and the rhetorical agenda of the science teacher to establish the consensually agreed scientific world view with the student, means that opportunities for dialogic discourse are minimized. Hence, introducing argumentation requires a shift in the normative nature of classroom discourse. Science teachers also have to be convinced that argumentation is an essential component for the learning of science. In addition, they are required to have a range of pedagogical strategies that will both initiate and support argumentation if they are to adopt and integrate this into the classroom.

At the core of such strategies is the requirement to consider, not singular explanations of phenomena, but *plural* accounts (Driver et al. 2000). Students must, at the very least, spend time considering not only the scientific theory but also an alternative, such as the common lay misconception that all objects fall with the same acceleration versus the notion that heavier things fall faster. Such contexts can also be social considerations of the application of science. These include, for example, the use of animals for drug testing, problem-based learning situations, or computer-mediated situations, for instance the material developed by the WISE project (Bell and Linn 2000).

Evidence suggests that argumentation is fostered by a context in which student–student interaction is permitted and encouraged. For instance, Kuhn *et al.* (1997), in testing the hypothesis that engagement in thinking about a topic enhances the quality of reasoning about the topic, found that dyadic interaction significantly increased the quality of argumentative reasoning, in both early adolescence and young adults. Likewise, the work of Eichinger et al. (1991) and Herrenkohl et al. (1999) found that bringing scientific discourse to the classroom required the adoption of instructional designs that permit students to work collaboratively in problem- solving groups.

Some of the research on discourse points, too, to the importance of establishing procedural guidelines for the students (Herrenkohl et al. 1999). The point to make is that *both* epistemological *and* social structures in the classrooms are important factors for designing activities that foster argumentation. One element, therefore, is the need to provide students with access, to not a singular world view, but to plural accounts of phenomena and the evidence that can be deployed in an argument. However, promoting multiplicity of explanations is not sufficient to nurture dialogic discourse. Instructional strategies, such as student presentations, role playing and small group discussions, are crucial in sustaining argumentation in the classroom.

Turning to the accounts

While the accounts outlined in this book highlight different innovative instructional strategies adopted by teachers, and hence may not have intended to promote argumentation, we have traced the accounts for their use of it. In our reading of the accounts, we wanted to identify if and how they made reference to arguments in terms of either a very broad definition of argument (e.g. link between claims and evidence) or more specific accounts illustrating the role of data, claims, warrants, backings and rebuttals in the structure of argument (e.g. Toulmin 1958). In other words, we sought for excerpts in the accounts where some definition of argument was suggested.

Likewise, we traced the acknowledgement of plural accounts of arguments and the notion of quality of argument, both important aspects of the nature of argument. We also investigated the extent to which accounts promoted strategies that enable argumentation to take place in the classroom. We examined the accounts for their use of instructional strategies such as role playing, group discussions and writing frames. Even though these strategies are not exhaustive, they provide a broad enough consideration of pedagogical tools (e.g. writing and talking) that can enhance the use of argumentation at the level of the classroom.

In the first part of the next section, we highlight our reading of the accounts with respect to the nature of arguments. Here, we consider issues that deal with the role and quality of evidence in argument. In the second part, we illustrate the pedagogical strategies that the accounts utilize and which promote argumentation in the classroom. Finally, we will summarize a set of recommendations that would enhance the use of argument in the accounts.

The nature of arguments

Defining argument

Our reading of the accounts has illustrated that some teachers are sensitive to establishing a definition of argument in their practice [2.1]. For example, in Account 9 (p. 73), in the context of describing skill development in science, Gabriel Ayyavoo implies that argument plays a role in his classroom: 'Having settled on an initial topic or goal, students are then faced with the often daunting task of designing a valid and reliable empirical investigation, which may provide evidence for various scientific or technological claims they might make.' Gabriel is pointing to the significant goal of coordinating evidence and theory in science, and the concerns over the realization of this goal in real classrooms. In the sense that he acknowledges and promotes the coordination of evidence and theory, Gabriel not only defines but also promotes the use of argument in his classrooms.

[2.1] Argument defined as a link between evidence obtained through empirical investigation and theoretical conclusions or claims *(see Account 9, p. 73)*.

Contrasting arguments

Argumentation does not occur with a single perspective on an issue. Typically, alternative and contrasting arguments about an issue provide the foundation for discussion [2.2]. In Account 6 (p. 46), Katherine Bellomo reflects on her reading of Stephen Jay Gould's (1989) book, *Wonderful Life: The Burgess Shale and the Nature of History*. She explains:

[2.2] Evaluation of evidence in contrasting arguments is a significant aspect of the nature of science *(see Account 6, p. 46)*.

> The book tells the story of the reinterpretation of the fossils from the Burgess Shale (British Columbia, Canada). These are fossils collected by Charles Walcott between 1909 and 1913. He examined them briefly and wrote about them. The fossils are of soft-bodied organisms from the Cambrian Period, which were covered in mud (probably from a landslide) and preserved.

> Walcott interpreted the fossils applying the view he held of evolution and diversification of organisms. Sixty years later, a different group of scientists re-examined these same fossils, interpreted them in a different way and drew a dramatically different conclusion. The reinterpretations give us a new iconography of the so-called 'tree of life', so often depicted in biology textbooks.

Katherine's reflection on the plurality of scientific explanations is indicative of the value she sees in nurturing in students an understanding of alternative arguments in science [2.3]. Her vision is consistent with the research evidence on effective pedagogical strategies that support argumentation through the evaluation of multiple explanations (Driver et al. 2000).

The wider context of Katherine's lessons provides further insight into her implicit use of argument as a theme in her classrooms. She begins her lesson by asking students to reflect on the nature of science and then proceeds to telling the story of the Burgess Shale. Katherine uses diagrams of fossils to speculate about possible classification of the organisms. In particular, she uses a diagram of Hallucigenia, 'an odd, weird specimen. I use it to show how difficult the process of classification is, and also to show the conclusion that this specimen might be a dead end is logical' (p. 49). In other words, Katherine especially chooses an open-ended problem that would generate uncertainty as well as alternative points of view from students. The problem includes an anomaly ('an odd specimen'), which creates a context for discussion in the classroom.

[2.3] The use of an anomaly can be an effective strategy for promoting argumentation *(see Account 6, p. 46)*.

Quality of argument

Argumentation literature recognizes the importance of immersing students in contexts where there is an opportunity to evaluate arguments (e.g. Pontecorvo and Girardet 1993). Engaging students in discussions where they generate or use criteria to evaluate arguments, not only enables students to understand other points of view, but also fosters the ability to critically assess the credibility of knowledge claims made by others as well as themselves [2.4].

In Account 9 (p. 74), Gabriel Ayyavoo creates opportunities for students where they can 'report the progress of the projects to their classmates thereby helping students to develop more critical perspectives on their methods and conclusions, oral presentation skills and ideas for future project work'. To facilitate students' participation along these lines, Gabriel frequently engages them in 'analytical discussions relating to science fair projects conducted by other students that I have previously videotaped' (p. 74). Likewise, in Account 10 (p. 85), James Johnston describes a project-based design task where he invites students to 'work in small teams' ... and then goes on to ... 'discuss logistical information for the challenge'. To facilitate students group work, 'information is given by way of *criteria* designed to provide students with assistance in making critical decisions and judgements about their design' [2.5].

[2.4] Reflection on other students' work provides a context for students to evaluate the quality of arguments *(see Account 9, p. 74)*.

[2.5] The use of criteria to evaluate arguments facilitates students' argumentation *(see Account 10, p. 85)*.

Strategies for supporting argumentation in the classroom

Role play

Role play is a popular technique that not only motivates students, but also enables them to view and evaluate claims from different points of view (Osborne et al. 2001) [2.6]. In Account 2, (p. 23), George Alex Przywolnik indicates that he finds 'the role-playing technique is particularly effective in teaching some aspects of astronomy'. Essentially, the content provides students with a claim that the Moon undergoes one rotation on its axis for every revolution around the Earth. The students find it difficult to understand that the Moon can rotate on its axis and always present one side to us. By inviting students to participate in role play, as the Earth and Moon, George helps students model the process and hence evaluate the evidence for the main claim.

[2.6] Role play promotes an understanding of different arguments and positions *(see Account 2, p. 23, Account 5, p. 41 and Account 7, p. 55)*

In Account 5 (p. 41), Karen Kettle describes role play in the context of historical vignettes. Some of her lessons explore the way in which 'dramatic tensions arise if students present scientists from opposite sides of a controversy'. In Account 7 (pp. 55–56), Susan Yoon describes a role-play activity in which students act as representatives from six special interest groups with specific concern about an ecological problem. For instance, students are asked to assume the role of local naturalists, farm owners, local residents, news reporters and town hall members to discuss whether or not to relocate a family of beavers that had moved to the area, given that their presence was creating some environmental changes in the forest ecosystem. Implicit in all these scenarios is the acknowledgement that each role assumes a different argument and that students are thus engaged in the modes of thinking that would construct and present that argument.

Group discussions

An important strategy for supporting students' participation in argumentation is small group discussions (Eichinger et. al. 1991). Since argumentation is by nature dialogic, the social making of a group provides the context whereby arguments can be generated, evaluated, contrasted and resolved [2.7]. In Account 1 (p. 16), Keith Hicks describes the role of group discussions in relation to learning:

[2.7] Group discussions encourage argumentation and active learning. They enable the structuring of knowledge and understanding *(see Account 1, p. 16).*

> It seemed clear that part of the problem was that the students were not taking an active part in their learning and were expected to 'soak up' knowledge presented in class through some sort of absorption process. The new lessons would encourage students to be more active in their learning and require them to take on

some responsibility for it. The students needed concrete models they could handle, and the opportunity to articulate their understandings through discussion in order to structure their knowledge.

One outcome of group discussions is that they enable learning from peers [2.8]. In Account 3 (p. 30), Josie Ellis describes her own learning situation:

> I got into the habit of working with a fellow chemistry student, going over each other's problems. One of us would ask a question and the other would try to explain the answer. This was a good indication of how well we understood what we were explaining, and helped determine whether we should seek a teacher's explanation if there was something we were finding particularly difficult.

[2.8] Peer interaction promotes learning (*see Account 1, p. 16 and Account 3, p. 30*).

In Account 4 (p. 35), Richard Rennie and Kim Edwards describe how restructuring groups can achieve different goals and learning outcomes [2.9]:

> Mostly, the students worked at their own pace within their own small group. Not surprisingly, students of similar ability often chose to team up. However, at times we would restructure the classes ... Sometimes, one of us took a small group of students into one laboratory to give instruction on a particular concept they were struggling to understand. The other teacher would then work with the rest of the group in the other laboratory. For example, in chemistry, one of us supervised those students who were coping well, while the other ran small, informal and intimate tutorials for those who found balancing chemical equations difficult.

[2.9] Restructuring of groups can help achieve different teaching goals and learning outcomes (*see Account 4, p. 35*).

Writing frames

Recent studies of science education have provided evidence for the importance of writing in developing students' understanding and use of scientific concepts (Keys 2000; Kelly and Bazerman 2003). Writing frames can scaffold students' structuring of their arguments and act as tools for reflecting students' own thinking about a particular argument [2.10]. In Account 7 (p. 57), Susan Yoon describes a sample worksheet where the pros and cons of an issue are highlighted to the students in the form of questions. For instance, students are asked to answer questions such as 'What are the risks to the environment?' and 'What are the benefits to the environment?'

Likewise in Account 8 (p. 65), Alex Corry uses a 'template for

[2.10] Writing frames scaffold students' generation and evaluation of arguments (*see Account 7, p. 57 and Account 8, p. 65*).

the students to help them develop their own hypotheses' in the form of the conditional: 'If – then – because'. The use of the writing frames in these examples illustrates an acknowledgement of the need to facilitate students' construction of an argument through particular written phrases and organizing statements.

Conclusions and implications

Our reading suggests that the accounts utilize features of argument and pedagogical strategies that support the learning of argumentation in the classroom. For instance, there are explicit references to the relationship between theory and evidence, as well as implementation of strategies such as role play and group discussion. The presence of these features of argument and strategies for fostering argumentation implies that, even when the teachers may not have explicitly intended to teach argumentation, some aspects of argumentation have manifested in their classrooms.

A significant aspect of our work in argumentation has been the identification of argument space through analysis of particular aspects of classroom discourse (e.g. Erduran *et al.* 2004). However, since the accounts did not include excerpts of real conversations between teachers and students (or students and students), it was not possible for us to investigate the nature of the arguments at more specific levels. For instance, we could not trace how teachers could be facilitating students' construction of argument through feedback on their use of warrants and backings. Future reporting of teaching accounts would not only be enriched by inclusion of transcripts based on actual classroom interactions, but would also acknowledge the significance of discourse in science teaching and learning.

With further and more explicit teacher training, as well as access to appropriate resources, teachers can then nurture other aspects of argumentation that may not have arisen in the accounts. For instance, we did not observe any reference to modelling the structure of an argument through use of everyday examples. In our current work, we are generating a set of training materials, lesson strategies and video-based exemplars of effective practice (Osborne *et al.* 2004). These will provide further guidance for teachers to incorporate such aspects of argumentation into their practice. Research on educational change shows that little will be achieved unless teachers develop a sense of ownership of any innovation (Ogborn 2001) and, in addition, are supported in a structured and systematic way while developing new strategies and approaches (Joyce and Showers 1988; Loucks-Horsley et al. 1998). The expertise of the teachers manifested in the accounts presented in this book suggests that they are well equipped for incorporating argumentation into their teaching. Furthermore, the enthusiasm demonstrated by teachers to challenge their teaching with new strategies illustrates their potential for transforming the contemporary calls for science education reform into actual classroom practice.

Analysis 3
STSE education: principles and practices

Erminia Pedretti

Introduction

We live in a rapidly changing world, where boundaries between science, technology, society and environment are constantly blurred. Genetic engineering, water and waste management, endemic disease, environmental degradation and so many other socio-scientific issues assail us everyday. Decisions about what is best and for whom confront scientists and citizens alike. One way of addressing these complex issues is through science, technology, society and environment (STSE) education. STSE education seeks to interpret science and technology as socially embedded enterprises, and promotes informed and responsible decision making (Aikenhead 1994; Alsop and Hicks 2001). Equipping students to understand science in its larger social, cultural and political context is a basic premise of STSE education.

STSE education is an umbrella term, supporting a vast array of different types of theorizing about the interface between science and the social world (Solomon and Aikenhead 1994; Pedretti 1997; Kumar and Chubin 2000). By its very nature, STSE education defies definition. There is no single, widely accepted road. Ultimately, teachers must choose the messages and methods that are appropriate to their educational context, and to their ideological tilts. At best, we can only chart a landscape that provides a spectrum of possibilities for thinking about and doing STSE education.

This chapter seeks to generate an analysis of the accounts from the perspective of the science, technology, society and environment movement. I highlight the possibilities for practice while simultaneously exploring underlying principles of STSE education through teachers' accounts. Their accounts illustrate the diversity of approaches to STSE education, and the potential for sponsoring creativity and imagination in the science classroom. Most of my analyses draw from Accounts 5, 6 and 7. I begin the chapter by providing a brief analysis of three approaches illustrated in the exemplary episodes: mainly the historical, philosophical/nature of science, and issues-based approaches. I then move to an analysis of STSE principles in practice that emerge across the teachers' praxis. These principles include: values and mindfulness; community and epistemological discourse; informed decision making; and personalization and empowerment. The chapter concludes with lessons learned from these accounts of exemplary practice.

STSE education: rhetoric and reality

We have all heard the STSE slogans before: 'science for all', 'scientific literacy', 'public understanding of science', 'citizenship education', 'science and social responsibility', 'democracy', 'stewardship', and the list goes on. Indeed, curriculum documents and policies endorsing the inclusion of STSE education have been written worldwide (Kumar and Chubin 2000; Pedretti 2003). However, in spite of widespread rhetoric in support of STSE perspectives, surprisingly little translates into classroom practice, often leading to its marginalization in the curriculum.

The special set of challenges in designing and delivering STSE education can be formidable. These challenges have been well documented elsewhere (see Hughes 2000; Pedretti 2003), and include for example, the role and appropriateness of action, student 'readiness', teacher confidence, the difficulties of integrating values education and moral reasoning, lack of time and the scarcity of useful resources. However, the spirit and message of STSE education remains strong for many educators, and provides continued incentive to teach students about citizenship, social responsibility, decision making, science and ethics. The exemplary accounts analysed in this chapter illustrate that barriers can be overcome and theory/practice gaps diminished. STSE education can be a reality in the science classroom.

Variations on the theme of STSE

There is a spectrum of possibilities for bringing STSE education to life in the classroom, none of which are mutually exclusive. Each approach has its own particular rationale, thematic virtue and pedagogical advantage. Ziman (1994) provides a brief survey of the different approaches to STS[E] education, including the use of historical dimensions, philosophical/nature of science explorations, and issues-based curriculum. I now turn to the teachers' stories as exemplars of how some of these approaches can be put into meaningful practice.

An historical approach

[3.1] The use of historical perspectives gives science a human face *(see Account 5, p.38 and Account 6, p. 47).*

An historical approach is one of the most natural mediums for humanizing science [3.1]. This is abundantly clear in Account 5: 'Science with a human touch: historical vignettes in the teaching and learning of science'. In this account, the teacher, Karen, draws upon the lives of scientists (such as Galileo, Currie, Einstein, McClintock, Fossey and Goodall) to help students better understand how science developed. She also uses these examples to help illustrate that science is conducted by people who hold particular views, attitudes, passions and prejudices. Through the use of historical account studies, Karen eloquently explains (pp. 38–39):

> The science came alive. It was no longer a logical sequential march towards 'truth'. There was tedious laboratory work to be sure, but there were also daring field studies, brilliant flashes of inspiration, serendipitous discoveries, false leads, creative collaborations, cut-throat competitions, political pressures and long lasting feuds. Science was much more personal and socially embedded than I'd ever realized. I'd discovered a world that would intrigue my students.

In Karen's class, historical accounts provided the fodder for students' dramatizations. Students researched the lives of scientists, wrote scripts, planned costumes and performances and prepared to answer questions in character from the audience. Through drama and role play, students began to explore the role and impact of context, politics and belief systems in the pursuit of science [3.2]. In researching and acting out particular episodes, traditional 'images' of science as cold, linear and unfettered by social relations were challenged.

[3.2] Drama and role play can challenge traditional images of science while addressing cultural, social and political contexts *(see Account 5, pp. 39–40, and Account 7, pp. 55–56).*

A philosophical/nature of science approach

One of the important components of STSE education is the inclusion of nature of science perspectives. A nature of science emphasis provides scope and breadth for exploring science in its wider social-cultural contexts and asks questions related to what science is, how knowledge is generated, how science works, how scientists operate as a social group and how society itself both directs and reacts to scientific endeavours.

Account 6, 'Exploring the nature of science: reinterpreting the Burgess Shale fossils', is a wonderful illustration of one teacher's approach to investigating murky epistemological questions about science with her students. Katherine uses the 'story' or 'historical account' of the reinterpretation of the Burgess Shale fossils to achieve her goals and address nature of science in her curriculum. She explicitly poses questions (p. 47) that challenge deeply entrenched views about the practice of science: 'What is science? What research was done to arrive at this knowledge? What questions were not asked? Is science about finding the truth or about constructing knowledge' [3.3]?

Such philosophical tactics assist students in moving beyond the 'canons' of science: canons that are typically presented as abstract, objective and monolithic. Although Katherine's story can be interpreted as a 'philosophical' approach, it is not directed towards the development of a purely intellectual conception of science 'where thinking somehow takes place outside a real world of thinkers, actors, and talkers' (Ziman 1994: 28). Rather, in trying to develop a meaningful epistemology of science, i.e. theory of nature, status and construction of scientific knowledge, it makes more sense that the approach be embedded within a social dimension. Katherine's account accomplishes just that.

[3.3] Inclusion of the nature of science perspectives allows for the exploration of complex epistemological questions *(see Account 6, p. 47)*

An issues-based approach

Another way of achieving the challenging goals proffered by STSE education advocates is through the exploration of socio-scientific issues (Ramsey 1993; Pedretti 1997, 1999; Alsop and Pedretti 2001; Roth and Desautels 2002). In issues-based learning, societal issues, such as waste management, reproductive technologies and so on, become central organizers for science curriculum and instruction. Watts et al. (1997) describe 'event centred learning' whereby real-life events or occurrences (global or local) trigger curriculum planning. Through issues and events, students investigate the interface between science and society, as they research multiple perspectives, engage in decision making, and possibly action.

In Account 7, Susan was inspired to use a real-life issue to create a powerful learning experience for her students [3.4]. The issue centred on the question of whether or not to relocate a family of beavers. Susan's students researched various viewpoints, constructed arguments based on research and evidence, and participated in the town hall meeting. Their field trip to the outdoor education centre was the catalyst for the role-playing strategy (i.e. town hall meeting) that would continue in their science class over a period of two weeks. This real-life issue became the curriculum organizer for Susan, as she planned socially relevant and personally compelling experiences for her students. Instead of the more common way of integrating STSE education where practitioners tend to teach content and then infuse applications or societal aspects as an add-on at the end of a unit, the process in Susan's class was reversed.

[3.4] Real-life issues create powerful opportunities for organizing science curriculum *(see Account 1, p. 16, Account 7, p.55, and Account 9, p. 81)*.

Similarly, in Account 9, students Vivien and Desmond explored issues related to biotechnology for their project work. Desmond's experience when he had a sore throat prompted his concern for being able to detect a person's illness in a fast, effective and inexpensive way. Hence, his inquiry into medicine, health and technology. These examples beautifully illustrate how real-life issues inspired inquiry and curiosity among students.

Enacting STSE principles and practices

In this section I draw upon some of the seminal STSE principles that emerge across accounts. These principles are discussed with respect to specifics of teacher instruction and student learning, and include: values and mindfulness; epistemological and community discourse; informed decision making; and personalization and empowerment.

Values and mindfulness

STSE education seeks to recouple science and values education, departing from the more traditional presentation of science as value free and objective. I borrow Aspin's (2002: 15) use of the term 'values' as referring to those 'ideas, conventions, principles, rules, objects, products, activities practices, procedures or judgments that people accept, agree to, treasure, cherish, prefer, incline towards, see as important and indeed act upon'. However, integrating values into the science curriculum presents educators with a slippery slope (Pedretti, 2003). Whose values are advocated? Whose interests are supported? Whose views and perspectives? Which stories are told? How are they told? Should teachers advocate particular positions? Can a 'balanced' curriculum be designed? In spite of the challenges inherent to the explicit inclusion of values in science curriculum, the teachers in these exemplary accounts persist, continually extending boundaries and repudiating the idea that scientific knowledge is essentially esoteric or value free.

Accounts 5, 6 and 7 attend to values in different ways. In Susan's story (Account 7), the notion of mindfulness – the process in which one views the same situation from several perspectives (Langer 1993) – is played out through the critical analyses of multiple viewpoints. In trying to resolve the issue of whether the beaver family should be relocated, Susan's students mindfully consider the ecological, environmental and economic implications of their decisions. These considerations are scrutinized through the lens of assumed roles, reflecting the pluralistic society in which science and technology operate [3.5].

Susan carefully structures the role-play activity so that the positions of various interest groups (Science Teachers' Alliance, Federation of Local Naturalists, Parks and Recreation Municipality, United Farm Owners, local residents, news reporter and town hall

[3.5] Students engage in consideration of multiple view points and critical analyses through role play in order to better understand various stakeholder positions and controversy *(see Account 5, p. 39 and Account 7, pp. 59–62),*

council members) are researched and represented. She assigns them roles, provides a short synopsis for each special interest group, and distributes a worksheet to guide their inquiries. Susan's pedagogical approach reflects Solomon's argument (1993), that only briefs should be prepared for role play. Ultimately, it is far more effective if students research and develop their own arguments and positions [3.6].

The notion of mindfulness is equally true in Karen and Katherine's respective accounts, as they probe with their students the instantiation of values in science and scientific practice. Through the Burgess Shale story, Katherine hopes that students begin to see that science does, in some ways, begin with a question, but that who gets to ask questions, and 'how those questions are researched, is *never* neutral' (p. 50). She is explicit in her goals to convey to students that who you are influences the work you do, the questions you ask and the lens you look through as you collect and analyse data. According to Katherine, this 'story' is the best example for illustrating science as a dynamic, changing and culturally determined practice, inculcated with values and judgements. Karen, in order to avoid a sterile chronology of dates and events, provides her students with a set of questions to assist them with their research [3.6]. These questions, for example, consider cultural, economic and political situations of the time. Set against a rich contextualized backdrop, the exploration of choices made by the various players begins; choices that are based on principles, rules, activities, judgements, preferences and inclinations and so on. Students' interpretations and analyses reinforce the value laden-ness of *all* thought and activity: '[Values] are embedded and embodied in everything we do, as part of the warp and weft of our and our community's whole form of life' (Aspin 2002: 15).

[3.6] Careful scaffolding assists students in developing their own arguments *(see Account 5, p. 42, Account 6, p. 47 and Account 7, p. 57).*

Epistemological and community discourse

Common to all three accounts – and to STSE education – is the centrality of talk. Talk serves many purposes. For example, through discourse one can begin to understand people's perspectives, engage with issues in the first person and model public debate. I refer to this as a kind of 'community discourse'; a strategy that allows students to participate in a distributed and democratic way with complex and often contentious issues. Through talk, students share their perspectives and articulations with one another, learn the art of argumentation and develop personal understandings of that knowledge (Mortimer and Scott 2000).

The notion of 'community discourse' is particularly evident in Accounts 5 and 7 [3.7]. In Karen's class students convey to peers, and sometimes parents, the nature of critical moments in scientists' lives through the use of enacted scripts and a question and answer session. Discourse through drama becomes a powerful tool for con-

[3.7] Talk can mediate student learning, allowing for shared perspectives and articulations *(see Account 5, p. 43 and Account 7, p. 61).*

structing and sharing their knowledge with others. Susan's students, in the role of various stakeholders, become deeply engaged in talk – ranging from debate about stewardship, to the role of zoos, to urban sprawl, to rights of living beings. In being able to 'discuss' these issues, students also had to understand scientific concepts embedded in the issues (i.e. environmental degradation, farming, water management etc.). According to Mortimer and Scott (2000), classroom talk can mediate student learning of science concepts. Talk was also particularly significant to Mitchell's meaningful participation. According to Susan (p. 54): 'For students like Mitchell, who had a greater oral capacity relative to other language modes, talking through concepts enabled him to relate both to his peers and with the content.'

Roth and Desautels (2002 p. 272) describe an 'epistemological' discourse whereby each construction of a scientific fact implies a particular epistemology: 'Discourse in the context of science courses, allows students to take a reflective and knowledgeable stance with respect to the nature of knowledge and the role of claims and evidence'. This is clearly illustrated in Account 6. In their exploration of the Burgess Shale story, Katherine's students deliberate over fundamental (epistemological) questions. Their talk gives rise to issues of evidence, claims warrants and theories, as they speculate on possible classifications of these fossils and reasons for the shifts in interpretation [3.8]. Social construction and reconstruction of claims about the nature of knowledge feature prominently in Katherine's use of the Burgess Shale.

[3.8] Students are learning not only to talk science, but also epistemology *(see Account 6, p. 49)*.

In summary, each exemplary episode utilizes discourse in different ways and for different purposes. Combined, these exemplary accounts can be used to construct an argument whereby students are learning not only to talk *science*, but also *epistemology*. Furthermore, through thoughtful talk, students create effective communities of discourse that promote exploration of the complexities of science and the social world.

Informed decision making

Informed decision making is often highlighted as one of the attributes of STSE education (Ramsey 1993; Aikenhead 1994; Pedretti 1999). However, decision making is an inherently complex process, encumbered by multiple perspectives and competing agendas. Given the centrality of being able to participate rationally and effectively in the social relations of science, various frameworks have been put forward to assist teachers in designing meaningful curriculum experiences. Cross and Price (2002), for example, advocate a number of epistemic tasks in the classroom that would enhance students' abilities: understanding the arguments, judging the expert, investigating the literature and the field, and democratic participation in decision making. Ratcliffe (1997: 169) provides a similar set of criteria to guide the decision making process in the context of socio-scientific issues.

Susan's approach (Account 7) reflects many of the epistemic tasks laid out by Cross and Price (2002) and Ratcliffe (1997), leading to a highly successful and meaningful experience for her students. In particular, Susan emphasizes understanding the arguments, gathering information, investigating and surveying, making judgements, choosing a position and participating in decision making [3.9]. As noted earlier, her students take on various roles to better understand competing interests, values and viewpoints. Students also meet with 'experts' at the Outdoor Education Centre to gather information on the history of the centre, topography and climate patterns of the region, statistics regarding population growth and density of urban residents and the flora and fauna of the region along with any unique environmental features. Later on, students walk through the grounds with a guide, collecting more information and data [3.9].

[3.9] Engaging in thoughtful decision-making requires consideration of multiple viewpoints, gathering of information and critical analyses (see Account 7, p. 58 and Account 5, p. 41).

It is commonly known that decision making activities, such as town hall meetings and such simulations, can quickly degenerate into superficial discussion or persuasive rhetoric empty of evidence. However, in Account 7, Susan skilfully avoids these pitfalls through thoughtful and systematic planning. To guide students' formulations and deliberations, Susan carefully scaffolds the unit. For example, when students travel to the beaver site to survey the surrounding environment to assess the risks and benefits to both the environment and society, and to gather evidence to be used later in the town hall meeting, it is not a vicarious, imagined experience: it is real. To help students organize their observations and arguments, Susan provides a worksheet. Throughout the process she stresses to her students the importance of critical analyses, understanding various viewpoints and the need for convincing evidence to back up arguments.

Personalization and empowerment

In the past few years, the 'personalization' of science has been a strong theme. Educators are calling for a science curriculum that promotes personalization through 'relevance', 'citizenship education', and more recently 'politicization', 'agency' and 'action' (see, for example, Hodson 1998b and Roth and Desautels 2002). STSE education is one way to accommodate many forms of personalization, as it seeks to design science curricula – often viewed by students as irrelevant and vicarious – that is meaningful and personal.

In Account 9, students Vivien and Desmond excitedly pursue inquiries to problems that emerge from their personal experience (for example, Desmond's sore throat!) In Accounts 5, 6 and 7, the 'personalization' of science permeates the curriculum and pedagogy. However, perhaps the most compelling example of this personalization of science is Account 7. Students participate in the resolution of a problem that is local, urgent and interesting. It is abundantly clear in reading through the account, that these students are highly engaged, passionate about the topic and very motivated [3.10]. The story of one particular student, Mitchell, identified as having a history of disruptive behaviour, is striking. His participation exemplifies what can happen when personalization and agency become enacted through the curriculum. Susan writes of the experience (p. 62):

> I am not overestimating when I say the atmosphere in class was one of sheer jubilance. I heard students laughing and talking about the meeting on their way out of the door and through the hallways. When I walked into the locker area, I saw one of the brightest students in 9B pat Mitchell on the back and say, 'Great job!' Mitchell's former science teacher, whose classroom was next door to mine, poked her head in the door after school and asked what the excitement was all about. We sat together for ten minutes and watched the video. She was truly amazed at Mitchell's level of engagement. Science turned out to be one of the most successful academic subjects for Mitchell.

Accounts 5 and 6 also have strong elements of the personalization of science, but from slightly different perspectives. Karen's curriculum story in Account 5 (p. 45) attempts to 'humanize' science through the use of scientists' histories and biographies. She hopes to inspire and empower her students:

> As my students perform on stage, I can watch them think, feel and respond from the perspective of an eminent scientist. Their answers shatter the myth that talent is an innate gift, and the diversity of characters illustrates the narrowness of stereotypes of scientists that appear in popular culture.

Katherine's account (p. 51), also puts a human face on the scientific enterprise, but she pushes the notion of empowerment even further. She is acutely aware that many students feel marginalized and powerless in the science classroom. In using the story of the Burgess Shale, Katherine describes her goals:

> My intent is also for students to see the possibilities within science, rather than only the barriers they face or the personal limitations they perceive. I want students to see that science is done by people, and that scientists are not so much exact and perfect as persevering. ... I suggest that many of these sorts of

[3.10] Through excitement and engagement in a topic, students become motivated to learn, and feel empowered (see Account 5, p. 45, Account 6, p. 49, Account 7, p. 61, and Account 9, p. 79).

examples show students they too are able to have questions that could be pursued, and can also potentially do science, become scientists and, therefore, generate knowledge themselves ... My goal, for this lesson, is to address the nature of science and how I, as a teacher, might portray it. What is the image of science in student-accessed resources? How is the nature of science examined and taken up for discussion within classrooms? How is it understood by my students regardless of their age, background or future aspirations? I want all of my students to see themselves as having the capability of entering into the culture of science.

In all three accounts, the affective component of STSE education is indisputable. One can 'feel' the engagement and excitement of students (and teachers) as they prepare for their dramatic performance in the town hall meeting, or delve into the story of the Burgess Shale fossils. In diverse ways, each of these accounts depicts a form of meaningful personalization that potentially leads to empowerment and action. For ultimately STSE education ascribes to some form of agency – personal and/or political in nature [3.11].

[3.11] Students participate in developing solutions for issues/problems that are relevant and meaningful *(see Account 6, p. 51, Account 7, p. 62).*

Concluding thoughts: what have we learned?

The exemplary accounts analysed in this chapter provide a kind of tapestry from which STSE practice might be viewed. Recoupling values and science, creating spaces for talk, addressing controversy, promoting informed decision making and empowering students are all part of the milieu of STSE teaching. In addition, the accounts reveal some useful lessons for educators interested in emphasizing social responsibility and ultimately participation in socio-political action.

First, the practice of STSE education must be explicit and considered. Casual infusion, or the occasional reference to science and its application to society is not adequate to achieve STSE education goals. In the accounts discussed above, teachers are clear about their goals and describe why they have taken a particular approach. They are deliberate about their curriculum planning, and place STSE education as an organizing theme from which different activities emanate. Second, STSE education needs effective scaffolding to support student learning. Each teacher has carefully crafted the curriculum so that students feel equipped and enabled to explore historical, epistemological and issues-based perspectives. Third, all three accounts suggest that STSE education is multidisciplinary, and that it extends outward, beyond the walls of the school, to include the community. Community involvement and resources allow students to better understand various stakeholder positions, gather information through different mediums (e.g. interviews, books, articles and the Internet), and explore science in a social-cultural context. Fourth, account analyses reveal that students can engage in activities that require empathy, understanding of multiple viewpoints and complicated relationships. Moreover, students can acquire competence in a diversity of epistemological stances, developing a reflexive and critical posture. Many will argue that students, particularly young children, lack the cognitive competence to do so, however these accounts suggest the contrary.

In conclusion, these accounts are exemplary in that they present a post-positivist, progressive vision of science education. Utilizing STSE education perspectives and approaches, these teachers challenge conventional science teaching with its heavily transmissive orientation. Instead, they convey an image of science teaching that reflects a more just, socially responsible and democratic science curriculum.

Analysis 4
Conceptual development

Keith S. Taber

Introduction

Much science learning is conceptual in nature. This is not to deny the importance of the affective (or even the aesthetic) in learning science, or the development of manipulative skills so essential for a laboratory scientist. Students will develop attitudes about the role of science in society, come to appreciate beauty in nature, acquire laboratory techniques, develop their social and group work skills and much more: but most science courses are traditionally largely concerned with 'learning science'.

For scientists and science educators, science is an evolving and dynamic body of knowledge that we use to make sense of, and – to some extent – control, the world in which we live. The *content* of science is not an archive of facts, but a complex set of related theories, laws, and so forth that we use to model the world. Science is a highly conceptual business, and learning science is about building – and developing – interconnecting frameworks of scientific concepts.

In Account 3, Josie describes how her initial perception of organic chemistry was of 'numerous reactions' to learn, to which she reacted with 'dread'. However, she came to see this area as a strength once she was able to see how the reactions fitted into a logical conceptual framework [4.1]. So the science teacher is charged with helping learners develop their conceptual frameworks in ways which reflect both the nature and content of science. This is a challenge indeed, and one which the exemplary science teachers whose work is reflected in the episodes reported in this book, have risen to.

[4.1] Learning is facilitated once students can see 'patterns' in the science content *(see Account 3, p. 29)*.

The nature of learning

Learning is a natural activity for human beings – we all acquire a wide range of knowledge without any conscious effort. However, teaching is concerned with directing the student's learning in specific directions, and doing this effectively is far from simple. As Keith points out in Account 1, expecting students to simply absorb knowledge in class is unrealistic [4.2]. Learning is highly constrained by a range of factors, relating to the cognitive abilities of the learner, their existing conceptual structures, their perceptions of learning and the learning context and the teaching context set up to facilitate conceptual development.

[4.2] Knowledge cannot simply be transferred from teacher to student *(see Account 1, p. 15, and Account 6, p. 51).*

The concrete and the abstract

Learning science is facilitated, and constrained, by the nature of the learner's perceptual and cognitive apparatus. Experiences in childhood and adolescence help trigger the development of increasingly abstract faculties of thought (Bliss 1995). Younger children need problems to be made 'concrete' before they can solve them [4.3]. For example, problems set in a familiar context make a lower cognitive demand on learners than formally equivalent abstract problems. In Account 1, Keith decided to reintroduce dissection into his teaching about the kidney. He felt that showing students nephrons from a real kidney would provide them with something concrete as a referent for class discussion of kidney function. In Account 3, Josie found that, for her, molecular models provided a way of making abstract ideas about molecular geometry and structure concrete.

[4.3] Making learning 'concrete' helps many learners relate to science concepts *(see Account 1, p. 18, Account 3, p. 30, Account 7, p. 58, Account 9, p. 76 and Account 10, p. 89).*

Limitations on information processing

It is sometimes *helpful* to think of the learner's brain as an information processing system (Taber 2000). Research has shown that the part of our brain, which might be considered the 'central processor' (sometimes called working memory), actually has a very limited processing capacity. This clearly has implications for the learning of complex material. When a learner perceives new information as 'overloading' the working memory there is little chance of the material being fully understood. A limited amount of novel material can be processed in a lesson, so the teacher needs to organize material into 'learner-sized' segments [4.4]. In Account 3, Josie reports how, when revising, she would review her notes on a single topic, and then change her activity to spend time testing and reinforcing her understanding, rather than trying to cover more material. Even when the new material does not seem too complex *in itself*, a learning task may still overload working memory, if additional material has to be recalled from long-term memory to process material. These limitations explain the problem identified by Keith in Account 1, where 'careful explanations' did not seem to help learners master knowledge about kidney function.

[4.4] The teacher needs to break the material to be taught into manageable 'learning quanta' *(see Account 8, p. 67 and Account 9, p. 73).*

People cope with such a low working memory capacity because our brains automatically 'chunk' information *that is familiar* into larger units. In Account 3, Josie was initially unable to see a pattern in the large number of reactions she was expected to learn in organic chemistry. However, when she learned about the different types of reaction mechanisms chemists conjecture to explain such reactions, it provided her with a way to classify the reactions. Her learning provided her with a series of mental slots ('schemata') to act as templates for sorting and conceptualizing reactions [4.5].

Utilizing information channels

One approach to maximizing learning is to involve several modes of input into memory. Different students have different learning styles, i.e. preferred ways of acquiring knowledge [4.6]. In Account 4, Richard and Kim used multimedia materials where students could select audio or written text. Some learners find the visual patterns in their notes helpful cues to recalling material – suggesting that patterned notes with plenty of colour and graphics, rather than volumes of uniform text, help these students. This may explain why, in Account 3, Josie found it helpful to rewrite worksheets in her own hand. Teachers should therefore both aim to cater for all learning styles and provide the experiences that will help learners *develop* their own repertoire of learning styles.

Motor memory seems to be largely independent of other forms of memory. For example, we can often remember a telephone number by dialling 'with our fingers' when we can't recall the number in other ways. Even for those who prefer visual and auditory modes of learning, physical activities provide a useful alternative, as Josie recognized when manipulating 3D simulations of molecules in Account 3 [4.7].

The time scale for forming memories

Once new information has been processed through the cognitive bottleneck of working memory, it still needs to be committed to a more permanent form of memory before any learning can be considered to have occurred – a process usually considered to *begin* some hours later [4.8]. New memories are initially only linked to existing memories to a limited extent. As Keith points out in Account 1, students commonly seem to have forgotten much that they understood in one science lesson by the start of the next. Accessing memories becomes more difficult over time unless they are reviewed. If memories are revisited regularly then they are increasingly integrated with other learning over a period of many months. The more a memory is linked to other learning, then the easier it is to access.

[4.5] The *perceived* complexity of new learning depends upon the way existing learning can be used to organize new knowledge (*see Account 3, p. 30*).

[4.6] Effective teaching is available to students with different learning styles (*see Account 3, p. 30, Account 4, p. 34 and p. 36, Account 8, p. 67–68 and Account 9, p. 77*).

[4.7] Physical manipulation of apparatus can provide an additional way of learning and recalling information (*see Account 3, p. 30, and Account 10, p. 86*).

[4.8] Learning is likely to be incomplete and fragile until reinforced (*see Account 1, p. 19, Account 2, p. 24, and Account 7, p. 59*).

Constructing learning

Science learning is both facilitated, and constrained, by the prior learning of a student. In any learning situation, *how much* is learned, and *what* is learned, are both highly contingent upon the existing knowledge that a learner already has available. The learner uses her existing conceptual frameworks as the basis for interpreting novel information: as the bedrock for anchoring new knowledge, the substrate for developing new understandings and the foundations for the construction of new knowledge [4.9]. In Account 3 (pp. 30–1), Josie found that interesting anecdotes, which brought out the human side of science (such as the origin of the name nylon), acted as useful targets to which she could anchor abstract learning. Similarly, in Account 5, Karen found that the biographies of scientists could provide the contexts for teaching students about the science. When planning instruction, the teacher needs to analyse the concepts being presented, both to make explicit the internal connections between component ideas and to identify the prerequisite knowledge that must be assumed if the new material is to make sense [4.10]. In Account 1, Keith identified a previous study of regulation of body temperature and blood-glucose levels as being reference points for explaining how the body regulates the water content of blood. That the identified prerequisite knowledge is available to learners can be checked through diagnostic assessment (Taber 2002).

[4.9] Prior experience acts as a substrate for new learning – for making sense of new ideas *(see Account 5, p. 45)*.

[4.10] Meaningful learning is only possible when the learner finds material relevant to previous learning *(see Account 1, p. 21)*.

However, when Keith taught about the structure of the kidney, he recognized that his students had no relevant experience to help them interpret the abstract structure (Account 1, p. 17). Schematic textbook diagrams were colourful, but could not be anchored to anything in the students' experience. In addition, a video animation that made sense to Keith was of little value to his students who did not appreciate what was being represented. Sometimes the teacher may decide that the students will not have the necessary experience to make sense of new material, *and* that providing direct experience is not a realistic option. In this situation, the teacher may find suitable analogies, models or metaphors to make a bridge between the new material and something that *is* available within the students' prior experiences. In Account 1 (p. 19), Keith modelled ultrafiltration, something that could not readily be demonstrated in an actual kidney. In Account 4 (p. 34), Richard and Kim provided students with an animation simulating electrical current.

Even when students have the necessary background knowledge, this does not ensure that they recognize its relevance – as James points out in Account 10 (p. 84). The teacher needs to make the connections explicit *and* show how the new information fits into the existing frameworks of knowledge. Alex, in Account 8 (p. 63), takes this process further, restructuring the curriculum to be taught around students' expertise and interests.

Students' ideas in science

Teachers do not just have to consider whether relevant prior learning is present and how to access it, but whether such prior learning sufficiently matches the accepted concepts of science. Research has revealed that in any science topic considered, regardless of the level of study, some learners are likely to hold 'alternative conceptions' or 'alternative frameworks': that is, understandings of the topic distinct from, and sometimes inconsistent with, the scientific models in the curriculum (Driver et al. 1994). Some alternative frameworks are found to be very common: most children seem to believe that the speed of an object is a measure of the force acting on it; most secondary students seem to develop a belief that chemical reactions occur to allow atoms to fill their shells. However, as all people are unique, and their experiences are somewhat different, many other alternative notions are found to be rare or idiosyncratic.

However limited, fragmentary and technically flawed a learner's existing knowledge of a science topic may be, it comprises the only conceptual resources available to the learner to understand new teaching. As existing knowledge and understanding act as foundations for new learning, students' *alternative* conceptual frameworks can be barriers to learning the accepted models of science. Our conceptual frameworks determine how we interpret new information, whether we are students, teachers or scientists – as demonstrated in the story of the Burgess Shale fossils discussed in Account 6. Although we may give up some ideas readily, others seem quite resistant [4.11]. In Account 2, George reports how some students retain a 'science fiction' view of space, despite being taught astronomical concepts. In Account 6, Katherine describes how students may hold on to an unrealistic notion of what 'proper' science involves.

[4.11] Ideas students bring to teaching may prove very tenacious *(see Account 2, p. 24 and Account 6, p. 49).*

Scaffolding learning

As the learner will have a limited capacity to process information, the teacher may need to show the students how to reorganize their knowledge into the most suitable form to support the new learning. As an example consider Account 2 (p. 24), where George describes how students were aware that the Moon presents the same side to the Earth, but could not see how this was consistent with the moon revolving on its axis. George used role play to help students shift their frame of reference to appreciate why the Moon must be revolving.

The order in which new material is presented is important in making it meaningful to learners. The optimum sequence will depend, both upon the prior experience available as a referent and the logical structure of the new content. In Account 5 (p. 45), Karen's students were only able to effectively plan an interview with a practising scientist because they had developed a suitable conceptual framework through their studies of scientific biographies. In Account 3 (pp. 29-30), Josie found that her teacher's decision to teach certain topics (isomerism and reaction mechanisms) early in the course, provided key ideas that could be used to organize subsequent teaching.

[4.12] Teaching materials often act as 'scaffolds' for student learning, helping to structure the learning process *(see Account 3, p. 30 and Account 5, pp. 41–42)*.

Teachers can often help learners by providing them with general structures to act as frameworks for knowledge [4.12]. Many teachers are familiar with writing frames to help scaffold written work, but in science there are many useful schemata. For example, Alex used such a schemata to represent cause and effect in Account 8 (pp. 64–65), to provide a general outline to help learners pattern information. The learner's grasp of new material will often be very delicate and fragile, and will not immediately be able to retain its structural integrity without the 'scaffold' of support provided by the teacher. Students who seem fully to understand new concepts may soon become totally confused, if expected to apply new learning without sufficient support. Also, part of the teacher's skill consists of judging how to withdraw the scaffold of support, at the optimum rate, to allow learners to become autonomous users of new ideas. The learner's knowledge becomes more robust as it becomes more familiar with use. As the new learning becomes better integrated into existing conceptual frameworks, it becomes easier to access from memory, and can be more effectively processed as a single 'chunk' of information. This is exemplified in Account 8, (pp. 65–66).

Incremental and mutational conceptual change

Conceptual change in science is often considered to be of two main types. Incremental learning would involve the addition of minor elements to an existing conceptual framework: such as learning that 'ash' is an additional example of 'tree' alongside 'oak', 'maple' etc; or that 'lustre' is an additional property of 'metal', along with 'electrical conductivity'. In principle, this is a relatively unproblematic process. Yet, even here the teacher must draw the learner's attention to relevant prior learning and help the learner to see *how* new information fits into their existing understanding.

In Account 1 (p. 19), Keith reports the use of a common teacher tactic at the start of a lesson: a recall of the learning objectives of the previous lesson. This draws attention to the prior learning which will form the substrate for the new understandings to be developed. In Account 3 (p. 29), Josie recognized how the organic chemistry she was taught related to her study of biology. Hence, she was able to develop a better-integrated conceptual scheme for her knowledge by adding new links [4.13]. Sadly, research suggests that such connections are not always so readily made by students (Taber 1998).

In contrast, mutational conceptual change requires modifications of, and not just addition to, the existing knowledge base – some form of restructuring of what has previously been learned. This is analogous to so-called 'scientific revolutions', such as the Copernican revolution. The reinterpretation of the Burgess Shale fossils, discussed in Account 6 (p. 46), requires this type of restructuring – reconceptualizing the data within a very different overall pattern [4.14]. This process of more radical conceptual change is not very well understood, but depends upon a natural tendency of the human brain to bring about greater coherence of conceptual structures. Knowledge structures in the brain are reorganized so that the overall pattern 'makes more sense'. Such restructuring results in new insight, such as Archimedes' 'Eureka' moment. Although the restructuring itself is an automatic and subconscious process, it is facilitated by conscious engagement with the subject matter.

Sometimes, conceptual development involves the independent formation of alternative conceptual structures relating to the same concept area. In this scenario, the new perspective is initially likely to seem less convincing to the learner. Here, the teacher's role is to make the new approach seem more logical, coherent, sensible etc., so that it may – in time – become the preferred way of thinking and the initial approach falls into disuse. We know from the history of science that such changes of mind require considerable time and effort (Thagard 1992). Here, the role of the teacher is to act as advocate and persuade the student that the curriculum model is a rational choice. Sometimes this may involve casting doubt about existing ideas. In Account 2, George describes how students find the logarithmic nature of the decibel scale counter-intuitive, and how he provides them with the empirical experiences to provide a 'cognitive conflict situation'. In this case, the evidence of their sense of hearing contradicts their expectations [4.15].

The importance of 'activity' in learning

What are always needed to bring about conceptual development are opportunities for students to explore new ideas, their meanings and their relationship with other concepts. We refer to this as 'active' learning, and in some accounts this may involve much *physical* activity. In Account 2 (p. 26) George's physics class actively take on roles within a scale model of the solar system, as well as playing ions in solution. However, it is mental activity which is the key. In Account 1 (p. 19), Keith recognized the importance of allowing students to discuss their ideas and provided a suitable teaching context through model building. This was an active learning task,

[4.13] Greater conceptual integration should be seen as a key objective for learning science *(see Account 10, p. 86)*.

[4.14] Sometimes conceptual change requires restructuring of existing knowledge *(see Account 6, p. 46)*.

[4.15] Sometimes teachers bring about conceptual change by challenging students' expectations *(see Account 2, p. 27, Account 5, p. 40, and Account 8, p. 64)*.

which encouraged students to share their ideas to achieve a common goal. Keith's class were set an activity that ensured students were busy, focused on the task, and necessarily exploring their understanding of the relevant ideas with their peers.

Keith described this activity in terms of chaos, fun and creativity – and as being intense. It seems that Keith's class were experiencing that state known as 'flow' (or 'optimal experience'), a condition where students find the learning activity motivating in itself, and learning seems to be effortless (Csikszentmihalyi 1988a) [4.16]. In Account 7, Susan describes how a role-play activity, which began at an outdoor education centre, engaged learners in a similar way – the students, working in roles, were able to absorb a great deal of information in a session. The assigned roles appeared to not only motivate students and help them maintain concentration, but helped provide a framework around which the students could structure their learning – some of Susan's students identified 'succession' as a potential organizing principle for their new learning. Similarly, when students are planning their own study activities, they would be advised – like Josie in Account 3 – to ensure they are actively engaged in restructuring the material to reinforce and help consolidate their learning.

To a significant extent, science education is about engaging with curriculum versions of models which have achieved some form of consensus acceptance in science. Understanding that science is developed using models should be a key learning objective of science education (Gilbert and Boulter 2000). As George points out in Account 2 (p. 24), it is important that pupils come to appreciate the limitations of the models used in teaching science, as well as their strengths. Clearly, involving students in the active development and evaluation of their own models can be a key part of their scientific education.

As discussed in other chapters, the learning process is usually mediated by the learner's own use of language – thinking through talking, listening, reading and thinking (Scott 1998) [4.17]. A particular feature of much of the exemplary science teaching presented in this book is that learners have been asked to use language in a particular way: to *plan* presentations for specific audiences. In Account 1, Keith's model-building activity provided opportunities for the students to explore and develop their fragile understandings, and then apply new knowledge to both building and defending their model to the class. The task included a planning stage, which required students to begin by *organizing their knowledge* in preparation for the model building. In Account 3 (p. 30), Josie describes how she would revise with someone able to perceive the science at a similar 'resolution'. In this case it was a fellow student. In Account 5 (p. 43), Karen not only had students brainstorm ideas, but also edit each other's written work.

[4.16] In most effective learning episodes, students experience an intense state of flow, where the activity is rewarding in itself *(see Account 1, p. 20 and p. 22 and Account 7, p. 62)*.

[4.17] Language is a key mediator of learning, and the means by which learners can explore new ideas *(see Account 1, p. 21 and Account 8, p. 65)*

The use of an audience can also provide learners with a more immediate purpose for learning. In Account 1, by suggesting that students would have to explain their ideas to the rest of the class, Keith was encouraging deep, rather than a surface, understanding of the task. Later in the sequence of lessons learning was reinforced by having pairs of students construct a mark scheme – again a context to explore and develop their understanding of the topic. The presentation of a model (Account 1), the defence of a debating position (Account 7) and the performance of a historical vignette (Account 5), all provide a rationale for constructing a 'product' of learning in a limited timescale, and are things that learners can relate to (i.e. concrete examples) and can work together to achieve, and which mimic the type of learning situations found in the world outside of school.

An overview of exemplary science teaching for conceptual development

Teaching for conceptual development requires teachers to start where the students are and to present new information in appropriate learning quanta – as seen from the learner's resolution. The new information is made as concrete as possible and clearly linked to available prior learning. Exemplary science teaching encourages active engagement of students and utilizes their different learning styles. In particular, students are given opportunities to explore new ideas with their peers in purposeful contexts. This is done to help them make sense of the new learning and so use it to construct new concepts. In this way the learner is able to develop conceptual structures that are more coherent, better integrated and so better represent the conceptual frameworks of science itself.

Analysis 5
Problem-based contextualized learning

Ann Marie Hill and Howard A. Smith

Introduction

In this chapter, we discuss the accounts from the perspectives of problem-based learning (PBL) and learning in context. Historically, both PBL and learning in context have served as the conceptual foundations for technology and how it is learned. Accordingly, an important feature of technology is that it 'depends on awareness gained during practical work, not only abstract knowledge' (Pacey 1992: 128) and places hands and hearts on a par with heads. This approach continues to define technology and technology education today and is also proving relevant to science education. Although PBL and learning in context possess distinct academic histories, they are conceptually interwoven.

In this chapter, the literature used for PBL interprets PBL as a *curriculum organizer* and *instructional strategy* that is grounded in constructivist pedagogy and is a subset of problem solving. The literature on learning in context offers further characteristics of PBL from the viewpoint of cultural psychology and of everyday or so-called authentic learning. Therefore, we examine each concept separately, beginning with PBL.

Problem-based learning

PBL can be traced to the work of John Dewey and inquiry-based learning, but is well known as a pioneer pedagogy originating in the Faculty of Medicine, McMaster University in Ontario, Canada in the 1960s (e.g. Camp 1996; White 1996). Today, PBL is evident in various forms in over 80 per cent of medical schools around the world. It has also spread beyond medicine to many other professions such as business, law, police science and education (Camp 1996). This growth in PBL has resulted in an enormous amount of literature that reports research, describes account studies, portrays character-istics and presents multiple definitions and models.

Torp and Sage (1998: 14) define PBL as 'focused, experiential learning (minds-on, hands-on) organized around the investigation and resolution of messy, real-world problems. It is both a curriculum organizer and instructional strategy, two complementary processes'. We also find numerous other characteristics of PBL in the literature (Boud and Feletti 1991; Barrows and Myers 1993; Savery and Duffy 1995; Camp 1996; Jones 1996; White 1996; Glasgow 1997; Fogarty 1998; Greening 1998). The following characteristics of PBL are most recurrent:

- PBL is based in constructivist philosophy;
- learners construct their own knowledge from real-life problems;
- knowledge acquisition is steeped in practice that actively engages learners in authentic activities and interdisciplinary environ-ments;
- problems are ill structured and solutions require an iterative process;
- learners negotiate socio-cultural meaning while solving problems in groups;
- PBL promotes higher order thinking as learners are encouraged to think critically, creatively and reflectively and, as such, improves the quality of learning;
- PBL is student centred, with students assuming responsibility for their learning, and
- PBL is faculty facilitated where faculty guide, probe and support group and individual learning.

In this section, we briefly discuss eight characteristics of PBL and relate them to the selected accounts. These characteristics of PBL are labelled constructivism, problem solving in real-life contexts, learning steeped in practice and authentic tasks, ill-structured problems, negotiated meaning, quality of learning, student centred and faculty facilitated. As these characteristics overlap in the literature, the dis-cussion below is derived from all citations above, unless otherwise indicated.

Constructivism

Philosophy frames educators' world views. It constitutes their para-digms or conceptual frameworks, which influence actions in class-rooms and in preparation for classrooms. Constructivism is one philosophical view. Savery and Duffy (1995: 32) provide a succinct overview of PBL within a constructivist framework. They put forward three primary constructivist propositions:

1. Understanding is in our interactions with the environment.
2. Cognitive conflict or puzzlement is the stimulus for learning and determines the organization and nature of the world.
3. Knowledge evolves through social negotiation and through the evaluation of the viability of individual understandings.

(Savery and Duffy 1995: 32)

They also propose eight instructional principles that evolve from the propositions:

1. Anchor all learning activities to a larger task or problem.
2. Support the learner in developing ownership for the overall problem or task.
3. Design an authentic task.
4. Design the task and the learning environment to reflect the complexity of the environment in which they will function in at the end of learning.
5. Give the learner ownership of the process used to develop a solution.
6. Design the learning environment to support and challenge the learner's thinking.
7. Encourage testing of ideas against alternative views and alternative contexts.
8. Provide opportunity for and support reflection on both the content learned and the learning process.

[(pp. 33–4)]

In Account 4, Richard Rennie and Kim Edwards offer an example of constructivist pedagogy. Students assume responsibility for their learning. The account demonstrates curriculum and instructional strategies that are consistent with constructivist propositions and instructional strategies [5.1]. Data presented in Table 2 (p. 37) clearly document that personal autonomy (Lebow 1993) is important to the students. Richard and Kim provide insight into the impact of constructivist pedagogy on the teacher. They describe the impact on teacher preparation and organization (see also Hill and Hopkins 1999).

[5.1] PBL is grounded in constructivism *(see Account 4, pp. 32–33)*.

Problem solving in real-life contexts

The dynamic of problem posing and problem solving in technology is most commonly known as 'the technological method'. In science the dynamic of inquiry is 'the scientific method'. When connected to real-life problems, it encourages problem posing, which they believe to be at the creative end of the problem-solving continuum. In PBL, students are not problem solving in an abstract way. They are solving problems that are central to what they are learning and the educational goals at hand.

One way to situate secondary school learning in real-life contexts is to link problem solving to projects needed in the community: what Hill (1999) has coined 'community-based projects', or to other relevant situations or issues in students' lives. When connections are made by students between what they learn in school and their own lives, they are more motivated to understand and remember. Connections provide a purpose to student learning in PBL because students need to acquire knowledge and skills to advance their projects and because learning is required to solve a problem relevant to their lives. Problems from real-life contexts also provide relevance to student learning, as projects reflect the intricate, holistic nature of the environment in which they will actually function. As such, students see value in what they are learning [5.2].

In Account 1, Keith Hicks's approach to student learning is to contextualize learning in real-life situations. He does this by using real kidneys to carry out investigation of the kidney and the nephron. Keith acts as a guide to probe and support learning. In Account 2, George Przywolnik engages students in familiar real-life outdoor experiences to contextualize the three concepts at hand. In the measurement of motion, learners negotiate meaning by pooling their times to create and discuss data patterns. The low-tech rocket activity also provides opportunities for group work, critical thinking and negotiated meaning. In Account 7, Susan Yoon examines how beaver populations affect ecosystems. Students visit an actual beaver site to engage in problem solving for the beaver problem. The structures that were built two years later represent what could be community-based projects in a technology class and an ideal situation to link science and technology.

[5.2] PBL uses real-world problems to engage student learning in the problem-solving process, and in the acquisition of disciplinary knowledge and skills *(see Account 1, p. 18 and Account 2, pp. 27)*.

Learning steeped in practice and authentic tasks

It stands to reason that if a problem is derived from a real-life context, the task at hand is authentic. In addition, research for information and the production of an artefact or product to solve the problem engages students in acquisition of both conceptual and procedural knowledge. This engagement of head and hand – theory and practice

[5.3] Community-based projects lead naturally to problem solving in real-life contexts *(see Account 7, p. 57)*.

– reflects problem solving as it occurs in the real world [5.3]. Arendt (1958: 169) crystallizes this position: '[T]he thought process by itself no more produces and fabricates tangible things, such as books, paintings, sculptures and compositions, than usage by itself produces and fabricates houses and furniture.'

In Account 10, Jim Johnston engages students in problem-solving activities that require both head and hand. Students are drawn into the exploration of components to produce a mousetrap car. In Account 1, Keith Hicks also engages students in both head and hand activities by exploring the kidney and building a nephron. He engages students in authentic tasks, and in doing so student learning is steeped in practice.

Account 2 demonstrates a situation where content taught in a school setting cannot reflect real-life, authentic tasks, and yet there is a focus on practice. Students cannot build the prototype of a real rocket. George Przywolnik's statement, 'the imprecision inherent in the technology obscures much useful information' (p. 28) describes teacher deliberation when deciding on the value of using simulations, or scale models instead of prototypes. Similarly, in Account 10, Jim Johnston uses the creation of a scale model car to engage students in theory and concepts of automotive technology. This is an introduction to senior courses where students can create a prototype of a car that uses electric power as alternative energy (see http://educ.queensu.ca/~techstd/gecr1999.html).

According to Savery and Duffy (1995), an authentic task does not necessarily mean that students need to work in an identical environment or tackle the exact task encountered in real life. An authentic task and authentic learning environment reflect the cognitive demands required in real life. We would add that physical skill and interpersonal skills are also required [5.4].

[5.4] PBL engages students in learning through practical activities where they use both head and hand to solve authentic tasks *(see Account 1, p. 20 and Account 10, p. 84)*.

Structured problems

[5.5] When problem solving is grounded in real-life, authentic contexts, real-life materials are frequently used to complete prototypes. *(see Account 10, pp. 84–85)*.

In PBL, problems derive from real-life contexts and are undertaken by students as exploration and experimentation. Hill (1998) posits that in the real world, technological problem solving is interactive, not linear and step by step. Knowledge, skills, materials and process are fundamental in technological processes [5.5]. The interactions between these factors are in flux until a final combination results in a solution to the problem. The problem-solving process, whether it originates with student or teacher problems, is iterative. While the process may seem linear on paper, the artefact is in a constant state of revision. Students constantly revisit prior phases. In Account 10, Jim Johnston fosters student recognition of this as they work through their mousetrap car project. In Account 1, Keith Hicks engages students in exploration, or what he describes as initial chaos.

Knowledge is most relevant to learners when they encounter a situation that requires additional knowledge to advance their activity. In Account 10, Jim Johnston practises this important feature of problem solving by teaching knowledge and skills when required to advance practice.

Negotiated meaning

Today, activities in the world outside of school are conducted in teams or multiple teams working together. PBL encourages group-based activities that require peer negotiation. The nature of the problems used is typically complex. They require students to gather knowledge from a variety of sources, negotiate meaning and consider others' points of view. As such, knowledge is socially negotiated. In Account 1, Keith Hicks's students work in groups and exhibit independent learning, construction of their own contextualized knowledge and social negotiation of meaning. In Account 9, Gabriel Ayyavoo encourages students to consult with professionals outside of school and this further enhances learning in real-life contexts.

Quality of learning

PBL promotes higher order thinking skills as learners are encouraged to think critically, creatively and reflectively. Reflection, an important metacognitive aspect of PBL, results in deep understanding as students retain knowledge for much longer. This retention of knowledge results in transfer of knowledge due to metacognitive activities [5.6]. In Account 1, Keith Hicks engages students in authentic tasks situated in real-world contexts. Reflection is also fostered resulting in a deep understanding of the kidney and the nephron.

[5.6] Problem solving used in PBL is an iterative process (see Account 10, pp. 89–90).

When problem posing precedes problem solving in PBL, ownership, creativity, engagement, motivation and enhanced learning are apparent in student learning. In Gabriel Ayyavoo's class (Account 9) student learning begins with student developed questions and continues with independent student exploration to answer their questions. However, problem posing by students can also occur throughout a teacher-posed problem, as demonstrated in Account 10, by Jim Johnston. The teacher-set project context is the mousetrap car, but students engage in problem posing and additional problem solving throughout the exploratory process of their car development.

Student centred

A problem can be assigned by the teacher or identified by students. In either case, once the problem is assigned or approved, all activities that follow and result in solving the problem are student driven in

PBL. Students are encouraged to take control of their own learning. They identify their own gaps in their understanding in the context of the problem at hand and go about independently learning required skills and knowledge [5.7]. Student motivation is greatly increased because of a sense of ownership. In Account 5, Karen Kettle uses an interdisciplinary, student-centred approach to research the lives of eminent people. Karen encourages students to follow their own interests and, in doing so, engages students in an ill-structured problem. Their learning is independent as they engage in exploration and the identification of gaps in their own knowledge. The peer editing of essays affords collaborative study. The examination of others' lives assists students with deliberations that they themselves face and places students in the shoes of others.

[5.7] In problem solving, discipline knowledge and skills are learned as needed to advance the solution *(see Account 10, p. 86)*.

Faculty facilitated

When students are directly involved in, and responsible for, their own learning in ill-structured but focused problems, there is obviously a need for a different kind of teacher role. Teacher instruction is focused on the development of skills of self-regulation so that learners can become independent. They act as role models in reflection, guiding students in their reflections about learning strategies and what was learned. The teacher also challenges and probes learner thinking [5.8]. In Account 1, Keith Hicks acts as a guide to probe and support learning. As 'creative consultant' in Account 5, Karen Kettle acts as a faculty facilitator. Gabriel Ayyavoo, in Account 9, guides and mentors students through problem posing, the identification of a real-life problem and possible solutions.

[5.8] In PBL learners negotiate socio-cultural meaning while solving problems in groups *(see Account 9, p.74)*.

Learning in context

Of course there is no such thing as non-contextualized learning, as all learning occurs in some context. However, major differences in perspective often exist between advocates of everyday learning and of school learning. In everyday learning, learning and context are inextricably linked as people engage in various forms of cultural activity. In this view, learning, ability, talent and intelligence are as much a part of the situation as they are of the individual (see Barab and Plucker 2002).

In traditional school learning, on the other hand, the focus of schooling agents is to decontextualize learning by emphasizing abstract concepts with little apparent relevance (for the students, anyway) to cultural activity. Nevertheless, a schooling context still exists, with its unique ways of being and knowing. Thus the relevant educational question becomes: which forms of learning are best supported by which contexts?

In this section we briefly discuss four of the complex factors linking learning and context, while simultaneously addressing the accounts. These factors are labelled: mediation, embodiment, distribution and situatedness. Since all the accounts exemplify these four factors, only a small selection of examples will be delineated for each factor.

Mediation

The view that learning is mediated originates with the notion that humans use cultural tools or mediational means when engaged in action of various forms (Vygotsky 1978). Examples of mediational means include language, musical instruments, hoes and hammers. The theory supporting mediation has several roots, but the works of Peirce, Dewey and Vygotsky are cited most frequently.

Although the secondary school student is usually treated as a passive recipient of knowledge, the mediated view of learning emphasizes the need for learners to engage in authentic cultural tasks using relevant cultural tools. As shown in the classroom studied by Hill and Smith (1998), where students constructed such items as bike-cars and a dome, human action is shaped by the cultural tools in use, including paper, pencil, drill presses and welding torches.

Hence, everyday (or authentic) learning exposes students to a wide range of cultural tools and their use in cultural tasks [5.9]. Each of the accounts in this book makes use of such tools. In Account 4, Richard Rennie and Kim Edwards prepare a variety of digital and written products to support student learning in their classes. Accounts 8 and 9 offer various examples of introducing students to the many tools of science, including its language and processes.

[5.9] Learning is mediated by tools of the culture *(see Account 4, p. 33 and Account 9, p. 73)*.

Embodiment

Everyday learning recognizes that learning involves the body as centrally as the mind and embraces cognitive, emotional, physical and social dimensions (see Johnson 1987). In embodied learning, cognition, perception, cultural tools and action all work together in the learning process [5.10]. For example, in building a bike-car in the manufacturing technology classroom (Hill and Smith 1998), students made key design decisions based on their own body structures and sizes in determining, for example, where to place the bike-car's seat, foot pedals and steering mechanism. Recognizing this element means separating students from the abstract verbocentric world of books in favour of bodily engagement – away from desks and even from the usual school setting.

In Account 1, Keith Hicks highlights the need for students to see, touch and actively work with real kidneys as opposed to merely

[5.10] All learning is embodied *(see Account 1 p. 17 and p. 19, Account 2, p. 25, Account 3, p. 30 and Account 7, p. 56)*.

looking at photographs of them. These students then build models of the nephron using familiar materials. Similarly, students in George Przywolnik's physics class (Account 2) use their bodies as props to learn about a variety of concepts, such as vibrations, waves and collisions between molecules. They also go outside the classroom to learn other concepts. Even preparing chemistry notes in one's own handwriting, as employed by Josie Ellis, supports the idea of embodiment. So does role play, as used by Susan Yoon in Account 7 for the town hall meeting on the beaver issue.

Distribution

Everyday learning claims that learning is not confined to the individual mind, but extends outwards to include the ongoing actions provided by cultural tools and other persons. The idea of learning as distributed also recognizes explicitly that many tasks cannot be completed by one person working alone, and that in the classroom, knowledge is distributed among all class members (Vygotsky 1978) [5.11]. This perspective conforms with that of most work places, where individuals must work cooperatively in pursuit of common goals, and where different abilities are needed to complete projects successfully (Hill and Smith 1998). Further, both individual and collective memories often reside in artefacts and actions that lie outside the brain.

[5.11] Learning is distributed across groups and situations *(see Account 5, p. 43)*.

In Account 1, Keith Hicks requires students to work in teams of three or four while producing models of the nephron. George Przywolnik (Account 2) uses three simultaneous screamers while studying decibel levels on the school grounds. In Account 5, Karen Kettle uses peer editors, prompters and drama coaches in class work on biographies. James Johnston, in Account 10, employs the whole class situation together with relevant cultural tools to teach a full spectrum of problem solving in technological education.

Situatedness

In contrast to the view that most learning is abstract and generalizable, research over the past two decades has emphasized the situated and contextually-grounded nature of learning (e.g. Barab and Plucker 2002) [5.12]. For example, Hill and Smith (1998) showed that involving students in genuine projects derived from community needs, such as garden tables for a retirement home and a spool rewind system for a major tyre manufacturer, provided specific contexts for engaged student learning.

[5.12] Learning is situated *(see Account 5, p. 38 and Account 6, p. 48)*.

Many of the accounts provide instances of situating learning for the students. For example, in Account 5, Karen Kettle works deliberately to situate science through compelling biographies of the scientists themselves. In Account 6, Katherine Bellomo provides a compelling example of situatedness in science through her lessons on the Burgess Shale fossils.

The learner

The preceding four factors on learning in context address various qualities of learning. An additional element involves the learner. Most people recognize that we differ from one another, often dramatically, in our abilities and interests. These observations have been supported by both theory and research, which have established that we possess an assortment of ability systems. These systems have been represented by Gardner (1983, 1999) as eight primary intelligences (linguistic, musical, spatial, logical-mathematical, bodily-kinaesthetic, intrapersonal, interpersonal and naturalistic) and by Smith (2001) as seven distinct signways (which parallel Gardner's array). Authentic learning recognizes a range of abilities and talents and seeks deliberately to foster them across a variety of contexts (Hill and Smith 1998). The assessment of such learning should also assume diverse forms.

Summary

In this chapter, the accounts have been discussed from the conceptually linked perspectives of problem-based learning (PBL) and learning in context. PBL has been interpreted here as a curriculum organizer and instructional strategy grounded in constructivist pedagogy and problem solving, while learning in context has contributed the additional elements of mediation, embodiment, distribution and situatedness of learning. For teachers, the two perspectives taken together emphasize *doing*, rather than abstract knowing, in culturally appropriate and culturally significant learning tasks.

Analysis 6

Motivational beliefs and classroom contextual factors: exploring affect in accounts of exemplary practice

Steve Alsop

> The day I went into a physics class it was death ... Mr. Manzi, stood in front of the class in a tight blue suit holding a wooden ball. He put the ball on a steep grooved slide and let it run down to the bottom. Then he started talking about let a equal acceleration and let t equal time and suddenly he was scribbling letters and numbers and equals all over the blackboard and my mind went dead.
>
> Sylvia Plath (cited by Claxton 1991: 21)

Introduction

Examples are everywhere. A primary impediment to learning is not cognition but affect. As Hidi and Harackiewicz (2000) suggest it is interest, not intellect that is the real pedagogical challenge for the twenty-first century. There is, of course, much more to science education than cognition. The presence of emotions in teaching is clearly documented: when science teachers talk about their work, they animate episodes of wonder, delight and excitement (Bell and Gilbert 1996), not only because of their love of science but also because of the emotional bonds, the relationships established, developed and maintained with children. It has been widely acknowledged that pedagogical practices are inextricably tied to emotions (Day and Leitch 2001). Hargreaves (1998), for instance, writes of the 'emotional geographies of schooling', the 'spatial and experiential patterns of closeness and/or distance in human interactions or relationships within the school' (Zembylas 2002: 80).

In Part 1, the ten accounts are all about classrooms; fragile and complex social worlds rooted in relationships, expectations, desires and anxieties. Learning science, at any level, is full of emotional challenges, setbacks and triumphs. It involves moving from the familiar – the known – to the unfamiliar – the unknown; traversing the feelings associated with success, self-doubt and identity. At an extreme level, emotions can swamp thinking and concentration such that intellectual efforts are rendered wholly ineffective. 'Cognition doesn't matter if you're scared, depressed or bored' as Claxton (1989: 155) writes. At the other extreme, feelings of enthusiasm, confidence and zeal are equally powerful motivators, so that learners are swept up in a flow of eagerness to learn. In the middle ground, learning is a place of mixed emotions, a balance of attitudes, beliefs, expectations and desires.

In science lessons it is every bit as much the role of the teacher to understand the emotions associated with education as it is to cover the curriculum. However, in research and practice the interaction of affect and cognition is largely understated. Affect is, more often than not, marginalized. In exemplary science teaching I suggest – quite simply – that it shouldn't be.

I can't get no satisfaction

There is presently a very real dissatisfaction with science education and this has an established history. Since the early 1960s off and on, people have worried about the lack of interest and achievement derived from science lessons. Curriculum reform has, for the large part, been built upon making science relevant, engaging and useful for all (Hodson 1998a). But evidence suggests that enrolment in scientific study is on the decline. Despite decades of research, it seems, many students still find science lessons mundane and rather dull (Osborne et al. 2003). Such sentiment is picked up in a comment made by Desmond Ngai in Account 9 (p. 79): 'In today's education system, there is a substantial percentage of students who think negatively about science.' His comments are reiterated from a teacher's perspective when Alex Corry (Account 8, p. 63) juxtaposes his enthusiasm with the tepid performance-orientated response of his students:

> Early in my career, the breadth of scientific knowledge fascinated me. This inspired me to want to infuse the desire for knowledge in my students. It soon became clear to me, that not all if not most, students shared my passion. Yes, they wanted to learn, but of greater importance was the achievement of a credit.

Over the years, there have been a multitude of studies of students' attitudes to science. The interested reader can find a comprehensive review of this work in Osborne et al. (2003). As these reviewers discuss, much of this work is beleaguered by a lack of clear definitions because different researchers see and monitor attitudes in quite different ways. However, some general trends do seem to surface:

- There is a marked decline in attitude towards science from age 11 onwards. Most evidence suggests that children enter school with a positive attitude but this becomes slowly eroded by compulsory education (Doherty and Dawe 1988).

- Girls' attitudes towards science are considerably less positive than boys' (Sjoberg 2000). Perhaps the single greatest travesty in science education is why girls choose not to pursue science studies even though they are now outperforming boys in most examination results.

- There is often a love–hate relationship with school science, which is labelled as either a favourite subject or a least favourite subject and rarely a subject of indifference (Hendley et al. 1995).

- Students' attitudes towards school science vary with specific sciences. Some subjects are considered more relevant than others. In a recent survey, biology, particularly human biology, was seen as addressing pupils' self-interest while the relevance of the physical sciences (less popular subjects) was difficult for students to identify (see Josie's comments in Account 3, p. 29). One topic that appears to attract universal antipathy is the periodic table – some suggest that this is because it is strongly associated with abstraction and memorization (Osborne and Collins 2000).

- A paradox exists between students' general interest in science and their specific liking of school science. Students, it seems, will happily rate science as interesting and relevant while in the same breath report that school science is boring. Some researchers suggest that a reason for this resides in the way school science is presented – as somehow separate and distant from society (Ebenezer and Zoller 1993).

While it is widely acknowledged that changing attitudes is essential, this is far from straightforward, of course. Although research has increasingly signified the magnitude of the problem, it has yet to indicate definitive solutions. Osborne et al. (2003) suggest that science educators could learn much from the literature on motivation and interest. We return to this literature shortly to comment on the accounts; but first, I offer some introductory comments about affect and the accounts.

The accounts

It should come as no surprise that affect is evident in the teachers' accounts. Indeed, in places the narratives positively bubble over with expressions of emotion: 'I am not overestimating when I say the atmosphere in class was one of sheer jubilance. I heard students laughing and talking about the meeting on their way out of the door and through the hallways' (Susan Yoon, Account 7, p. 62). 'Educational chaos, with great fun, creativity and intense learning' (Keith Hicks, Account 1, 20). 'The first year I tried this, I became so enthused by the results and the students' obvious enjoyment of the exercise, that I expanded the data gathering to include students on bicycles on the same track' (George Przywolnik, Account 2, p. 27).

Early on, perhaps, it should be recognized that talking about teaching in such emotive terms is actually both uncommon and controversial. The current education system seems to have been formulated in a detached, mechanistic way to ensure cognitive accountability, efficiency and productivity. Little time is given to considering attitudes. Indeed, teachers' and students' feelings are largely absent from lesson plans and evaluations, which more often than not have a rather dry, factual, anodyne style. The Office for Standards in Education in England and Wales (Ofsted), for instance, offers the following description of exemplary practice (Ofsted 2000: 2):

> Pupils were asked how they pictured electric current and resistance. Suggestions included the flow of water in pipes or a river, cars in roads of varying width, people crowding through stadium entrances, a chain-gang, and eels swimming through a swamp. The class discussed the strengths and shortcomings of each of these as representations of electric current. Pupils demonstrated a good understanding of electricity when questioned and used a variety of analogies to explain particular points.

Elsewhere, I have advocated the use of analogical discussion-based activity as an effective pedagogical technique, and I believe this to be a good example of such an approach. However, this efficient description of practice, I believe, is lacking because it fails to acknowledge affect. I have some additional questions: are pupils enjoying themselves? Are they comfortable with these discussions? Is a sense of humour evident? Do pupils demonstrate an increased interest in electric currents? Which analogies do pupils prefer and why? This serves as one illustration. In more general terms, it seems that although prominent in teachers' lives, affect is often forgotten when discussing exemplary practice.

Teachers' 'enthusiasm for teaching' and 'love of their subject' are

[6.1] Teachers' relationship with their subject infuses their practice *(see Account 3, p. 31, Account 4, p. 36 and Account 5, p. 38)*.

two factors that have become associated with students' attitudes to science (Woolnough 1998) [6.1]. As Josie (Account 3, p. 31) notes about her teacher's positive attitude to chemistry and how it impacted on her lessons: 'An enthusiasm for the subject was transfused onto the students and, as a result, lessons were interesting.'

Woolnough (1998) suggests that teachers' subject confidence is a key feature here. Consequently, he suggests, teachers should be actively encouraged to teach in subject areas that they feel more confident with (often their specialist areas). Perhaps an interesting feature of the accounts is the way in which our teacher-authors have tended to describe lessons in their specialist subject areas, lending, perhaps, some support to Woolnough's claim?

In general terms, the ten accounts raise a number of interesting features about affect in science classrooms. There are tinges of personal expression and the feelings associated with the challenge of teaching. Some evidence is also presented of the emotional climate, the social and emotional setbacks, and rewards faced by individuals in their evolving relationships with their teachers, classrooms and knowledge. It is to these general features that we now turn, albeit with a particular focus.

The lens of analysis

There is a considerable body of work, largely external to science education, which has sought to explore how various motivational constructs influence the quality, quantity and speed of cognition. Here, psychological models abound – attribution theory, self-efficacy theories, goal theories and many others. The literature on motivation is indeed vast. Over a decade ago, a very influential paper was published by Paul Pintrich and colleagues at the University of Michigan (Pintrich et al. 1993). The paper sought to challenge the overly rationalistic and cold image of learning dominating science education. Using this analysis, I focus my exploration of the accounts on hot, motivational beliefs and classroom contextual factors. My analysis has two components, summarized in Figure 3. The first explores learners' beliefs about their *reasons* to perform a particular task. Here, I discuss the accounts with respect to the value components, goal orientation, interest and utility. Another important aspect of motivation is learners' belief about their *ability* to perform a task, in other words, their expectations of success. This is my second section, which I explore with a self-efficacy focus.

My overriding assumption is that effective science education is an experience that learners want to be part of, rather than something that they have to be part of. Given this premise, for me, a key feature of the accounts is how the teachers seek to encourage and promote a positive relationship with science. Or phrased differently, how do the

| The learners beliefs about their *reasons* to perform a task | Task value | Goal orientation Interest Utility |
| The learners beliefs about their *ability* to succeed in a task | Task expectancy | Self-efficacy |

Based on Pintrich et al.'s (1993) analysis.

Figure 3 Motivational components

teachers help learners to become part of, and care about, their science education?

Discussions of motivational beliefs usually focus on the learner, and seek to understand why (or why not) and how learners engage with particular tasks. In contrast, my analysis has a more social emphasis, exploring how the learning environment might serve to actively motivate learners. In this instance my interest is primarily pedagogical. That is, how do the account authors describe classroom activities that are potentially motivating? Or, phrased slightly differently, how are extrinsic classroom-based factors utilized to increase academic motivation?

Learners' beliefs about their reasons to perform a task

People arrive at any learning task with a series of attitudes, expectations and desires, which in conjunction with the task itself and the classroom environment shape their learning. The *achievement goals* that individuals set themselves, their *interest* in the learning task and the *usefulness* they associate with a task are three factors which have been recorded as significant in shaping task engagement.

When discussing achievement goals, a distinction is often drawn between two extremes: task mastery and performance orientation [6.2]. Students with a task mastery goal orientation view learning as largely a means to fully comprehend a task; in this regard their motivations are often described as intrinsic or personal. In complete contrast, those who adopt performance orientation goals overly focus on grades/credits and outperforming others, essentially extrinsic or external values. Evidence suggests that learners with mastery orientations are more likely to use deeper cognitive strategies (including meta-cognition) when compared with students who adopt performance orientations, who often rely mostly on memorization and rote learning.

Classroom environments influence goal orientation. It emerges that tasks which promote student choice are challenging, collaborative and relevant, in terms of their application outside of school, and can

[6.2] Learners often co-exhibit task mastery and performance orientation goals. Take for example, Josie's comments in *Account 3, p. 29 and p. 31*. She describes her interest in learning organic chemistry as well as her *goal* to perform well in examinations.

promote the adoption of mastery goals (Dweck 1986). These features are evident in the accounts presented in this book.

Take, for example, Accounts 8 and 9, in which students are actively encouraged to participate in the setting of learning objectives [6.3]. In these classrooms, the teachers provide learners with considerable flexibility of project focus and as a consequence, as noted by Susan Yoon (Account 7, p. 61), 'incredible motivation and excitement that had been generated'.

[6.3] Promoting learning autonomy promotes mastery orientation *(see Account 4, p. 32 and Account 8, p. 67)*.

I hasten to add that this should not be taken to mean that pupils should be left to do it all on their own. Instead, a delicate balance is struck between self-direction and teacher mentoring. In Account 9, for instance, a specific technique used to support pupil independence is to provide exemplars of previous successful projects, thus effectively increasing familiarity while setting clear expectations. As a consequence, Gabriel reflects: students appear to 'become less stressed and more motivated' (p. 72). Effective practice, I suggest, should promote, structure and nurture student independence and choice.

The authors of the accounts in this book offer a variety of activities that foster collaboration rather than competition and comparison [6.4]. These lessons are not about 'teaching for the test' and tend to steer clear of evaluation procedures that promote comparison, competition and performance orientation goals. The classrooms offer supportive nurturing environments in which pupils work together on particular projects. Their learning is closely and systematically evaluated while in progress and not artificially dissected in post-learning examinations.

[6.4] A collaborative environment helps promote mastery orientation *(see Account 7, p. 54)*.

For instance, Susan, in Account 7, describes the basis of her pedagogy in terms of 'cooperative learning and community building' (p. 54). Her thought-provoking role play, in which participants act as representatives from special interest groups, provides a structure for discussing different ideological perspectives. Significantly, the goal of this discussion is 'consensus' building (pp. 59–62) and not outperforming (or besting) others. Often a weakness with classroom debate is the way in which it fosters competition (rather than collaboration), where each group sets out with the goal of winning the argument. What I found particularly refreshing about Susan's account was the notion that each group had something to offer the overall discussion, and that the goal was to reach consensus based on different points of view (p. 61). This approach, I suggest, encourages the mastery of complex issues, using higher order reasoning – analysis and synthesis – to understand and compare different perspectives, rather than arguing from a singular point of view [6.5].

[6.5] A Mastery Orientation Goal encourages higher order reasoning skills *(see Account 7, pp. 59–62)*.

Interest and utility value

Interest and utility value are two other motivational constructs associated with increased student performance. Research suggests, that these deep-rooted personalized constructs have the potential to mediate cognition in fundamental ways (Pintrich et al. 1993).

Quite simply, effective teachers make lessons interesting. Paradoxically, however, by the time students reach secondary school, surveys suggest that their interest in science is often waning (Doherty and Dawe 1988). In the accounts, our authors use a variety of situational teaching techniques to 'buck' this trend. George, Karen and Katherine (Accounts 2, 5 and 6, respectively), for instance, make science more enticing by relating it to people, a humanist tradition [6.6]. Attitudinal research suggests that many students find abstract dehumanized scientific content difficult to digest (Ebenezer and Zoller 1993).

[6.6] Relating science to people *(see Account 5, p. 38 and Account 6, p. 48)*.

In Account 1, Keith teaches human biology, a popular subject. Adolescent girls and boys, perhaps unsurprisingly, seem to like things to do with human bodies (Sjoberg 2002). Moreover, I suggest that Keith's use of real kidneys serves to make this lesson more authentic, sensational and provocative. George, in Account 2, seeks to build a relationship with a more remote and esoteric object, physics – more specifically waves and dynamics – by using role play. Quintessentially, again a humanizing teaching technique. Students become projectiles, planets and waves and wet rocket scientists. There is also the added tension of the starter pistol and Mr Przywolnik in his car: unorthodoxy, of course, promotes interest.

Karen and Katherine also help their students identify with humanistic values. Karen (Account 5) uses techniques more commonly associated with other areas of the curriculum to personalize, and I might add, 'socialize' and 'emotionalize' learning. She expresses this beautifully in her reflection (p. 45):

As my students perform on stage, I can watch them think, feel, and respond from the perspective of an eminent scientist. Their answers shatter the myth that talent is an innate gift, and the diversity of characters illustrates the narrowness of stereotypes of scientists that appear in popular culture. The audience gains an appreciation of different creative lifelines and the wide variety of forms scientific research can take. They also appreciate that individuals control many of the choices concerning purpose, prolonged work and repeated encounters with tasks that allow them to become productive. Should we put science and theatre together? Why not? It comes alive. Everyone learns!

In this lesson, scientists are presented as real people, not distant, remote geniuses. Katherine's use of the Burgess Shale fossil story in Account 6 offers a more grounded historical approach. Her use of explanatory stories serves to entangle students in a foreign culture. Like other analysis authors, I particularly enjoyed her reflection (p. 51):

> Why do some students love biology (or science) and some hate it? Why does 'scientist' become a career choice for so few? For many students, the experience of school science is foreign and difficult. It involves memorization and little of the interpretative features of science practice. ... Students feel lost and alienated. Most don't see scientists as real people, and they don't see scientists as 'like themselves'. Many students see themselves as 'not smart enough' or 'not good at memory work', and so not fit to be scientists.

[6.7] Making science more interesting and relevant *(see Account 5, p. 45, Account 6, p. 51, and Account 9, p. 72 and 77).*

What seems to surface in Katherine's account is the importance of learners' relationships with science [6.7]. In this sense, learning science is more than acquiring content, but also includes a feeling of involvement and attachment with a subject. Helping learners identify with science is fundamental to their success; as Pintrich et al. (1993: 183) comment: 'If a student sees himself or herself as becoming a scientist – that is, a scientist is one of her possible selves – then science content and tasks may be perceived as being more important, regardless of his or her mastery or performance orientation to learning' [6.8].

[6.8] Developing a positive relationship with knowledge is axiomatic in learning *(See Account 6, p. 51).*

[6.9] Utility value is an articulated feature of this pedagogy, *(see Account 8, p. 63).*

Utility value concerns a learner's perception about the potential usefulness of content (or tasks) in helping them achieve some goal, e.g. getting into university, getting a job, solving a problem at home, and so on [6.9]. These values seem to be an important feature of Alex's pedagogy (Account 8, p. 63), he writes: 'I now believe it's not what the students know, but rather how they use their knowledge that is most important. Therefore, I structure lessons around what students currently know and want to know and, then, piggyback the "curriculum" on exploring their beliefs.'

Discussions of this type, within science and technology education, are often explored in terms of 'relevance'. The desire for 'relevance for all' has emerged as a rallying slogan for contemporary educational reform – and like many slogans it is probably not as clearly defined as it might be. One associated problem, of course, is the difficulty of making material 'relevant' for large groups of learners with a spectrum of different goals, interests and aspirations, particularly as research presents a rather gloomy picture of children's decreased valuing of school science activities, especially in secondary school (Wigfield and Eccles 1992).

While most pupils view science to be useful in everyday life, the significance of school science is often found wanting (Sjoberg 2002). Recent evidence suggests that by situating school science activities within the context of authentic socio-scientific issues (concerning health and the environment) can serve to increase relevance (Schreiner and Sjoberg 2003). Keith's and Susan's accounts (1 and 7 respectively) exemplify this approach (further discussion of this issue can also be found in Analysis 3).

The interested reader might wish to explore a different approach to promoting relevance, as proposed by Langer (1993), which she claims might actually be longer lasting. Her proposal is to change students' attitudes to materials by helping them to make material meaningful to themselves. In this account practice takes on a more active role in developing 'attitudes to study'. Rather than teachers attempting to adapt content, pupils are encouraged to look at and explore subject matter in different ways depending on their interests. Langer proposes that too often teachers develop learning environments that compel children to look at material in the same way and from the same perspective as they do. In this case, it is the teachers' interests, values and beliefs that dominate classrooms and not children's. There is much merit, I suggest, in the promotion of emotional learning autonomy.

Learners' beliefs about their *ability* to succeed in a task

While goal, interest and utility beliefs explore some of the reasons why learners engage with particular tasks, another widely recognized feature of motivation is learners' beliefs about whether they can accomplish a task. Central to these considerations are self-efficacy beliefs, which refer to the learners' perceptions or judgement about their cognitive capabilities to accomplish a specific academic task or obtain specific goals (Pintrich et al. 1993).

Research suggests that many secondary school children view ability as an inherently stable entity, one that is not open to change. Children, for example, who view themselves as doing poorly in a subject, such as science, readily believe that their poor performance is due to a lack of innate personal ability in this area of study. As a result, they come to the decision that science has little value to them personally and socially. Hence, they invest as little time and effort as possible in trying to understand it.

Much work on developing self-efficacy is based on increasing the affective construct *confidence*. It is not appropriate, as all successful teachers know to create tasks which promote confusion and then leave students entirely on their own to resolve this. A number of instructional techniques have been proposed in the literature which assist learners to resolve conceptual conflicts and ambiguities and in so doing, it is hoped, increase their, for instance, confidence in learning.

Schunk (1989, for instance, maintains that modelling of conflict-solving strategies by teachers and other students is the key. The approach is based on classroom environments containing a great deal of teacher–pupil interaction, such that an abundance of opportunities exists for pupils to work with other pupils to overcome conceptual difficulties. It is significant to note that our account authors, without exception, describe lessons that involve considerable social interaction.

The skill of the teacher in this setting, Schunk suggests, lies in the selection and support of appropriate tasks that are challenging but not beyond the level of comprehension of learners or, significantly, beyond their self-efficacy beliefs about their ability. This latter point is important, since to develop confidence, task selection should be based on the premise of self-efficacy beliefs and not just conceptual ability. If pupils have robust beliefs about their abilities, they are likely to have the confidence and persistence to succeed at even extremely changing tasks. In contrast, if pupils lack confidence and feel a sense of failure they are likely to abandon relatively straightforward tasks. As Susan Yoon succinctly suggests in Account 7 (p. 54), cognition will not occur if students have a negative opinion of themselves as learners [6.10].

[6.10] Developing learners' opinions of themselves as learners (*see Account 7, p. 54*).

In this light, the role of the teacher is to create a pedagogical environment that nurtures self-efficacy as well as, and alongside, concept formation. Common notions of scaffolding (see Analysis 4) take on a more affective realm as practitioners aim to create and structure activities in which pupils gain a sense of personal satisfaction and achievement. In practical terms, for instance, a clearly structured task, broken down into a series of negotiable, achievable and identifiable short-term goals has been shown to increase success and build confidence. This approach is demonstrated well in Accounts 8 and 9.

Effective practice needs to bear the stresses and strains associated with learning. Motivation theorists often discuss this in terms of a cost-benefit analysis, where learners are conceptualized as rationally appraising and re-appraising learning with a view to determine a safe (and profitable) level of engagement (Wigfield and Eccles 1992). The costs of engagement include, for instance, performance anxiety, fear of failure (and fear of success), as well as the amount of effort that will be necessary to succeed at the task. Teaching, in this way, takes on a more therapeutic theme. A therapeutic practitioner is skilled at promoting the benefits and reducing the costs associated with learning [6.11].

[6.11] A therapeutic practitioner is skilled at promoting benefits and reducing the costs of learning (*see Account 4, p. 34 and Account 5, p. 44*).

Examples of this are scattered throughout the accounts. Karen Kettle, for instance, allows nervous students to go first so that their part was over quickly (p. 44). Moreover, she describes her role as a 'creative consultant' (p. 43), encouraging some students to take risks while supporting others who are less comfortable with science.

Richard and Kim in the SCOT project (Account 4, pp. 32) seek to deploy technology to create learning environments that are comforting and supportive for all. Susan teaches a topic which 'resonated with an aspect of the students' lives' (p. 54). Katherine wants her students to 'see the possibilities within science, rather than only the barriers they face or the personal limitations they perceive' (p. 51). Keith, in Account 1, describes a successful example of learning through doing. His pedagogy seeks, in some ways, to balance motivation against distress. Some, I have no doubt, will find the gory kidney dissection fascinating. For others, of course, it will be a turn-off. Keith's challenge is to make such an activity palatable and conceptually challenging for all (Alsop 2000, Alsop & Watts, 2003).

In the longer term, of course, learners need to learn to tolerate and enjoy the emotions associated with the uncertainty of learning. As their confidence increases, teachers need to thoughtfully and carefully remove the amount of support given, and encourage and nurture a sense of emotional independence and autonomy.

Descartes' dream

Rene Descartes, it is commonly told, initiated the formation of modern science with the severance of mind and body – divorcing emotions and feelings from knowledge and knowing. Strangely, some 250 years on, his legacy lingers on in science education. Curricula outcomes are typically stated in terms of acquiring concepts, skills and processes, only occasionally (if ever) in terms of exploring feelings or displaying compassion or sentiment. The Ontario Science Curriculum (OMET 1998: 9) for instance, lists what seems like a dictum of 'conceptual outcomes' and then interprets *attitude* solely in cognitive terms, habits of mind, e.g. commitment to accuracy, precision and integrity in observation; rather than affective terms such as interest, wonderment, fascination and excitement (Simpson et al. 1995).

In science education, by and large, we promote an image of intelligence as individuals thinking quickly and rationally about clearly defined depersonalized things which have certainty (i.e. right or wrong answers) [6.12]. This approach, some suggest, needs to change. It is now widely lamented in academic circles how the very nature of school science might serve to disengage learners. One reason offered as to why many girls find science so unappealing is because of its form. This, theorists suggest, is at fundamental odds with feminine values associated with human and affective aspects of knowledge (see Analysis 9 for more detail).

I am delighted to say that the teachers who have written accounts

[6.12] Refuting stereotypical images of scientists *(see Account 5, p. 40)*

[6.13] Science is more than an emotion-free objectification of the world (*see Account 6, p. 51*).

in this book, point to a different image of science [6.13]. Take for instance, Katherine (Account 6) who blends thought and feeling in her explanatory stories (p. 48):

> Harry Wittington, Derek Briggs and Simon Conway Morris tell of their amazement as they opened drawers at the Smithsonian. The scientists could not believe their eyes as they took in the spectacle of hundreds and hundreds of well preserved soft-bodied animals in fossil form.

She goes on to comment (p. 51): 'The science that students learn (often from a textbook) seems to have been born in the text, not in the mind, work, sweat, tears, frustrations and pleasures of the working scientist.'

Reversing declining attitudes to science, I believe, requires a shift not only in teaching but also in the image we present of science in our classrooms. By ignoring affect, science educators might be culpable on two counts: of actually turning some learners away from understanding and enjoying science, and of misrepresenting science. As Gallas (1995: 20) writes, 'Science does not originate from distance and objectification of the world: it begins with wonder, imagination and awe.' The same, I feel, should be thought of science education.

Science education with a sense of self

Science education is complex. The processes involved in teaching and learning certainly cannot be reduced to a series of algorithms, universally applicable in all educational settings. Our accounts serve nicely to illustrate the insuperable complexity of teaching and learning, and how our teachers' work is grounded in an intricate balance of affect and cognition. This chapter might be thought of as describing teaching in perhaps more varied terms than normal by underscoring the relationship that learners develop with science. It is the quality of this relationship which, I propose, has a lasting effect on their achievement and enrolment. I have briefly highlighted how attitude, interest and motivation play a fundamental role in teaching and learning, lest we forget, as Osborne and colleagues (2003: 1074) remind us, 'that attitudes have an enduring quality while knowledge is more often than not ephemeral'.

In more general terms, I think and feel that there is a spectrum of possibilities for practice by looking at science education through the lens of affect. In the past, theory and practice has largely focused on how students acquire knowledge, rather than conceptualizing learning and doing science as an activity through which one develops a sense of intellectual and personal identity. It is my hope for the future that science educators prioritize the challenge of affect, for as

Csikszentmihalyi (1998a: 115) writes, 'if educators invested a fraction of the energy they now spend trying to transmit information in trying to stimulate the students' enjoyment of learning, we could achieve much better results'.

Analysis 7
Instructional technologies, technocentrism and science education

Jim Hewitt

Introduction

Progress in education can be painfully slow. In many respects, teaching is not a significantly different profession today than it was several decades, or even half a century ago. In other fields, such as medicine, there is a greater sense of advancement over time. Rarely a day goes by without a newspaper announcement of a new vaccine, a new means of diagnosing illnesses, or a new treatment for a serious disease. However, in education, the story is quite different. News-papers rarely mention the results of educational research. It is probably fair to say that most people do not see the field of education advancing at the same rate, or in the same disciplined fashion, as the field of medicine. In fact, some critics openly question whether the quality of schooling is improving at all from year to year.

Interestingly, in spite of the public's difficulties perceiving pro-gress in education, there nevertheless exists a popular belief that learning in tomorrow's schools may be a more efficient and enjoyable process than it is today. Technology plays a central role in this line of thinking. Advocates of technology-rich classrooms feel that compu-ters, camcorders, the Internet, digital video and various electronic devices have the potential to transform schooling in fundamental ways. Indeed, this belief is so strong, and so widely felt, that school boards have already invested deeply in instructional technologies – often using monies that could otherwise be used for textbooks, teaching assistants and library resources (Armstrong and Casement 1998; Robertson 1998). This large-scale investment in technology is perhaps not surprising. Given that technology is transforming the rest of society, it is not unreasonable to believe that it may transform schooling as well.

Will technology revolutionize schooling? So far, there has been little hard evidence that it will have a significant impact. Some published studies support the popular belief that technology offers educational benefits, but the research literature is frequently contradictory in this regard. For example, in 2002 the *Economic Journal* published a paper that raised concerns about the educational value of computers. The study, conducted by Joshua Angrist from MIT and Victor Lavy from the Hebrew University of Jerusalem, examined the educational impact of Israel's Tomorrow-98 initiative, an ambitious technology infusion programme that took place in Israel during the mid to late 1990s. Funded by proceeds from the state lottery, Tomorrow-98 involved the large-scale deployment of computers in elementary and middle schools coupled with an extensive technology training programme for teachers. Angrist and Lavy's (2002) longitudinal analysis of standardized test scores in Tomorrow-98 classrooms suggested that the programme had no discernible effect on language or mathematics learning. In fact, the programme was associated with a slight, but statistically significant decrease in fourth grade mathematics scores.

Obviously, there is still considerable uncertainty regarding the potential of technology in education. In an effort to bring some clarity to the matter, it is proposed that we need to move beyond broad generalizations of technology as inherently effective or ineffective and, instead, develop a deeper sense of the kinds of situations in which technology is best used. What applications of educational technology have the most promise? How can experienced teachers leverage technology to create richer learning experiences and foster deeper student understandings? In an attempt to make headway on these questions, this chapter examines some of the more compelling uses of technology in the ten accounts presented in this volume. A review of these accounts suggests that technology can be an effective support for: (i) concretizing abstract concepts; (ii) providing students with tools for analysing scientific processes; and (iii) supporting connections between people. Each of these applications is discussed in turn and illustrated with reference to both the account studies and other educational research.

Technologies for concretizing abstract concepts

One compelling use of technology in education involves turning artefacts that are normally intangible into artefacts that are tangible. This allows them to be studied in greater depth. In Account 3, Josie Ellis's recollection of organic chemistry offers a non-technological example of this phenomenon [7.1]. Through her use of molecular model kits in high school, Josie was able to create physical models of molecules that could be manipulated, examined and analysed. This led to a deeper understanding of the concept of geometric isomerism

[7.1] Models help comprehension *(see Account 3, pp. 29–30)*.

– a much deeper understanding than she likely could have acquired from reading textbooks or viewing 2-dimensional illustrations of molecular structures. The physicality of the model contributed to her learning.

Computers and other technologies can also be used, to some extent, to concretize abstract concepts. In Account 4, 'The Science Class of Tomorrow?' by Richard Rennie and Kim Edwards, computers were used in this fashion [7.2]. During a unit on electricity, teachers produced a computer animation video that showed the movement of electrons around an electric circuit. In effect, it allowed students to look inside the battery and bulb circuits that they had built on their desks. In this fashion, an important concept that was not open to simple inspection was turned into something more concrete. It is important to note that the use of the computer video did not replace student experimentation with actual bulbs and batteries, but rather served as a complement to those experiences.

There is considerable variability in the degree to which an abstract object may be concretized. For example, a word processor turns words, sentences and paragraphs into objects that have some of the properties of physical objects. Screen objects, like sentences, can be grabbed with the cursor and moved around with a mouse. This offers significant advantages over handwritten text. In essence, objects on a computer screen (e.g. written text) exist at an intermediate level of abstraction. They can be studied and manipulated somewhat, but they have no physicality.

Given the intermediate level of computer-based abstractions, teachers must think carefully about whether it is worthwhile to use technology in a particular learning situation. In some cases, computer-based representations offer perhaps the only way of turning complex, abstract ideas into something tangible (e.g. a teacher might use a computer simulation to examine the effect of relativistic speeds on mass and time). However, in other cases, computer-based representations may be unnecessarily abstract relative to other possibilities. For example, it would be more educationally valuable for elementary students to dissect a real flower than a virtual one. Computers provide certain possibilities for making abstract concepts less abstract, but where feasible, real-life experiences tend to be preferable. Thus, when deciding whether to incorporate technology into a lesson, teachers have to decide whether the intermediate level of abstraction provided by computers offers advantages over alternative approaches.

Sometimes, the best pedagogical decision is *not* to use technology. Keith Hicks, in Account 1, seized upon the importance of concretizing abstract concepts while planning his lessons about kidney function and dysfunction. Recognizing that students in past years had difficulty grasping the notion of a nephron, he felt that some of

[7.2] Computer animation illustrates movement *(see Account 4, p. 34).*

the problem might have been caused by the abstract images used in textbooks and videostrips:

> The diagrams in the text, which are similar in nearly all modern day texts, struck me as very abstract compared to the photographs. This had also been pointed out to me by students. However, the diagrams were very colourful and the textbooks looked much more inviting than the old black and white tomes of the past. But what did the diagrams mean to students who had never seen a real kidney (except perhaps in a steak and kidney pie), or seen the magnified photographs of nephrons? In other words, without a frame of reference, the diagrams were meaningless to the students. I therefore took the decision that it was time to reintroduce dissection into the classroom. I wanted to ensure that all students actually saw a real kidney, and that a teacher (but preferably one of the students) tease out a nephron or part of a nephron from the kidney prior to viewing any schematic diagram.

> (pp. 16–17)

Keith stopped using the video in favour of bringing real kidneys into the classrooms for students to analyse. He chose not to abandon the textbooks entirely. Following the kidney dissection, students were referred to the textbook diagrams again. However, after observing the extraction of a nephron from a kidney first hand, it was easier for them to make the connection between the real-life object and the more abstract representations in the text [7.3].

[7.3] Connecting real-life objects to representations (see Account 1, p. 19).

As a follow-up to the kidney dissection, Keith challenged groups of students to build a model of a nephron, and then present their models to the class. Each model, in this account, served as a shared artefact around which group members could articulate their own understandings of kidney function. Students also had opportunities to learn from each other, since Keith had set up the task in such a way that group members were required to come to consensus regarding the structure of the model [7.4].

[7.4] Learning through collaboration (see Account 1, p. 20).

In sum, technology can be a useful tool for concretizing abstract concepts. However, it is important for teachers to be aware of the alternatives open to them. One of the problems with instructional technologies is that it is usually impossible to make broad generalizations, such as 'simulations help students learn'. The value of a particular technology depends heavily on the instructor's goals, the needs of the student and the context of the lesson. Sometimes, technologies can offer views on natural processes that would otherwise remain invisible (e.g. electrons moving through a wire). However, as the Keith's account illustrates, technologies such as computers and videotapes, which present concepts at an intermediate level of abstraction, are not always the best alternatives. If the teacher has a choice, real-life experiences are often preferable.

Technologies for analysing natural phenomena and scientific processes

Perhaps one of the most important, yet under-utilized, uses of technology in educational settings involves the analysis of natural phenomena and scientific processes. A variety of sensors are widely available that allow students to take field measurements of such variables as temperature, the acidity of a liquid, or the height of an object. Other technologies allow learners to take audiovisual records for later analysis. For example, a simple video camera can be used to slow down time so that learners can study the wing movements of a bird in flight, or speed up time so they can watch a flower come into bloom. George Przywolnik, in his account: 'Episodes in physics', described some uses of these technologies in his physics class. In one lesson, he invited students to yell as loudly as possible into a sound meter and to record the decibel level. He then prompted them to predict what would happen if two people yelled simultaneously. Some of the students thought that the decibel level would double and were surprised to discover that this was not the case. George reports that this was a useful technique for helping students understand how sound is measured and how a logarithmic scale works [7.5].

In addition to lessons about sound levels and logarithmic scales, George's account also describes several activities organized around the topic of motion. For example, his students plotted the speed of a moving car with data collected from stopwatches [7.6]. In another lesson, video cameras captured the launch of a student-constructed rocket, thus affording an opportunity to study parabolic flight paths in slow motion [7.7]. These kinds of technology-supported activities offer a number of obvious educational advantages: they are engaging, they are meaningful because of their connection to the real world, they provide new ways of looking at natural phenomena and they usually provide opportunities for hypothesizing, testing and analysis.

Mitch Resnick is another researcher who has used sensors and portable electronic devices in educational contexts. In one recent experiment, Resnick gave wearable temperature sensors to elementary school children (Resnick et al. 2000). These sensors, which were created in MIT laboratories, not only measure the current temperature, but also retain a record of temperature over time. Resnick's students took these sensors with them on a school trip. Upon returning, they plugged them into computers to plot a minute-by-minute temperature profile of their journey. The students found they were able to trace the times they entered and left buildings or vehi-

[7.5] Using sound meters *(see Account 2, p. 27)*.

[7.6] Tracking motion with stopwatches *(see Account 2, p. 27)*.

[7.7] Tracking rocket flight *(see Account 2, p. 28)*.

cles, and they noticed a distinctive spike in the graph on those occasions where their sensor touched something hot or cold (e.g. a cup of hot chocolate that they purchased as a snack). This kind of activity illustrates how portable technologies can be used as a support for student investigations of the world around them. It makes science personal and meaningful.

Sensors and portable recording devices offer many exciting possibilities for Science Technology Society and Environment (STSE) education, and significantly expand the realm of possibilities for the kind of independent scientific inquiry that Alex Corry discusses in Account 8. The premise of Alex's account is that students should spend at least part of the curriculum engaged in authentic, scientific investigations [7.8]. Unfortunately, teachers are sometimes reluctant to allow students to engage in authentic inquiry, preferring instead the kind of recipe/cookbook laboratory experiments where results are predictable and known in advance. However, when cookbook laboratory activities are practised exclusively, they convey a misleading notion of scientific practice. One of the strengths of STSE education is that it engages students in more realistic science – science in which the data are messy, conclusions are difficult to reach and no one knows what those conclusions will be. In a properly designed lesson, new technologies can play an important role in supporting these kinds of authentic activities.

[7.8] Developing scientific inquiry skills *(see Account 8, p. 64)*.

Technologies for supporting connections between people

Increasingly, technologies are used to support new forms of interaction between learners, or between learners and domain experts. Email is perhaps the simplest and most widespread form of electronic communication. Richard Rennie and Kim Edwards in Account 4 report that email plays an integral role in the 'Science Class of Tomorrow' (SCOT) project [7.9]. Using Apple iBooks® and home Internet access, learners can send messages to their teacher or their classmates at any time of the day. Email serves a variety of purposes for these students: they use it to help each other with schoolwork, to collaborate with their peers on joint projects, to receive notification of school-based events and for socializing. In essence, it provides them with a powerful way of communicating and working with others, one that removes time and location as constraints on their interactions.

[7.9] Using email to share information *(see Account 4, pp. 33–34)*.

Other kinds of electronic communication technologies have also shown educational promise. For example, the Acid Rain project is a large-scale data gathering and data analysis effort that spans significant portions of North America. It represents a joint effort among students in classes across the United States to measure levels of acidity of local waterways. It begins with a class trip to local rivers or lakes to measure the pH levels of the water. This data is then uploaded to the Acid Rain website. Using the uploaded data from many school sites, a national map can be created that provides a detailed account of regions of high and low acidity. This map, in turn, can be used to draw connections between levels of high acidity, the presence of air polluting industries, and the effects of prevailing winds. Educationally, such activities are valuable in a number of respects: they help students learn about science, they engage learners in an authentic scientific inquiry and they produce findings that make a genuine contribution to society. Initiatives like the Acid Rain project are almost impossible to orchestrate without technology.

In Account 9, Gabriel Ayyavoo, Vivien Tzau and Desmond Ngai offer a different but equally compelling vision of how technologies can support educationally productive collaborations. They describe how high school students prepared their science fair experiments with the help of mentors at American and Canadian universities. Most of these mentoring relationships took place over great distances. Although the students experienced difficulty finding experts who would help them (Desmond Ngai estimated that it took 100 requests to find a single mentor) one cannot help but be impressed by Ngai's enthusiastic narrative in which he describes how his collaborations with these research professionals contributed to his own growth as a scientist [7.10].

[7.10] Learning with mentors (*see Account 9, p. 80*).

Another project, Writers in Electronic Residence (WIER), makes similar use of mentoring relationships. In WIER, high school students post their written compositions on the Internet and receive online feedback and advice from well-known professional Canadian writers. Typically, this inspires students to further improve their work. WIER represents another exciting example of how the power of the Internet can be tapped for educational purposes.

The Knowledge Forum project (Hewitt and Scardamalia 1998; Hewitt 2002; Scardamalia 2002) takes the idea of online communication a step further. 'Knowledge Forum' is a learning environment that supports collaborative inquiry. Typically, a Knowledge Forum activity in an elementary or secondary classroom begins with the generation of problems of understanding. For example, fourth grade students who are studying light might ask, 'Where does colour come from?' or 'How does water refract light?' These questions are stored as notes in the Knowledge Forum database and serve as the foundation for subsequent investigation. As students pursue these problems, they create more notes that contain theories, descriptions of experiments, discoveries, and any new questions that arise. Other facilities allow them to link together related notes, or organize them in different configurations against a graphical backdrop. The entire contents of the Knowledge Forum database can be accessed by anyone in the class, so students can easily share ideas and learn from one another. The power of this system derives from its ability to support a degree of knowledge sharing among learners that would not be logistically feasible in classrooms without computers.

Technologies that support communication and collaboration are potentially revolutionary in the sense that they open the door to new educational possibilities. Through the Internet, students can interact with domain experts, receive one-on-one assistance from volunteer mentors, or work on joint projects with students in other schools. Email software and collaborative learning environments allow students to access more easily the surprisingly broad knowledge base that their peers bring with them to the classroom. The teacher is no longer seen as the sole source of knowledge. Students now have opportunities to tap the expertise of a variety of people, both within and beyond the classroom walls.

Discussion and conclusions

The previous sections described three broad ways that technology can add value to education by making possible new ways of thinking and learning. The first category consists of applications in which technology is used to turn previously abstract concepts into more tangible artefacts that students can analyse. The computer animation of electron movement in Account 4 serves as an example [7.11]. Simulation software is also often used in this capacity. The second category consists of applications that support the measurement and analysis of natural processes, such as George's sound meter [7.12], stopwatches [7.13] and video camera [7.14] in Account 2.

Finally, the third category is concerned with the use of the Internet and other communications technologies to connect learners to other learners, or learners to mentors. Technologies like those used by the SCOT project in Account 4 [7.15] and the mentoring arrangements in Account 9 [7.16] have the potential to extend the classroom by involving parents, domain experts, and external mentors in day-to-day school activities.

In considering the preceding three categories, it is important to emphasize that the success of any educational technology application hinges on the design of the accompanying instructional framework. For example, scientific sensors and probes are less likely to be of educational value if they are not part of an inquiry-driven instructional agenda. Similarly, the Internet is a flexible communication technology, but this does not mean that any kind of computer-supported interaction is necessarily worthwhile. Teachers must ensure that there is an authentic purpose for online interaction, one that exposes students to new ideas and challenges them to push forward the boundaries of their own understanding.

The notion that teachers should consider carefully their instructional uses of technologies – and in particular the situations in

[7.11] Computer animation illustrates movement *(see Account 4, p. 34)*.

[7.12] Sound meters *(see Account 2, p. 27).*

[7.13] Tracking motion with stopwatches *(see Account 2, p. 27).*

[7.14] Video camera *(see Account 2, p. 28).*

[7.15] Email *(see Account 4, pp. 33–34).*

[7.16] Mentors *(see Account 9, p. 80).*

which their application may or may not be appropriate – seems almost self-evident. However, matters are not that simple. It is an unfortunate reality that teachers are often under considerable pressure from both parents and school administrators to incorporate educational technologies in their lessons. This push to add technology to the curriculum can foster ineffective and shortsighted pedagogies. For example, in some classrooms, putting children on computers becomes a goal in and of itself, rather than a means to a particular educational end. The teacher's objective should not be to rush to implement educational technologies, but rather to use them selectively, keeping in mind their effective and ineffective applications.

The tendency to oversimplify the role of technology in education has a long history. In his (1985) book, *Teachers and Machines: The Classroom Use of Technology Since 1920*, Larry Cuban argues that past efforts to introduce new technologies into the classroom (e.g. television, radio, motion pictures) have followed a common pattern. Initially, there is great enthusiasm for the new technology and predictions are made that the technology will transform education. Inevitably, the promised improvements fail to materialize. At first, people try to explain away these failures by pointing to such factors as insufficient funding, teacher resistance, or lack of administrative support. Later, as failures continue to mount, the technology itself is blamed. Interestingly, computers do not follow Cuban's pattern perfectly. They appear to have had more staying power than previous technologies, such as television or radio, probably because they are continually re-inventing themselves. Over the years, a variety of different computer applications – computer-assisted instruction, Logo, learning environments and now the Internet – have taken their turn in the educational spotlight. It appears that just as the public tires of one incarnation, computers present themselves in a new guise and again there is enthusiasm for purchasing hardware and software for schools.

It is proposed that the cycle of technological disillusionment described by Larry Cuban is, in large part, a by-product of elevated expectations brought about by a 'technocentric mindset' in our society. The term 'technocentric mindset' refers to a tendency to fixate on technological solutions to schooling and the belief that technology alone can improve the quality of learning. For example, in the 1920s, Thomas Edison predicted that motion pictures would revolutionize the school system by providing students with videos of exemplary lessons taught by outstanding teachers. Similar predictions were later made about radio and television. These claims failed to pan out. Today, people are making similar comments about the Internet. The issue is not that technology cannot contribute in important ways to educational reform. Indeed, technology may play a supporting role in such efforts. Rather, it is argued that it is simplistic to believe that technology will drive reform. Improving the quality of schooling requires, above all else, a focus on rethinking and reworking instructional practices.

One of the ways that the technocentric mindset often manifests itself is through a tendency to reduce the classroom impact of technology to simple cause and effect statements. For example, when the Angrist and Lavy (2002) study was published in the *Economics Journal*, some newspapers reported the findings with headlines such as, 'Research discovers computers have no effect on learning'. Angrist and Lavy, of course, made no such claims, but the headlines resonate with the popular belief that it should be possible to scientifically measure the effect of computers on learning, perhaps through controlled experimentation. This kind of thinking is fundamentally misguided. Trying to determine the effect of computers on learning is meaningless; it is akin to assessing the educational impact of a bulletin board, or the contribution of classroom chalk to standardized test scores. It is based on the false assumption that technologies have an intrinsic educational value that can be measured by swapping them in and out of classrooms and determining changes in student performance. Such experiments are not feasible, since the utility of a particular technology depends upon the nature of the instruction, the goals of the students, the role of the teacher and many other factors.

Computers, or any other technology for that matter, can be used in both effective and ineffective ways. They are neither a panacea for education's problems, nor are they expensive, over-hyped teachers' aids. Rather, their value, or lack thereof, is inextricably tied to the particular instructional situation in which they are used. As Salomon (1995: 17) observes:

> The meaning of the configuration, Gestalt, composite or constellation of factors is qualitatively different from that of its components. It is the composite that students and teachers experience; it is that composite which they interact with, not each of the ingredients taken one at a time; and it is that composite that we should be studying.

Expressed another way, the value of any educational technology cannot be understood through conventional scientific techniques of controlling all variables except for the one under investigation. Classrooms are too complex for such methods. Instead, it is necessary to take a holistic perspective, one that looks at how technologies *in combination with* certain classroom practices can productively support learning. Under the right conditions, technology can open the door to completely new educational possibilities. In other situations, uses of computers may be educationally questionable or may even subvert learning (e.g. if students spend hours surfing the web looking for information that could be more easily accessed in an classroom encyclopedia or in the school library).

In general, the decision to employ a technology should be driven by something more than a belief – or hope – that exposing students to technology is a worthy goal in and of itself. Rather, such decisions should be based on a rationale of how the technology, in conjunction with certain instructional interventions, can improve the breadth or depth of student learning. The accounts presented in this volume provide us with a starting point for thinking about technology in this capacity.

Analysis 8

Reading accounts: central themes in science teachers' descriptions of exemplary teaching practice

John Wallace

Introduction

In framing my reading of the accounts in this book, I have taken as a starting point the editors' brief to analyse the accounts from a teaching perspective. As much as possible, I have tried to take the teachers' and students' accounts at 'face value'. While understanding the risks and shortcomings of interpreting accounts in this way, and being aware of my natural tendency to critique as much as analyse, I have worked from the assumption that the teaching described herein is exemplary. My approach has been to construct eight central themes related to the teaching of science, based on the teachers' (and students') descriptions and my inferences as to the reasons behind teachers' actions. In the hermeneutic tradition, I have attempted to create meaning from the texts in the light of my own preconceptions, interests and research frames (Wallace and Louden 1997).

In constructing the themes, I have tried to reinforce that which is most apparent in the accounts, to accentuate that which is less apparent and to provide some accompanying theoretical analysis. The eight themes are:

- the tenacity of teaching
- the immediacy of input
- the centrality of content
- the plurality of pedagogy
- the expedience of epistemology
- the legacy of the laboratory

- the disguise of dilemma and
- the motive of morality.

The central themes

The tenacity of teaching

One feature, which stands above all others in these ten accounts of exemplary practice, is the tenacity of teaching. That is, the teachers in these accounts are primarily occupied with their own role in the teaching/learning process rather than the role of students. In other words, teachers are concerned with teaching rather than with what Fenstermacher (1986) called studenting. Perhaps this feature is an artefact of the process of account writing. That is, when teachers are asked to describe exemplary classroom practice, they place themselves, rather than the students, at the centre. Perhaps it has something to do with the word exemplary, with its obvious connotations of high levels of teaching accomplishment. Or perhaps, as many other commentators have observed, classroom practice, even exemplary practice, is overwhelmingly a teacher-oriented endeavour.

And so we have, with a couple of interesting exceptions, a set of accounts with the teacher in the middle. Three examples particularly illustrate the tenacity of teaching [8.1]. In the first account, Keith Hicks describes a series of lessons on kidney function, where he led the students through a sequence of activities including dissection, demonstration, model building, presentation, and display and reviewing examination questions. In Account 2, George Przywolnik describes his use of role play in helping students to understand some abstract concepts in astronomy and physics – concepts such as astronomical distance, wave motion, molecular collisions and the speed of sound. In each example, George guides the students through a structured activity to assist them to 'experience' the phenomenon, drawing their attention to the parallels between the role play and the concept.

[8.1] The tenacity of teaching *(see Account 1, p. 17, Account 2, p. 23 and Account 6, p. 47)*.

In Account 6, Katherine Bellomo tells how she uses the story of the reinterpretation of the Burgess Shale fossils to teach students about the cultural underpinnings of the nature of science. She employs whole-class presentation and discussion to raise questions, present material, brainstorm ideas, challenge thinking and generally stimulate debate about the nature of science.

In each of these three accounts, the teacher determined the central theme of the lesson/s and directed the students through a series of largely pre-planned activities and discussions. Each lesson was structured to achieve well-defined content and process goals while enhancing students' attitudes to school science. In other accounts, we might have the teacher less concerned with the minute-by-minute control of the lessons but the impression of a strong teacher orientation pervades all but two of the accounts. This observation about the tenacity of teaching in exemplary practice may sound surprising in the light of recent moves towards more student-centred approaches. My own view is that even so-called student-centred classrooms demand the strong hand of a teacher in the middle.

Teachers must always be concerned with teaching. The key issue is not about teacher or student centredness per se, but about who has responsibility for what. It is the teacher who is primarily responsible for teaching, setting broad goals, structuring activities, scaffolding learning, promoting communication and assessing outcomes. It is the student who is primarily responsible for learning. Exemplary teachers, I propose, understand this distinction and work actively, purposefully and tenaciously to *teach* students to take responsibility for their own learning.

The immediacy of input

A second, and related, observation about these accounts is that they reflect the immediate importance of teaching inputs in the way that teachers organize and conduct (and hence represent) their work [8.2]. In Account 1, for example, Keith Hicks leads us through a tightly structured series of lessons on kidney function. In Account 7, Susan Yoon describes an environmental impact role-play activity during a class visit to a local outdoor education centre. Alex Corry (Account 8), tells how he uses the idea of researchable questions to promote student inquiry. Account 10 lays out a five phase teaching activity for students to design, construct and test a mousetrap car.

[8.2] The immediacy of input *(see Account 8, p. 64 and Account 10, p. 84).*

Clearly, when asked to write about exemplary practice, most of the teachers chose to emphasize input activities or strategies for teaching rather than student outcomes, or strategies for learning or assessment. Student learning in most of the accounts is treated as an assumed flow on from the teaching activity. While students are frequently referred to as a group, there are very few examples where the experience of individual students is described. One notable exception is Mitchell in Account 7. It is interesting to note, then, that the word 'student/s' appears more than 500 times in the ten accounts. This is more than twice the frequency of the next most used word, 'science'.

What does this tell us about exemplary practice? It is possible that exemplary teachers, like teachers of all kinds, start to think about practice at the beginning, that is, with inputs. They are concerned with what Lortie (1975) called 'presentism'. They deal first and foremost with the immediacy of preparing lessons, designing activities and keeping students occupied.

A preoccupation with inputs is another way of building routine into lessons, a way of having teachers and students feel comfortable with particular patterns of practice (Wallace and Louden 1992). It is not that these teachers are unconcerned with learning and assessment. Indeed the word 'learn/ing' appears more than 100 times in the ten accounts. Rather, I suspect that for these lessons, many of which might be considered innovative as well as exemplary, learning seems to have been backgrounded rather than foregrounded. Nonetheless, it is worth (re)emphasizing the importance of balancing pedagogical inputs with monitoring learning outputs (teaching with assessment). Exemplary science teachers are those who manage to hold both in an appropriate dialectic tension, so that each informs the other.

The centrality of content

A third feature of the accounts is the central place of content knowledge in science teaching and learning. To a greater or lesser degree, in each of the ten accounts the teachers and the students display a deep concern for content [8.3]. Once again, this feature could be an artefact of the account writing, or it could be the case that, as some scholars suggest, content knowledge stands as a central feature of secondary school science teachers' sense of themselves and their work (Siskin 1994).

[8.3] The centrality of content *(see Account 4, p. 34 and Account 9, p. 80)*.

In Account 4, for example, Richard Rennie and Kim Edwards describe an online curriculum development project. These teachers relate how they tried to embed the curriculum materials into the students' laptop computers, with links to various interactive software packages, the web and other digital materials. However, throughout their descriptions of the process are references to content, e.g. wave patterns, electron movement, blood pressure, formation of ions, balancing chemical equations, electron shells and so on. The teachers also describe the role of this content in organizing the curriculum.

In Account 3, Josie Ellis's description of learning organic chemistry as a student is infused with images of content. Josie wasn't just in school; she was in school to learn the intricacies of organic chemistry. She describes in some detail the order in which the content was presented – first isomers, then mechanisms and then reactions – and the kinds of activities that assisted her to learn. Such activities included model building, visualization, practical work, note taking and regular tests.

In another account, Desmond Ngai (Account 9) writes of his experience as a 16-year-old high school student and the assistance received from teachers and scientists as he worked on various science fair projects. At the heart of his account is Desmond's growing and passionate interest in genetics, particularly the use of computer-assisted DNA analysis to diagnose disease-causing pathogens. Alex

Corry (Account 8), refers to the importance of students' prior knowledge of science concepts such as molecules, bonding and chemical change when investigating a researchable question about dissolving Alka Seltzer™ tablets in water. Katherine Bellomo (Account 6) calls on students' understandings of fossilization and natural selection to tell them the story of the Burgess Shale fossils.

Knowledge of, and a passion for, science and its methods is a common and foundational feature of the exemplary practice described in these accounts. While there is evidence of students learning science, learning about science and learning to do science (Hodson 1998b), content knowledge seems to be a cornerstone of all three. The evidence from these accounts is that exemplary teachers are convinced of the value of science knowing, sure of their own science content knowledge and understand something of the complex, and often perplexing, relationship between science and the nature of science.

The plurality of pedagogy

A striking feature of these accounts of exemplary practice is the wide range of pedagogical techniques employed [8.4]. Three examples serve to make the point. Keith Hicks's description (Account 1) of teaching a series of lessons on the topic of kidney function contains several pedagogical techniques. These include direct instruction, kidney dissection, model building, group presentations, poster making and practising examination questions. Josie Ellis (Account 3) describes the teaching strategies that helped her to understand the intricacies of organic chemistry. The teaching strategies included direct instruction, model construction, individual revision, practical work, note taking, regular tests and completing past examination papers. In Account 5, Karen Kettle describes her use of historical vignettes to build students' appreciation of the human character of science. Over several weeks she had students prepare for and present a public performance of an historical scientific event. She employed techniques of individual research, essay writing, script production, role play and reflective analysis.

There are many other examples of pedagogical plurality in these ten accounts. For example, student role play of physics phenomena (Account 2), individualized student e-learning (Account 4), student participation in a town hall debate (Account 7), student inquiry using researchable questions (Account 8) and students' involvement in a technology-based project (Account 10).

Notwithstanding the wide range of pedagogical techniques in evidence in these accounts, the following three elements seem to be present, to a greater or lesser degree, throughout. Most of the above lessons, for example, contain some aspect of 'messing about' (Haw-

[8.4] The plurality of pedagogy *(see Account 1, p. 17, Account 3, p. 31 and Account 5, p. 39)*.

kins 1974), or 'experience first' (Munby and Russell 1994), where students and teachers draw on their own backgrounds to explore prior understandings, play with ideas and generate possible lines of inquiry. The 'draw a scientist' exercise in Account 5 (p. 40), is an example of a messing about activity.

A further element is 'guided inquiry' where students engage in some kind of focused science-related activity. For example, recording data, synthesising notes, designing models, developing hypotheses or explaining phenomena. The kidney dissection in Account 1 (p. 17), or the vibrations and waves student role play in Account 2 (p. 24) are examples of guided inquiry.

Finally, a feature of many of these accounts is the element of 'culminating performance' (Wiske 1998). Examples of this include: a project, role play, product, essay, reflective analysis, summary discussion or other performance task designed to demonstrate student understanding of the goals of the topic. This element is found in several accounts, including the review and answering examination questions exercise (Account 1, pp. 21–22), the town hall debate (Account 7, p. 59) and science fair projects (Account 9, p. 71), among others. Taken together, these three elements provide focused opportunities for teachers and students to build on prior experience, learn new things and demonstrate what they know.

What can we make of this pot-pourri of strategies? Conventional wisdom (supported by a considerable body of literature in recent years) would suggest a certain distinction between more desirable, 'constructivist' strategies versus less desirable 'traditional' strategies. For example, small group work is seen to be more desirable than direct instruction. A closer analysis would suggest that this dichotomy is unhelpful, and that exemplary practitioners have a repertoire of strategies, although some teachers may have a distinct preference for some strategies over others. What is more important, however, is how exemplary teachers incorporate and intertwine different elements of teaching into their practice to promote and have students demonstrate understanding.

The expedience of epistemology

[8.5] The expedience of epistemology *(see Account 6, p. 51 and Account 8, p. 63)*.

A further feature of these accounts is the diversity in the representations of the nature of science. These exemplary teachers seem to take an expedient or pragmatic view of epistemology, rather than adopting an ideological stance [8.5]. The accounts of Alex Corry (Account 8) and Katherine Bellomo (Account 6) serve to illustrate this point. Alex, for example, uses the idea of researchable questions to teach his students the standard skills of scientific inquiry. For the most part, his lessons are conducted in a routinized manner, such as, developing the question and the hypothesis, designing the experiment, controlling variables, observation, measurement, analysis and reporting, etc. He explains (p. 63):

> Before grade 9 students begin to learn about particular scientific concepts, such as structure and behaviour of atoms and molecules, they learn several scientific skills, including: question and hypothesis development, measurement, graphing, data analysis and reporting. At the same time it is important that they learn such skills in relation to particular topics. So I start their course with an inquiry unit that gets them to focus on biological, physical, chemical, and earth science concepts related to the general theme of water.

Katherine, on the other hand, deals with nature of science issues by examining the controversy surrounding the interpretation and reinterpretation of the Burgess Shale fossils. By telling this story she aims to show students that science is conducted within a social milieu. In her words (pp. 50–51):

> I think the students see that science does, in some ways, begin with a question and who gets to ask questions, and that how those questions are researched is never neutral. I believe that students begin to see that it *does* matter who does the asking. I also believe that they begin to see science as socially constructed and culturally determined.

At first glance, these two positions appear to be in stark contrast with one another, suggesting a dualism of the empiricist versus the social constructivist view of science. Closer inspection reveals that there are elements of both views of science in each account. Alex, for example, warns students against adopting a linear approach to scientific inquiry and incorporates discussion of controversial scientific issues such as smoking and lung cancer. He refers to 'culturally specific methods of sharing knowledge' (p. 67). Katherine incorporates a discussion of experimental design, data collection and results in her lessons on the nature of science.

What conclusion can we come to about exemplary practice? Which epistemological position should be promoted in science lessons? The best teachers, I would suggest, are those who take a pragmatic line and are able to show their students that science is *both* empirical *and* social, thus adopting what Tobin (2002) calls a *both/ and* perspective. These teachers demonstrate to their students that science is empirical, and that it provides a systematic way of researching interesting questions. They teach about the importance of careful methods of data collection, interpretation and reporting, and attend to issues of validity and reliability. But they also emphasize the social character of science. They remind students that observation, data collection and interpretation are value-laden activities and that the theories generated are tentative. An expedient or pragmatic view of epistemology, therefore, attends to, and makes visible, both views of science. Exemplary science teachers, I suggest, are those who encourage their students to participate in disciplined scientific inquiry, while helping them to develop attitudes of informed and healthy scepticism.

The legacy of the laboratory

[8.6] The legacy of the laboratory *(see Account 8, p. 64)*.

A further characteristic of these accounts is the important legacy of the laboratory in the teaching of school science [8.6]. Indeed the word 'lab/oratory' appears more than 50 times and the word 'experiment' more than 40 times in the ten accounts. To a greater or lesser degree, bench laboratory work is described in Accounts 1, 3, 4, 8, 9 and 10. In the first account, for example, the students used the laboratory to conduct a kidney dissection and to draw a 'standard diagram' of the kidney and label the parts. In Account 3, Josie Ellis recalls her experience as a student and how practical work assisted her to understand the theory behind the structure and reactions of organic compounds. Much of Account 8 is centred on the use of the laboratory to investigate researchable questions.

At first glance, it would appear that there is little in these accounts that is different from the legacy of routinized school laboratory work, often criticized in the literature (Hodson 1993). A deeper analysis indicates that the work of these exemplary practitioners has some elements of the kind of 'authentic' laboratory practice advocated by commentators such as Arzi (1998) and Roth (2002).

For example, the dissection in Account 1 is conducted in the context of a follow-up activity where students work in groups to construct kidney models and explain their understandings of concepts to each other. Similarly, in Account 3, Josie Ellis describes how practical work was used as one of a series of teaching and learning strategies to help scaffold the development of her knowledge about organic chemistry. In Account 8, questions are formulated, investigated and the results reported in a classroom environment characterized by brainstorming, discussion, peer assessment, evaluation and justification.

Two aspects of exemplary laboratory practice emerge from these and the other accounts – social context and relevance. The first aspect addresses the need for laboratory practice to proceed and develop in a social context of persuasion, negotiation and argumentation, requiring an atmosphere of accountability rather than rightness. As Roth (2002: 48) argues, 'we need to bring about contexts in which producing reasonable accounts guides student activity rather than some purported "right" answer'.

The second aspect concerns the relevance of the activity and importance of connecting the laboratory with 'real-world' issues and scientific problem-solving contexts. Authentic, and hence exemplary, laboratory activity, I suggest, attends to both aspects. It is conducted within a vigorous social milieu employing a variety of techniques to inquire into interesting and relevant scientific problems.

The disguise of dilemma

Exemplar-focused accounts, such as those found in this volume, are designed to accentuate the positive, to describe the things that work in teaching rather than the things that don't. Consequently, exemplar accounts make teaching seem easier or more seamless than it really is. In other words, these kinds of accounts are designed to disguise rather than highlight the problems and dilemmas of practice, and the management thereof [8.7]. Although largely hidden from view, dilemma management remains an integral part of the minute-by-minute, day-by-day classroom activities of exemplary teachers.

[8.7] The disguise of dilemma *(see Account 6, p. 50 and Account 7, p. 54)*.

An episode from Account 6, written by Katherine Bellomo, serves to illustrate the importance of dilemma management in teaching. Towards the end of her series of lessons on the interpretation of the Burgess Shale fossils, Katherine asks students to consider what the story tells them about the nature of science. She comments that the results are often unpredictable depending on the mix of students. Some students, for example, appreciate the tentative and social nature of science. Others, she says, reject the message, preferring to hold on to an algorithmic view of science. Katherine, it appears, is faced with a dilemma at this point. She can either insist that her own view prevail, or respect individual differences in interpretation of the story. Katherine's approach, consistent with her views about the social nature of science, is to tolerate this diversity. She concludes (p. 50) that she cannot expect all her 'students to have "nature of science epiphanies" from one example, but this is a wonderful story and without fail, it gets them thinking'.

Katherine manages the dilemma by challenging students' ideas while, at the same time, acknowledging that different students will draw different conclusions, depending on their own reading of events.

The story of Mitchell (Account 7, p. 54), provides another example of dilemma management. The teacher, Susan Yoon, describes her experiences with class 9B. Mitchell, one of the students with special educational needs in Susan's class, is loud and articulate with a history of disruptive behaviour. The dilemma for Susan was how to engage all the students in the class, including those such as Mitchell who, when faced with difficult concepts and language, would readily give up on learning and disrupt others. In other words, how could she keep the whole class involved in learning while attending to the special needs of the individual?

Susan's approach to this dilemma is to design her lessons around topics of interest to the students. She encourages her students to use familiar vocabulary, to exchange and negotiate ideas based on their experience and make decisions based on a range of beliefs and real-world evidence. In the example of the field trip and town hall debate, Susan employs these strategies to engage all of her students, particularly Mitchell, in a highly successful learning experience.

These two episodes serve to illustrate that teaching is a complex business, rich with dilemmas (Lampert 1985; Wallace and Louden 2002). Teachers are required to balance many competing educational demands: for example, between attending to the individual *and* the rest of the class, between respecting students' naive science understandings *and* promoting canonical knowledge, between listening to students *and* telling them the answer, and so on. The best science teachers, such as those described above, are those who manage their way through these apparently irreconcilable alternatives, with diligence, good humour and respect for all involved in the teaching and learning process.

The motive of morality

Not often seen in accounts of science teaching is the notion of moral motive or purpose. The focus is usually on practical classroom routines and strategies rather than the underlying motivations for teaching. Similarly, in these ten accounts, we see an emphasis on matters such as the teachers' actions, content knowledge, classroom inputs, teaching strategies, the nature of science and the operation of the laboratory. We need to search a little more deeply in the texts for some of the moral dimensions of teaching [8.8].

[8.8] The motive of morality *(see Account 2, p. 23, Account 3, p. 31, Account 8, p. 63 and Account 9, p. 75)*.

Mostly, these dimensions seem more evident in the students' accounts than the teachers'. Josie Ellis (Account 3, p. 31), for example, referring to the enthusiasm and encouragement of her teacher, says that the reassurance that she could 'get help almost anytime of the day was very supportive'. In Account 9 (pp. 71–83), students Vivien Tzau and Desmond Ngai refer to the enthusiasm and deep commitment of their science teacher, Gabriel Ayyavoo. His 'programmatic mentoring' (p. 75), assisted them to compete successfully in national and international science fairs and influenced their decisions to pursue careers in science. Another student of Gabriel's said to him, 'I love discussing findings with you because it makes me feel important'.

While the teachers were not so forthcoming, aspects of moral purpose were also evident in their accounts. Keith Hicks (Account 1) refers to the importance of students taking responsibility for their learning. George Przywolnik (Account 2) aims to help students acquire skills to help them succeed in society. Such skills include communication, modelling, decision making and problem solving. Richard Rennie's and Kim Edwards's teaching (Account 4, p. 32) operates from the fundamental premise that 'all students can learn'. Katherine Bellomo (Account 6, p. 51) wants students to 'see themselves as potentially able to enter science in spite of the barriers they face from race, class and gender'. Susan Yoon (Account 7, p. 55), says that students should achieve success. In her account, she refers to the importance of engaging all students and providing them with 'appropriate and timely' scaffolds to learning. Alex Corry (Account 8, p. 63), wishes to instil in his students a 'desire for knowledge'.

To summarize, in all of these accounts of exemplary practice there appears an underlying moral dimension. This dimension seems to have two aspects. First, these exemplary practitioners believe that *all* students can learn science and that students should take more responsibility for their learning. Second, and perhaps more importantly, these teachers demonstrate practices congruent with their espoused beliefs. Such practices include mentoring, respect for students and their knowledge, patience for students' pace of learning, compassion for students and sincerity in their relationships with them. Primarily, morality is about how students are to be treated (Kilbourn 1998) and morality in teaching lies beyond the technical (Tom 1984). In these accounts of exemplary practice, moral motives permeate the teaching of science, underscore teachers' relationships with students and form a springboard for all pedagogical decisions.

Conclusion

In this chapter I have tentatively stepped into the world of exemplary practice. Given that many others before me have also trod this ground, I do so with some trepidation. Exemplariness is a tricky concept, defying a formulaic definition. What one teacher or observer may see as exemplary, another may not. However, more to the point, teaching is an uncertain and complex domain of knowledge. It is uncertain because much of its structure and complexity, hence its exemplariness, lies hidden below the surface of events as they are observed and described (Kilbourn 1998). In narrating teaching events, for example, teachers may only be tacitly aware of the reasons behind their decision making. The accounts may provide some guidance about teachers' intentions and actions, but the rest is hidden from view and can only be inferred.

What I have come to understand, after reading and rereading these accounts of exemplary practice and my thematic analysis, is the importance of balance in teacher's work. What these exemplary science teachers have managed to do is strike a productive balance among competing educational demands, strategies and epistemologies. For example, they maintain a strong teacher presence while encouraging students to take responsibility for their learning. They balance students' needs to learn science, do science and learn about science, and have strong content knowledge themselves. They connect teaching inputs with learning outcomes. The teachers also employ a balanced mix of teaching strategies, incorporating elements of exploration, guided inquiry and performance. They represent science as being both empirical and social. They use the laboratory as a place where different views about the nature of science are played out in authentic activities. Exemplary teachers manage the dilemmas and tensions inherent in these competing demands by balancing, and where necessary trading off, one course of action against another.

In many respects, this volume serves as a celebration of diversity, incorporating a view of exemplariness which emphasizes 'multiple and flexible conceptions of teaching excellence' (Hargreaves 1994: 61). Here, teachers' decision making is provisional and context dependent. Rather than rely on singular models of teaching, the teachers in this volume employ a wide repertoire of teaching strategies. Direct instruction, classroom debate, small group work, structured activities, open-ended investigations and examination review sit alongside one another with equal legitimacy. The choice of strategy depends on the teaching circumstances and learning objectives. Its successful use relies on the teacher's wise pedagogical decision making.

Finally, and importantly, I am struck by the moral dimension of the teaching in these accounts. Once again, this dimension is often hidden from view, but is strongly inferred by the high levels of emotional involvement, trust and cooperation among participants. These behaviours suggest that exemplary science teachers are motivated by a concern for learning, and a deep respect for students and the knowledge they bring to the science classroom.

Analysis 9
Equity in science teaching and learning: the inclusive science curriculum

Léonie J. Rennie

> I wanted to move toward a more inclusive science curriculum but needed to ask myself: how do I understand inclusion, and how do I include all students? Do all students see themselves in the curriculum so that individuals do not feel marginalized? Is school science honest in how it portrays the nature of science and the philosophical underpinnings of the process of knowledge construction? Could I show science to be – as I believe it to be – biased, human and idiosyncratic? Could I address issues of race, class and gender, that block some students from entering into the culture of science – or at the high school level into the subculture of the science classroom?
>
> (Bellomo, Account 6, p. 47)

Katherine Bellomo's questions in this excerpt from Account 6, capture the essence of this chapter. She draws attention to an inclusive science curriculum, to the nature of science as a process of knowledge construction, and to the issues of race, class and gender that sometimes block students' access to science. What does inclusion mean? she asks. How can I be sure all students feel included in the curriculum?

The term 'inclusive science curriculum' is a relatively recent one. It builds upon changing ideas about equity, and many educators and researchers refer to an 'equitable science curriculum' to mean much the same thing. However, equity in science education has had different interpretations as research in the area has evolved. This evolution is seen most clearly in the literature relating to gender equity (Rennie 2001) and Parker and Rennie (2002: 882) point out that: 'In terms of instructional strategies, the accumulated wisdom of researchers and practitioners from virtually every continent of the world has resulted in the development and refinement of an approach which has become known as "gender-inclusive".'

In this chapter, and following Katherine Bellomo's account, I will use the term 'inclusive' to describe the kind of science curriculum that provides equity in science teaching and learning by including students from different sub-groups, based on socio-cultural variables such as gender, race and class. In the following section, I provide a definition to enable us to come to an understanding of inclusivity and to identify the essential components of an inclusive science curriculum. With these components clearly in mind, we have a means of answering Katherine's questions. We can then turn to the accounts and highlight some of the ways that teachers are making science at school more inclusive of all students.

The components of an inclusive science curriculum

The Western Australian Curriculum Framework (Curriculum Council 1998: 17), offers a definition of inclusivity that can be used to build a description of an inclusive science curriculum:

> Inclusivity means providing all groups of students, irrespective of educational setting, with access to a wide and empowering range of knowledge, skills and values. It means recognizing and accommodating the different starting points, learning rates and previous experiences of individuals or groups of students. It means valuing and including the understandings and knowledge of all groups. It means providing opportunities for students to evaluate how concepts and constructions such as culture, disability, race, class and gender are shaped.

In terms of this definition, then, an inclusive science curriculum has three components. The first component refers to appropriate science-related knowledge, skills and values. In an inclusive science curriculum, all students have access to a wide and empowering range of science-related knowledge, skills and values. For students to be able to acquire and make use of them, these knowledge, skills and values must be relevant and meaningful to the students, whoever they may be and wherever they attend school.

In her keynote address to the annual meeting of the National Association for Research in Science Teaching in 2003, entitled 'I used to like science and then I went to school: the challenge of school science in urban schools', Professor Gloria Ladson-Billings (2003) described how, as a young science student, she was unable to make a Cartesian Diver (see Account 9 for discussion of this device) for a homework assignment. This was because she did not have access to the equipment needed to assemble it. Although she was an enthusiastic and able student, this assignment was discriminatory in terms of her home circumstances. It also denied her access to the relevant science concepts. Professor Ladson-Billings's experience as a science student demonstrates the overlap of the first with the second component of the inclusive science curriculum. This is because it is difficult to ensure that all students can access the appropriate knowledge, skills and values unless account is taken of their diversity as individuals.

Thus, the second component of the inclusive science curriculum requires accommodation of diversity by recognizing, valuing and including the kinds of learning styles and background experiences of all students. This means that students are provided with a wide range of activities for learning and tasks for assessment so that they can progress, and demonstrate that progress, in ways that suit them as individuals. During the 1980s, significant investment was made in developing resources for teaching science from a gender-inclusive perspective (e.g. Ditchfield and Scott 1987; Gianello 1988; Canadian Teachers' Federation 1992). Although aimed at gender, it was found that the large variety of inclusive, participatory activities suggested in these resources were effective for males as well as females. They were also inclusive for other minority groups, especially those related to race and class (Kenway et al. 1998).

The main reason for this seems to be that variety allows for students with different needs to find something that works for them. Importantly, it means that students are included because their individual needs are being met. While some of these needs may be associated with their being female, or being members of particular religious, cultural, geographic or other social groups, each individual's needs are unique. As I have argued elsewhere (Rennie 2001, 2002), an inclusive science curriculum deals with individuals according to their needs, not what their needs are perceived to be on the basis of their membership of some socially defined group. On almost any variable associated with learning, it can be demonstrated that there is more variation within a subgroup (such as males or females) than there is between those subgroups (i.e. between boys as a group or girls as a group). For example, Fennema (1987) demonstrated this quite clearly for cognitive differences more than two decades ago. Gipps (1996) noted the need to recognize difference among girls and women: one approach does not suit all girls, nor does it suit all members of a particular socio-cultural subgroup.

Finally, an inclusive science curriculum requires that students have opportunities to examine critically the culture of science and the stereotypes and myths about the people who do science. Therefore, students can think about science as a discipline that can include themselves, regardless of their gender, culture, race or other social roles. This third component challenges the construction of science and scientific knowledge in terms of concepts such as gender, race and class.

The traditional representation of science as male, white, Western and middle class has been challenged from different theoretical standpoints. Willis (1996), writing about mathematics education, refers to a socially critical perspective for achieving equity, one that is readily adaptable to science education (Rennie 1998). Roychoudhury et al. (1995), describe a feminist science which is based on similar premises. Bianchini synthesized various perspectives representing science as personal, social and political activity as background for her course for beginning science teachers on the nature of science and issues of equity and diversity (Bianchini and Solomon 2003). She found that beginning teachers rarely moved their thinking across these perspectives, a demonstration of the difficulty of challenging the science curriculum. Bianchini and Solomon concluded that considerations of all three perspectives held 'greater promise for achieving a science education that was inclusive of all students' (p. 53).

In turning to the accounts in the next section, we find that most demonstrate the first and often the second of these three components. Accounts 5 and 6 clearly demonstrate the third component, and thus offer students the kind of science curriculum that fully reflects the definition of inclusivity given above.

Turning to the accounts: creating an inclusive science curriculum

Nearly all of the accounts have something to say about equity or inclusivity, although most of them do not mention these terms explicitly. Of course, the accounts were not necessarily written with these features in mind, but they provide wonderful examples of good teaching that results in learning for all students. If we examine each of the three components of an inclusive science curriculum in turn, the accounts can be used to illustrate some of the strategies that build an inclusive science curriculum.

Access to appropriate science-related knowledge, skills and values

According to the definition of an inclusive science curriculum, the knowledge, skills and values to which students are exposed need to be wide ranging and empowering. Empowerment cannot occur unless the student can understand and see meaning and relevance for themselves. Returning to Account 6 (p. 51), we find Katherine describing how 'students see science as a foreign culture' [9.1] and do not see scientists as real people similar to themselves. She uses the story of the Burgess Shale fossils to bring science and students closer

[9.1] Scientists are real people *(see Account 6, p. 51)*.

together. Katherine's lesson begins by having students talk about the meaning of 'science'. After the story and discussion, the class generates a list of characteristics of scientists. Katherine is then able to point out that because scientists are much like the students themselves, they too can have access to science.

Another example of promoting access to knowledge comes from Account 2 (p. 23). George Przywolnik describes a few of the activities he has devised to bring the principles of physics home to his students and to 'expose students to as wide a range of experiences as possible, so that students with "non-standard" learning modes can learn effectively' [9.2].

The example of screaming to demonstrate the nature of the decibel scale to measure sound is especially compelling (Account 2, p. 26). The activities selected illustrate George's commitment to having students learn skills beyond physics. These include a range of generic skills to promote success outside of school.

As an aside, it is interesting that his students arc all female, and show no embarrassment at being involved in the very active role plays and other activities described. Research in co-educational schools (AAUWEF 1998; Parker and Rennie 2002), often indicates that many girls of this age (16 years) are passive compared to boys and less willing to participate in 'public' activities such as these in the company of male students. Here is one example that exploits the flexibility of single-sex schools!

Where the science syllabus is difficult and not very flexible, it is a challenge to ensure that all students can access the knowledge they need. In Account 3, student Josie Ellis reflects on her learning of organic chemistry at an advanced level. Here, an enthusiastic teacher provided a variety of resources to promote student understanding. Although the content was fixed, the order of presentation was rearranged, something that helped Josie to grasp the fundamentals of the course (p. 29). In addition, students' participation by explaining things to each other, working together and sharing different viewpoints enhanced their access to organic chemistry (p. 30).

Recognizing and accommodating diversity

Access is also enhanced by taking steps to ensure the inclusion of diverse groups of students. Richard Rennie and Kim Edwards designed their Science Class Of Tomorrow (SCOT) project, the basis of Account 4, explicitly to be inclusive. Recognizing the diversity of the school's population (urban and rural students, and many others from different countries whose first language is not English), Richard and Kim rejected 'the "one size fits all" approach' [9.3] and individualized their ninth grade curriculum. They exploited the flexibility afforded by students having immediate Internet access via their own

[9.2] Making science personal and real-world *(see Account 2, p. 23).*

[9.3] Individualizing the curriculum *(see Account 4, pp. 32–33).*

laptop computers. The pedagogy, assessment and science curriculum were all changed.

As Richard and Kim discuss in their account, their goal was to put the students online, not just the curriculum materials they write. They also describe how the outcomes-based science curriculum incorporated digital multimedia to present material in a variety of ways to accommodate students' different learning styles, skills and abilities (pp. 34–36). For example, the audio buttons to read definitions aloud could be used by poor readers, students who learn aurally and English as second language students, but be ignored by others. Students' responses to the evaluation survey (p. 36), indicate an appropriate spread, suggesting that this was working well. The individualized, self-paced mode allowed students to plan a course to suit themselves, with the teachers taking supportive and mentoring roles.

The SCOT project presented an individualized curriculum but students usually chose to work in small groups, something that seemed to suit their learning needs. Properly organized group work, where the purpose and outcomes are clear, is a powerful tool in an inclusive curriculum [9.4]. This is largely because it offers opportunities for students to appreciate, and learn to value, the diversity among group members. With group tasks requiring a variety of skills, quiet students or those whose behaviour can be problematic have the chance to shine and gain confidence from their contribution to the science lesson.

Susan Yoon notes that Mitchell, the 'problem' student highlighted in Account 7, was congratulated by one of the brightest students for his part in the town hall meeting [9.5]. Of course, the grouping of students into teams to prepare for the meeting was central to the success of the lesson sequence. By giving teams different positions on the beaver issue, Susan ensured that students were able to explore the priorities and values from a range of perspectives. They could also take opportunities to examine the beaver issue in ways that were new to them.

Keith Hicks also used group work to advantage in Account 1. Keith thought carefully about the reworking of the curriculum on kidney function, targeting his changes to achieve more active participation of the students. A central activity was building a nephron representation in groups, enabling the complementary mixing of students' skills and abilities to produce the model [9.6]. Offering students a choice to participate in the kidney dissection showed acceptance of students' sensitivities.

Keith also mentions that an old videotape about dialysis and kidney transplant would be 'retired', but he doesn't mention its replacement. Organ transplants are a great way to introduce the values and ethical dilemmas related to science and medicine, as Hildebrand

[9.4] Group work and valuing diversity *(see Account 4, p. 35)*.

[9.5] Different abilities and perspectives are highlighted in group work *(see Account 7, p. 62)*.

[9.6] Group work to increase participation and mix skills *(see Account 1, p. 20)*.

(1989) demonstrated clearly in her hypothetical scenarios requiring students to decide who, of six deserving people, should receive a liver transplant. Such discussion brings to the fore some of the ethical and value-laden aspects inherent in an inclusive science curriculum.

Alex Corry provides another approach to accommodating variation among students, the central plank of this component of an inclusive curriculum. In Account 8, he describes how he is able to 'structure lessons around what students currently know and want to know and, then, piggyback the "curriculum" on exploring their beliefs' in teaching about scientific inquiry [9.7]. His list of alternative methods, including cartoons and dance sequences, for students to report science investigations is a good illustration of variety in assessment methods that allow students to demonstrate what they have learned, in a way that is comfortable for them.

[9.7] Alternative assessment *(see Account 8, pp. 67–68)*.

Opportunities to examine the culture of science

'All of a sudden the science was not separated from people who created it' writes Karen Kettle in Account 5 [9.8]. Her love of scientists' biographies led students to open up their ideas about science and scientists in the creative drama work described in Karen's account. Karen's approach gave her students opportunities to 'live' science as a scientist, as they researched and performed a snippet of a scientist's life story.

[9.8] Making science human *(see Account 5, p. 38)*.

Students began Karen's 'Science and Society' course by drawing pictures of a 'scientist at work' and then used these pictures to explore cultural stereotypes of scientists (p. 40). By making the stereotypes visible, students were able to think through their sources and challenge their validity. Later, after students had developed and presented their performances, Karen returned to the original drawings to emphasize the narrow stereotypes featured in the media. Wrap-up and consolidation is crucially important, allowing students to reflect upon and drive home the significance of what they had learned [9.9].

[9.9] Reflection and discussion *(see Account 5, p. 45)*.

In her lessons, Karen explored the diversity of people's lives as scientists, particularly the physical adversity and cultural and social barriers they overcame to achieve success. This creates a compelling challenge to the idea of the rational, objective truth that is often portrayed as science. Karen encouraged students to read a biography, aided by focus questions and supplemented by other sources, enabling them to engage closely with their scientist's life (pp. 41–42).

She also employed a range of supportive strategies for her students. Screening videos of last year's class (also a technique used by Gabriel Ayyavoo in Account 9), peer editing of essays, taking scripts on stage as a safety net, and practising as much as time allowed gave students confidence and assuaged uncertainties about performing

[9.10] Building
students' confidence
(see Account 5, p. 43).

[9.10]. Further, this long period of engagement is reminiscent of Rosser's (1990) notion of personal bonding with the subject matter, a part of her 'female-friendly' approach to science. As a result the students were, as Kettle puts it, 'extremely familiar with the lives of the eminent scientists they had studied' (p. 44). This familiarity gave students the tools and techniques to analyse, among other things, the scientists' careers and the associated expectations and social responsibilities that form an essential part of the world of science.

Karen's Account 5 and Katherine's Account 6, stand out as challenging the nature of science and the science curriculum. In Account 5, Karen's approach to the science curriculum was genuinely inclusive. Every student was engaged in the performance and there was enough variety in resources and support from both the teacher and their peers, for all students to achieve success.

Furthermore, the understanding gained about science and scientists, the stereotypes that pervade our thinking and how these arise, equip students to think critically about how they might engage in science themselves. Of course, Karen's enthusiasm may be awakening 'the actor' in students as well as 'the scientist', but students' career choices will be better informed!

The quotation from Account 6, used to introduce this chapter, also reflects the need for students to understand how science is constructed in a socio-cultural sense. Katherine states her belief that science is biased, human and idiosyncratic. She recognizes that issues of race, class and gender are potential blocks for students entering into the culture of science, even the subculture of the science classroom. She goes on to describe the difficulties students have in accessing science at school, regarding it as foreign and therefore alienating to themselves [9.11]. Katherine shuns the 'parading by minority groups or women scientists' as 'a weak attempt to be inclusive' (p. 51) and searches for something more involving.

[9.11] Socio-cultural
construction of science
(see Account 6, pp. 51–
52).

In her lesson about the Burgess Shale fossils (p. 46), Katherine focuses on Gould's (1989) recounting of the interpretation of the story and implications for understanding the evolution of life. Most importantly, she draws attention to the people involved and the prevailing social context. Walcott's original interpretations, nearly a century ago, were consistent with the contemporary understanding that these creatures could be classified within modern phyla. Whittington, Briggs and Conway Morris, 60 years later, decided that this approach did not work well, and had sufficient insight to suggest a major change in evolutionary thinking.

[9.12] Students think
about the construction
of scientific knowledge
(see Account 6, p. 49).

It seems that Katherine has two objectives, apart from teaching 'real science' [9.12]. First, she wants students to realize that scientific knowledge is constructed in the context of current knowledge and beliefs. Also, knowledge and beliefs change as the accumulation of evidence requires shifts in how the world is interpreted. Second, this evidence is accumulated and new understanding built by people not much different from the students themselves. Katherine admits that not all students embrace these ideas but it 'gets them thinking' (p. 50).

Like Karen's drama-based approach in Account 5, the lesson described in Account 6 satisfies all of the criteria for an inclusive science curriculum. The students have access to scientific knowledge and the values associated with it. Katherine's telling of the story, instead of making it assigned reading, ensures that all students can be engaged, and the ensuing discussion enables recognition of their experiences and ideas.

Finally, the opportunity provided for students to examine a real story about science, the scientists involved and the construction of understanding brings to the fore the way science works. And that way is often dynamic – the argument continues about the interpretation of the Burgess Shale fossils and its evolutionary implications (Conway Morris 1998).

Concluding comments

It is tempting to draw a parallel between the interpretation of equity in science teaching and learning and the interpretation of the Burgess Shale fossils. Teachers want to do their best for all of their students, just as scientists want to make the best interpretation of their fossils. Paleontologists make their decisions based on their experience and contemporary theories and understandings in their field, just as teachers draw on educational theories and their understanding of how to teach and how students learn.

When Walcott made his initial interpretation of the Burgess Shale fossils, equity was an entirely different concept than it is now. As pointed out at the beginning of the chapter, thinking about equity has evolved, but different interpretations remain. Unlike the dormant fossils, however, students are active participants in the interpretation of teaching and learning. We have realized the importance of dealing with diversity among students' individual life circumstances and learning styles.

The accounts in this book document some of the ways in which teachers are dealing with issues of equity. The teachers are also promoting an inclusive science curriculum, in terms of providing access to knowledge, skills and values and accommodating variation among the students in their classrooms. Challenging the nature of science and the science curriculum is a further step addressed in some of the accounts.

It is likely that achieving an inclusive science curriculum will continue to challenge science educators in the foreseeable future. In Australia at least, ethnic and cultural diversity among the members of science classrooms has been increasing for some time, as political upheavals in various countries encourage emigration to Australia and elsewhere. While the resulting diversity among students challenges teachers, the accounts in this book demonstrate a variety of strategies that teachers have used to make science more accessible.

The lessons reveal the excitement and rewards in understanding the concepts and nature of science, chipping away at stereotypes of science, scientists and science students. This in turn breaks down the barriers associated with gender race and class. As Katherine Bellomo (Account 6, p. 51) concludes, 'I wanted all of my students to see themselves as having the capability of entering into the culture of science'. It is difficult to have a more inclusive aim than that.

Analysis 10
School science for/against social justice

Larry Bencze

Introduction

Around the world, it is now common to hear people using and, apparently, accepting language typically found in business, including terms such as: competition, individualization, standardization, efficiency and accountability (e.g. Dobbin 1998). Indeed, Gabbard (2000: xvii) suggests that business now 'subordinates all other forms of social interaction to economic logic'. Given the importance of education in shaping societies, some suggest that businesses are encouraging governments to engineer school systems in ways that 'utilize sophisticated performance measures and standards to sort students and to provide a relatively reliable supply of ... adaptable, flexible, loyal, mindful, expendable, "trainable" workers for the twenty-first century' (Noble 1998: 281).

Since professional science and technology play prominent roles in industrialized and, more recently, in knowledge-based societies, it follows there may be significant ways in which school science assists in such social engineering. It is, indeed, apparent that school science systems function primarily to generate a society's knowledge producers and, as a side-effect also beneficial to business, a large mass of knowledge consumers.

More particularly, schools that over-emphasize the selection and education of the relatively small group of students who may work as engineers and scientists to help companies develop and manage mechanisms of production (and consumption) of goods and services may also generate large groups of citizens who may function best as compliant workers and as enthusiastic purchasers of products and services of business and industry. Where this is happening, it is an unjust use of school science. Citizens who mainly function as knowledge consumers are less able to think and act independently, since each consumer product carries with it a set of instructions for thought and behaviour.

In this chapter, segments of the accounts of exemplary practice in this book are used to illustrate ways in which teachers can provide a more democratic science education; that is, schooling that aims to enlighten and empower all citizens in ways that allow them to lead personally fulfilling lives. The discussion below is divided into two major sections. The first illustrates ways in which aspects of the accounts can help subvert discriminatory effects of schools' search for potential knowledge producers. The second demonstrates how aspects of the accounts can help subvert consumerist effects of some school science characteristics.

Towards a more democratic science education

Subverting discriminatory school science: promoting more inclusion

Rather than being an opportunity to be educated in science, school science is often like a selection and training camp for identifying and educating the relatively few students who may become scientists or engineers. In this kind of environment, 'lessons' are less about learning than about being *tested*. It is a survival of the fittest experience. To succeed, students must be able to quickly understand large volumes of abstract ideas – such as laws and theories – that are rapidly transmitted to them using didactic methods such as lecturing and question and answer sessions.

Moreover, students often must try to understand abstractions with few opportunities to apply them in personally meaningful problem-solving situations. Through this kind of education, students may be sorted along a continuum, largely dependent on their *cultural capital*, i.e. intellectual and social wealth that comes from advantaged experiences such as: speaking in the abstract, reading important works of fiction and non-fiction and use of new technologies (Henry et al. 1999). Cultural capital is associated with financial well-being. Apparently, one of the greatest determinants of (overall) academic success is parental income: '[T]he myth of equal opportunity therefore masks an ugly truth: the educational system is really a loaded social lottery, in which each student gets as many chances as his or her parents have dollars' (McLaren 1994: 220–1).

Although such discriminatory school science is undemocratic, it seems to serve corporate interests. The relatively few students experiencing success in school science are likely to work in professions such as engineering, science, accounting, business management and law, through which they could develop and manage mechanisms of production and consumpton of goods and services on behalf of financiers of business and industry. Generally, they would be a society's main knowledge *producers*. Meanwhile, it is apparent that the scientific literacy of most other students is compromised and, as a consequence, many of them are left to fulfil roles as knowledge *consumers*. How this seems to occur is discussed below (next page), along with ways in which episodes from the accounts can undermine consumerist effects of school science.

Teaching and learning scenarios depicted in the account documentaries in this book can, however, help to promote a more *inclusive* school science curriculum (refer to Analysis 6). Several ways in which episodes from the accounts can help more students to be engaged in the science curriculum are discussed below.

One way to promote inclusion is to avoid inductive activities for teaching particular predetermined concepts and, instead, use deductive ones [10.1]. In an inductive activity, students are expected to 'discover' (induce) general principles by observing specific phenomena. Students who sprinkle iron filings on a sheet of acetate that is positioned over a magnet may be, for example, expected to discover magnetic lines of force. This is difficult, if not impossible, unless students already have a notion about invisible lines of force. Even Josie Ellis (Account 3), a high-achieving student, noted that the abstract nature of school science can make it difficult to learn (p. 29).

[10.1] Avoid induction; promote deduction *(see Account 1, p. 18, Account 2, p. 24, Account 8, p. 68 and Account 10, p. 85)*.

Therefore, if educators intend to help all students to develop understandings of specific pre-determined conceptions (e.g. laws and theories), they should *present* them more directly to students. At the same time, those ideas should not remain abstract [10.2]. Learners generally need opportunities to evaluate abstract claims (e.g. laws and theories), through empirical tests (deductions) in contexts having relevance for them. There are, indeed, several instances of deductivist instruction in the accounts. Keith Hicks (Account 1, pp. 17–18), for example, demonstrates how to dissect basic kidney parts before students are asked to do so. Moreover, in discussing results of their dissections, he de-emphasized induction by noting with them how difficult it was to 'discover' nephron structure.

[10.2] Make the abstract concrete and, where appropriate, contextualize it *(see Account 7, p. 58)*.

A key element in the success of such deductive activities is for teachers to use concrete phenomena to illustrate abstract ideas. Often, this will contextualize the abstraction, bringing in more 'real-world' variables and making the idea more relevant to learners' everyday experiences. This is apparent in many of the accounts, including when Keith Hicks contextualizes highly schematic kidney drawings with a freshly butchered kidney (p. 18), using a porous rubber hose to demonstrate kidney function (p. 19) and by asking students to construct a model nephron using common materials (pp. 19–20).

Teachers also can have much success by contextualizing concepts through use of role play. For example, George Przywolnik in Account 2 (pp. 24–25), encouraged students to mimic particles, videotaped them and then discussed more abstract models of particle behaviour. Even when teachers are careful to clearly present ideas and give students various opportunities to evaluate them in meaningful contexts, some students are still likely to have difficulties and, ultimately, feel or be excluded. This may be particularly true for students who, for example, tend to lack self-confidence, are alienated from school or for various reasons tend to be discriminated against. For these individuals, teachers need to implement appropriate adaptations [10.3].

[10.3] Accommodate for difference *(see Account 1, p. 21 and Account 5, p. 43)*.

For example, when some of his students were unable to complete their model kidneys on time, Keith Hicks allowed them to take a bit more time, and also adapt their model to demonstrate effects of Anti-Diuretic Hormone (ADH) on nephrons (p. 21). Similarly, Karen Kettle in Account 5, allowed students with differing acting abilities to play different roles and/or to be in roles suiting their abilities (p. 43). On a more systemic basis, meanwhile, Richard Rennie and Kim Richards point out that the multimedia nature of the SCOT project allows students with different learning styles to learn the same material (p. 34).

[10.4] Problematize science *(see Account 5, p. 41 and Account 6, p. 51)*.

Finally, students can become more engaged in science if they realize that its practices and claims are potentially problematic [10.4], (refer also to Analysis 1). The human face that Karen Kettle puts on science through emphasis on historical accounts of scientists and inventors is an excellent example of this (p. 41). More explicitly, Katherine Bellomo (Account 6), points out that, when students see each scientist's perspective can influence the direction of scientific thinking, it can be considered more inclusive, meaning that anyone can be a 'scientist' (pp. 50–51).

Subverting consumerist school science: promoting more self-actualization

Where school science systems focus on identifying and educating a few potential scientists and engineers, the education of most other students may be compromised. While there are many possible causes, several aspects of such schooling can generate large groups of citizens best suited to become consumers of knowledge; which, as argued above, often involves consumption of labour instructions and products, and services controlled by business and industry. Clearly, in a democracy, students deserve the right to develop abilities and attitudes that enable them to self-determine their thoughts and actions. This is in addition to gaining access to the intellectual riches (e.g. laws and theories of science) of their forebears (Beane and Apple 1995).

The accounts in this book provide several approaches science teachers can take to help students to self-determine their thoughts and actions. These approaches are discussed below, in terms of ways in which they can undermine six mechanisms that seem to promote consumerism.

Promoting more self-motivation

While sharing with students many of the achievements of science and technology, such as laws and theories, is essential for their participation in decision making in societies greatly dependent on science and technology, an excessive emphasis on these can lull students into habits of passive consumption. Indeed, it has been suggested that the 'medium [of school science] is reinforcing the message ... that science education is about remembering the results of other's [professional scientists' and engineers'] research ("facts") rather than developing the ability to conduct one's own' (Claxton 1991: 28). A steady diet of conclusions may stifle students' self-motivation to ask questions, to critique claims, to criticize those who control knowledge and to develop their own conclusions.

Among ways educators can avoid pacifying effects of saturating students with achievements of science and technology is to create a kind of knowledge 'vacuum'. That is, reducing pre-determined expectations for student learning, leaving room for the possibility of new knowledge development. As the American Association for the Advancement of Science (AAAS 1989) recommended, school systems need to help students to *do more with less* (knowledge expectations). While none of the accounts in this book are explicit about this, most seemed to create conditions that promoted proactive perspectives on knowledge development [10.5].

[10.5] Promote proactive perspectives on knowledge development *(see Account 1, p. 19, Account 5, p. 44 and Accounts 7 to 9)*.

For example, although kidney models made by Keith Hicks's students had to be based on real kidneys, they had considerable flexibility in how they constructed them from the materials provided (pp. 19–20). Similarly, while Karen Kettle's students drew from others' historical accounts, they had a great deal of flexibility in how they *dramatized* them (pp. 43–44). Such creativity, based on existing knowledge, was also exemplified in the STSE simulation initiated by Susan Yoon (Account 7).

The accounts that perhaps best illustrate a proactive perspective on knowledge are those of Gabriel Ayyavoo (Account 9) and his students, and that of Alex Corry (Account 8). For example, in the latter (pp. 67–68), the validity of knowledge claims is questioned and students are encouraged to develop their own scientific and technological knowledge through projects under their control.

Promoting more skill development

To ensure students develop understandings of the many achievements of science and technology that often dominate government curricula, teachers may 'over-manage' students' thoughts and actions. For example, teachers commonly engage students in practical activities that resemble experimentation, but take steps to ensure the activities support conclusions of Western science and technology (Hodson 1996). Such over-regulation can prevent students from developing expertise for important knowledge development activities, for example, skills such as: question asking, empirical test design, graphing and debating.

While students can 'discover' skills for doing science by being involved in activities, such as projects involving experimentation similar to those used by scientists and engineers, it also is helpful for teachers to provide students with a kind of *apprenticeship* [10.6]. Here, students are shown particular strategies, given opportunities to practise them and, then, are encouraged to use them in their own knowledge-building activities (Bencze 2000).

[10.6] Provide students with an apprenticeship for development of expertise for knowledge creation in science and technology *(see Account 5, p. 42, Account 7, pp. 55–57 and Accounts 8 to 10)*.

Given their goals are to explicitly promote students' development of such expertise, apprenticeship activities provided by Alex Corry (Account 8), Gabriel Ayyavoo (Account 9) and James Johnston (Account 10) are appropriate. Especially helpful, given the idiosyncratic, contextual nature of knowledge development, would be those forms of assistance set within students' problem-solving endeavours. For example, in Account 7, Susan Yoon provided a role-playing framework that culminated in the town hall meeting (pp. 59–62). In Account 9 (pp. 79–82), we see how experts demonstrated various relevant techniques in molecular biology to help Desmond Ngai with his science fair project.

Promoting more social learning

In school systems that focus on identifying and educating those students who are likely to become knowledge producers (e.g. scientists and engineers), there can be a tendency to individualize learning and, especially, assessment practices. Students often are assessed and graded individually, rather than as cooperative groups. This limits the extent to which students learn from others and can develop knowledge. Like a *Gestalt* experience (Mullet and Sano 1995) this knowledge is, different from, and possibly greater than, knowledge developed by students when left to their own devices.

Indeed, it is apparent that meaningful learning is promoted through engagement in social learning systems and, in particular, *communities of practice*. These are groups of individuals who, through their involvement in common knowledge-processing activities, develop a rich repertoire of skills and strategies, often speak in similar ways and identify with each other (Wenger 2000). Students, as newcomers to a particular field, can learn from people with different amounts and kinds of expertise within the community [10.7]. A good example of learning based on such communities of practice is found in Account 9. Desmond Ngai describes various authentic practices and ideas he received while interacting with different scientists and technicians working in his field of interest.

[10.7] Promote social learning and assessment *(see Account 5, p. 43, Account 9, pp. 78–79)*.

Although the contexts are less realistic, similar sorts of ideas and strategies are demonstrated by teachers with procedural expertise in Accounts 8 and 9. On the other hand, Karen Kettle (Account 5) and Katherine Bellomo (Account 6), provide related expertise but, in their accounts, demonstrate more the nature of scientific practices than procedures used in scientific knowledge building. In addition, there are numerous instances in which peers with differing kinds and levels of expertise collaborate in learning activities. These include when groups of students role-play aspects of an STSE problem (Account 7), negotiate kidney modelling (Account 1), cooperate in various practical practice activities (Account 2), engage in peer editing (Account 5) and team-based problem solving (Account 10).

Promoting more enlightenment

In efforts to attract students to careers in science and technology, teachers may, inadvertently or otherwise, idealize products and practices of science to an extent that school science functions like an 'infomercial' for professional science. Achievements of science (e.g. theories) are made to appear certain, and methods of achieving them are portrayed to be efficient and objective. In addition, the sciences are depicted as unproblematic in their relationships with fields of technology, societies and environments.

Among the myths perpetuated through school science are that observation provides direct and reliable access to secure knowledge and that scientific inquiry is a simple, algorithmic procedure (Hodson 1999). Such naïve views about the nature of science can lead students to become uncritical consumers of products of science and technology, and in turn, less able to generate scientific and technological knowledge. Educators, therefore, need to promote realistic conceptions of the nature of science(s) (refer to Analysis 1) and relationships among sciences, technologies, societies and environments (refer to Analysis 3) [10.8]. Generally, this can be accomplished using *implicit* (inductive) and *explicit* (deductive) approaches (Abd-El-Khalick and Lederman 2000).

[10.8] Promote realistic conceptions of the nature of science(s) and relationships among sciences, technologies, societies and environments *(see Account 2, p. 26, Account 5, p. 39, Account 6, p. 51, Account 7, pp. 55–56 and Account 9, pp. 76–77)*.

An excellent example of such approaches from the accounts is provided by Susan Yoon when she points out (explicitly, pp. 55–56) the nature of common stakeholders, yet encourages students to 'discover' (implicitly. pp. 57–58) other characteristics through their engagement in a realistic problem-solving activity. Similar strategies are used in other accounts, showing science to be, for example, idiosyncratic (p. 41), theory limited (pp. 47–50 and p. 64), culturally mediated (p. 40), subject to measurement errors (pp. 26–27), and assisted by, although sometimes limited by, models (pp. 19–21 and pp. 76–77).

Promoting diversity

Recently, governments have tended to standardize curricula and measure student achievement to ensure teacher compliance. Governments claim such curricular consistency will guarantee all learners equal opportunities, regardless of their learning situations (e.g. DfEE 1999). Another perspective, however, is that standardization engenders societal *conformity* (Elkind 1997).

[10.9] Promote *naturalistic* (as well as rationalistic) curricula and instruction *(see Account 5, p. 39 and Accounts 7 to 10)*.

While it is important that all students have access to the same set of societal knowledge in a democracy, curricula and instruction should also be adapted to individual students' needs, interests, perspectives and abilities. In other words, education should be *naturalistic* (situational), as well as rationalistic (e.g. pre-specified) (Guba and Lincoln 1988) [10.9]. This implies that more opportunities be provided for student-directed (SD), open-ended (OE) activities (as well as more teacher-directed (TD), closed-ended (CE) ones (Lock 1990). Open-ended activities allow conclusions to be derived from specific situations, rather than being pre-determined (as with CE activities).

A more naturalistic form of education is exemplified by Susan Yoon's account (Account 7). Although she provided a framework for the town hall debate (including general descriptions of its participants), 'in role play and simulation activities, students were given full control of . . . decision-making processes with the resulting learning outcomes being highly successful' (p. 57). In comparison, all the other accounts illustrate important forms of preparation for more naturalistic education. While those of Karen Kettle (Account 5), Alex Corry (Account 8), Gabriel Ayyavoo (Account 9) and James Johnston (Account 10) represent more direct preparation for this sort of education.

[10.10] Rationalize curriculum expectations, thus leaving time for increased quality of learning *(see Account 5, p. 39)*.

Dramatizations of eminent scientists and inventors, although based on written biographies, were created by Karen Kettle's students in Account 5. As she says, 'the course was unfettered by a tradition of how it "should" be taught. Therefore, it was easy to convince the young people that this was a logical way to learn about creative productivity' (p. 39), [10.10]. Such experiences can help students develop *self-efficacy* towards more SD/OE knowledge development.

The teaching and learning scenarios depicted in Accounts 8–10, meanwhile, are excellent for helping students to develop expertise for more naturalistic education. Using methods described in the accounts, students can learn, for example, approaches to *problem posing* (e.g. for developing cause-result questions and hypotheses, pp. 64–66), *problem-solving* (e.g. for using models in developing theoretical perspectives, pp. 76–77 and for techniques such as welding, p. 87), *peer persuasion* (e.g. for reporting techniques and critiquing written reports, pp. 67–68) aspects of knowledge building (Johnson and Stewart 1990).

Lastly, but not necessarily of least importance, are instances in which teachers provide students with *motivation* for SD/OE inquiry and technological design (e.g. starting a unit by encouraging students to explore their pre-instructional conceptions in a topic, p. 64 and by being shown exemplars of previous students' projects, p. 40 and p. 74).

Promoting greater understanding

While professional science and technology have been successful in developing products such as laws, theories and inventions, over-emphasizing these in school science can be problematic. Given the wealth of accumulated scientific and technological knowledge, being a student of school science can be like trying to take a sip from a fire hose! Where curricula over-emphasize achievements of science and technology, teachers may try to teach them so rapidly, and with so few opportunities for application in personally meaningful contexts, that many students are left confused or only capable of rote learning (Claxton 1991). Millar (1996) claimed, for example, that most studies of students' understandings (by age 16 years) of fundamental laws and principles of science (e.g. about the particle theory of matter) are either simplistic or quite different from those of scientists.

As argued above, school systems need to be encouraged to 'do more with less' (AAAS 1989). That is, rationalize (reduce and group) pre-specifications for learning, thus making room for development of deeper understandings of required concepts, skills etc., and for students' development of new knowledge.

Karen Kettle (Account 5, p. 39), for example, was explicit about the freedom afforded by the 'open-ended' nature of the grade 9 interdisciplinary studies class in which she implemented her drama-based science programme. Such freedom for more in-depth teaching and learning is implied in several other accounts; for example, in the time Keith Hicks (Account 1) took to reinforce ideas about kidney structure and function and in the many different time-consuming, but effective, practical applications and role-playing techniques George Przywolnik (Account 2) used to teach physics. Other examples include, Josie Ellis's teacher (Account 3) choosing to teach reaction mechanisms, rather than every reaction on the syllabus (p. 30), and the time for collaborative problem solving provided by Karen Kettle (Account 5), Susan Yoon (Account 7) and James Johnston (Account 10).

Accordingly, there is ample evidence in the accounts of students' development of deep understandings about scientific knowledge. Examples of this include: kidney structure and function (pp. 21–22), the nature of space travel (pp. 23–24), the human element in science and invention (pp. 41–42), the theory-based nature of data interpretation (pp. 50–51), particular factors affecting STSE decisions (pp. 59–62) abilities for developing causal questions and experiment design (pp. 65–66), and analysis and critique of scientific inquiries (pp. 67–68).

Summary and conclusions

While the nature of teaching and learning depends on contexts involving particular teachers and students in particular learning environments, there are also many 'beyond the school' influences on educational processes. Currently, it is apparent that school systems are under enormous pressure from powerful individuals and groups promoting 'the *new capitalism*' (McQuaig 2001: 22, original emphasis). This is an ideology that promotes globalized production and consumption in environments that give greater priority to corporate profit making than to individual and community rights and interests.

Under this influence, many school systems have engineered science programmes so that they efficiently identify and educate potential knowledge producers. This includes scientists and engineers, who can help business and industry develop and manage mechanisms of production and consumption. Often compromised by this selection and training process is the scientific literacy of most students. As a consequence, their thoughts and actions may be excessively regulated through labour instructions as well as the goods and services they consume.

In this analysis, excerpts from the accounts are used to illustrate how science teachers potentially can help all students become more enlightened and empowered to live personally fulfilling lives. Based on the accounts, it is apparent that specific approaches can be taken to make school science more inclusive. Also apparent is how, in efforts to enable greater self-actualization, such approaches help students become more self-motivated, skilled, enlightened and diverse, for example. With more teachers using the kinds of approaches highlighted in this book, perhaps school science will be of greater service to those being educated than to those controlling education.

PART 3

Possibilities, accounts, hypertext and theoretical lenses

Part 3 has two chapters. These explore the nature of the text as: (i) a representation of exemplary practice, (ii) a research project and (iii) a model of teacher professional development. Our intent is to take stock, provide an overview, and then point to future possibilities.

The first chapter, 'Voices and viewpoints' grapples with exemplariness and all its bombastic overtones. The final stage of the project offered teachers the opportunity to reflect on the accounts and analysis. More specifically, we asked them to contemplate the image of teaching that emerged and the role this might have in shaping future practice. Their written comments shape the opening discussion, which is organized by curriculum categories (teaching science, teaching about science and doing science, Hodson 1993). Rather than seeking generalizations, comments are drawn to a meta-analysis – a higher order consideration of what and why: why do science teachers select particular exemplary strategies? What knowledge, beliefs and affections underpin teachers' choice of practice?

The following section extends the teaching theme by exploring professional growth. Throughout this project, our goals have been unreservedly utilitarian – driven by a very real-world question: what might teachers' accounts and their analysis offer teachers? From the beginning, it was never our intention to add to obscurity, or to produce a theoretical treaty languishing in the world of academia. The penultimate chapter concludes with some thoughts about the model of professional development permeating the text and how this might translate into action. These reflections underscore the significance of quality conversations about particulars rooted in a broader situational understanding and critical reflection.

The final chapter focuses on research; more specifically the nature of the book as a research project. We turn to methodology and in the tradition of the social sciences to reflect on and justify an empirical approach (in our case, the use of teacher narrative and layered multiple analyses). The tone has a more academic feel as we delve into considering validity and reliability. At a time when the merit of qualitative educational research seems in question, we offer our voice in its support. Indeed, science education might provide a unique venue to comment on such debates by virtue of being a social science routed in science.

Our suggestion is that we can learn much from a rich, in-depth exploration of the particular and it makes little sense to judge this in normative terms. We contend that our text is inherently *trustworthy* on the basis of: (i) those who participated (our sample of experienced practitioners); (ii) the richness of its attention to the particular and the theoretical depth of the subsequent analysis; and (iii) our use of triangulation (exploring a particular phenomenon from a multiplicity of perspectives).

The final section returns once again to our overarching epistemological theme – theory and practice. We feel unable to end discussion of research without some comment on the pragmatics of the real world, the classroom. In this regard, we feel it important to extend the traditional debate of validity to one of functionality and utility. Not only do we seek to justify our approach methodologically (in terms of its empirical validity) but also practically. We are ever conscious of pedagogical validity (the purchase that the accounts and analyses might hold to create future teaching possibilities). We conclude our conversation with a reflection on agency: an extended warning of the dangers associated with plunking-and-deploying facets of the text in search of a pedagogical enlightenment or a quick fix. Rather, we claim, the utilitarian fruitfulness of the book resides in the extended conversation; the stimulus that it might provide in engaging ongoing collaborative re-negotiation of praxis. Our image of teacher growth is inextricably embedded within a conceptual framework of social justice and empowerment. Throughout our journey we have sought to preserve the voices of teachers and academics, recognizing their considerable expertise, while offering a framework, which we hope brings facets of this expertise together.

Reflection 1

Voices and viewpoints: what have we learned about exemplary science teaching?

Erminia Pedretti, Larry Bencze and Steve Alsop

Introduction

This book, for us, has been a foray into exploring and celebrating exemplariness in secondary science teaching. Although we were deliberate in our methodology – our quest to combine accounts of authentic *exemplary* science classroom practice with educational theory – the construct of 'exemplariness' has not been so easy to pinpoint. How and why do teachers choose particular episodes as exemplary? What does a science teacher consider when determining how to teach a particular concept? Why does a science teacher use a particular strategy for some concepts and not others? What reasoning underpins the science teacher's practice? As Roth (1998) suggests, perhaps the subtleties of quality teaching defy analysis, yet we believe that through this collaborative venture we can illuminate practice so that it can be viewed, analysed and explored by others.

In the first half of this chapter, we revisit the notion of exemplary science teaching, in an attempt to understand the landscape of 'exemplary' *science* practice and its relationship to theory. In the latter part of this chapter we look back at the experience of framing and writing the book, to consider the nature of accounts and their axiomatic role in professional development and teacher education. Specifically, we describe quality professional development as attending to the specifics of teaching, situating teaching within broader theoretical ideas, promoting quality conversations and setting up contexts in which these quality conversations can happen. By way of bringing the book to a close, we invited contributing teachers to read and respond to the collection of accounts and analyses. Their voices and viewpoints are interwoven into this final commentary.

In search of a common place and practice: what constitutes exemplary science teaching?

In the introductory chapter, we problematize the nature of exemplary teaching. What might it mean? Is it a useful concept to explore? What might constitute exemplary practice? What do good teachers do? While we pose these questions and attempt to provide some response, we are acutely aware that a single vision of teaching (in this case termed exemplary) is problematic. Exemplary practices are diverse, highly personal, and occur within a contextually rich tapestry. There is no single, virtuous road, no grand blueprint or narrative. Teaching itself is complex, messy and multifaceted: 'the notion of science teaching as a rational technical process of identifying problems, applying theory to interpret the situation, and behavioristically enacting a prescribed solution greatly underestimates what it means to teach' (Barcenal in Koballa and Tippins 2004: 2). Karen Kettle, in her written feedback to us, describes exemplary teaching as the following:

> Teaching is a balancing act. On a daily basis teachers attempt to balance the cognitive, emotional and social needs of students; strategies for teaching, assessment, evaluation and classroom management; content concerns; equity issues; ongoing professional development goals, integrating technology; laboratory safety; communication with parents; and change initiatives. What sets exemplary practice apart may be the ability of some teachers to thrive in this chaotic environment and maintain their hope that they can make a difference in the lives of their students.

Katherine Bellomo offers the following:

> Writing the case and then reading the analyses has made me think about exemplary practice ... Exemplary practice is context specific, sometimes student driven (one student might connect with this material and another not). It is an intellectual and emotional and personal manifestation of what in the hands of another teacher could well be a good and competent lesson but not necessarily an exemplary one. It is based on preparation, awareness of student needs, acknowledgement of teacher needs, experience, luck and overall passion for the work!

Not surprisingly, teachers' accounts span a range of pedagogical practices, each embodying some aspect of what we might call 'exemplary' pedagogical content knowledge (Shulman 1987). In other words, teachers have a lexicon of 'successful' activities and practices from which they draw to create teaching situations that help learners make sense of particular science content. The accounts provided in this book portray an amalgam of content knowledge and teaching knowledge, ranging from the tried-and-true and familiar, to the unexpected and unconventional.

From the seemingly simple question: 'Could you describe an aspect of your practice that you consider exemplary?', we received accounts of teaching as diverse as teachers themselves. Yet, in spite of the range of teaching approaches described and subject areas covered, are there threads that can be extracted across stories, across continents? Are there principles at play that guide sound pedagogical practices in science teaching? We think so, although we hasten to add again that these paradigmatic ways of knowing are not prescriptive, but rather very 'situated' and contextualized. We use the term 'principles' as did Dewey (1960: 137) when he argued that principles are not rules to be blindly followed, but 'guides for suggested courses of action'. As Karen Kettle explains, 'exemplary practice is ... not one, but the selection of a constellation of appropriate science experiences'. It is to these experiences that we now turn.

Teaching abstract scientific content in creative and meaningful ways (learning science)

In thinking about teaching science, content (understood as not merely a collection of facts, but a complex set of related theories, laws and models that help us to understand the world: see Keith Taber, Analysis 4) plays a predominant role. For the learner, however, an emphasis on content is not always alluring. It conjures up memories of formulas, abstractions, rote and often decontextualized learning (Solomon 1994; Hodson 1998b). However, teachers' accounts suggest differently. For example, in Account 1, Keith Hicks teaches about kidney function through dissection, diagrams, model building and displays, while George Przywolnik, in Account 2 teaches longitudinal and transverse waves through role play and demonstration. In Account 4, Richard Rennie and Kim Edwards showcase technology mediated instruction that is the bedrock for teaching the grade 9 science curriculum, while in Account 7, Susan Yoon's students learn about the environment through their direct connection with the outdoors. Exemplariness in science teaching clearly has something to do with bringing potentially abstract concepts to life through diverse and creative approaches, acknowledging students' different learning modalities, and promoting high student engagement. These themes are brought to the fore across all analysis chapters, and beautifully captured in John Wallace's notion of the 'plurality of pedagogy' (see Analysis 8).

George Przywolnik, in his final reflection to us shares a similar insight: 'I was completely surprised and then bowled over by Josie Ellis's case study [Account 3] ... I found myself ticking off a mental checklist of those practices that I believe encourage real learning and understanding: using molecular models to make the abstract more concrete; emphasizing the underlying structure of a discipline rather than focusing on surface features; integrating the practical with the theoretical; peer instruction ...'. There is much we might learn from listening to students' reflections on pedagogy.

Katherine Bellomo, in her final analysis about teaching the Burgess Shale, makes the point that content knowledge is important (see also Analyses 4 [Taber] and 8 [Wallace]), but that, so too, are excitement and passion for the subject:

> I chose this case because I love this story. I use the word love purposely. I love the story; I loved how Stephen Jay Gould told it in his book *Wonderful Life*; I love how much it affected my own thinking and teaching and I love teaching about the Burgess Shale fossils and of their later reinterpretation. Writing the case and then reading the analyses has made me think about exemplary practice. Perhaps exemplary practice in some instances (or perhaps for me) arises from a strong emotional attachment and a deep understanding of content!

Across most accounts, expressions of emotion and enthusiasm for the subject and for students' learning prevail. Stories and analyses (see, for example, Analysis 3 [Pedretti], and Analysis 6 [Alsop]) strongly suggest that affect mediates cognition and learning in fundamental ways, and that quality pedagogical practices are inextricably tied to emotions.

Teaching science as a human construct (learning about science)

Hodson (1998b) describes learning *about* science as 'developing an understanding of the nature and methods of science, an appreciation of its history and development, and an awareness of the complex interactions among science, technology, society and environment' (p. 5). However, historically, these perspectives are often marginalized and delegated to a peripheral position in the curriculum, an 'extra' if you will (see, for example, Hughes 2000; Pedretti 2003). It is significant that some teachers chose, as their exemplary episode, lessons that explicitly celebrated 'learning about science'. In Account 5, for example, students study the lives of scientists within a rich social, cultural and political fabric using role play and research. Account 6 illustrates the story of the reinterpretation of the Burgess Shale, while

Account 7 explores students' participation in responsible and informed decision making through a town hall meeting. Other accounts address 'learning about science' implicitly through careful attention to nature of science key points (for example, scientific knowledge while durable, has a tentative character, there is no one way to do science; observations are theory laden; science is part of social and cultural traditions). Similarly, analyses chapters referent 'learning about science' perspectives through various theoretical lenses (i.e. argumentation, affect, conceptual development, equity and inclusivity, and social justice). It would appear then, that exemplary science teaching attends to learning *about* science, in many forms and manifestations.

If we return to teachers' final reflections, Karen Kettle highlights the importance of 'learning about science' (although she doesn't explicitly label it as such):

> The realization that science is deeply affected by culture, economics, politics and human nature, surprises many students and disappoints others, but it provides a more realistic picture of the discipline they may choose to enter ... Students become aware that people from both genders and all cultures and classes contribute to science, critically examine the nature of science, and debunk myths and stereotypes about scientists. This makes the science curriculum more inclusive.

Karen's words reinforce yet another common thread throughout the book – that of inclusivity and equity as fundamental to exemplary practice. Léonie Rennie (Analysis 9) elegantly describes components of an inclusive science curriculum, components that are also echoed by Hodson [Analysis 1], Pedretti [Analysis 3], Wallace [Analysis 8] and Bencze [Analysis 10].

Teaching science through doing science

Laboratory investigations and benchwork have long been a mainstay in the science classroom. Often this amounts to students following recipes and algorithms to arrive at what is perceived as predetermined and unfathomable outcomes. However, our collection of narrative accounts suggests a much broader interpretation of what it means to 'do science'. We borrow Hodson's (1998b) suggestion that 'doing science' involves engaging in and developing expertise in scientific inquiry and problem solving in many contexts (i.e. designing experiments, undertaking correlational studies or engaging in technological problem solving). For example, in Accounts 7, 8, 9 and 10, students and teams of students engage in problem-based learning and open-ended scientific inquiry in the classroom and in the larger community. Students engage in messy real-world problems, asking questions, seeking solutions, designing experiments, playing with the unknown (see Hill and Smith [Analysis 5] and Bencze [Analysis 10] for more detail). Karen writes about the excitement and ambiguities of open-ended inquiry:

> Students who love the tentative and exploratory nature of science or technological design thrive on these open-ended, minds-on and hands-on projects. These students are not deterred because there is no simple right answer. The ambiguity of the unknown engages them. Students learn how to ask scientific and techno- logical questions, ponder hypotheses, devise experiments to generate data, tinker with equipment, observe, analyse, report and repeat. They engage in science, not to conduct the steps of a carefully designed laboratory exercise, but to answer their own questions and construct their own knowledge.

Accounts suggest that there are many variations on the theme of what it means for students to 'do' science. Sometimes engaging in inquiry and problem solving requires outreach to the larger com- munity – seeking expertise or perspectives from various stakeholders (Accounts 6 and 8 for example). Many worthwhile scientific inquiries can be conducted in outdoor venues such as field centres, forests, museums and zoos. At other times, explicit teaching of scientific and/ or thinking skills, in order to enhance students 'doing' of science, is required. Consider Karen Kettles' reflections as she identifies the importance of developing such skills:

> Examples of students using fundamental scientific skills appear through the case studies. These include making observations, reviewing the literature, developing research questions and hypotheses, designing experiments, managing equipment, sol- ving problems, manipulating variables, analysing data, detecting bias, criticizing knowledge claims, collaborating, reaching con- sensus, and communicating their understanding in a variety of forms. Exemplary practice requires that we do more than provide occasions to think. We must explicitly teach students how to use a selection of thinking tools and when to apply them. The most complete examples of guiding students through the development of skills appear in Cases 8 and 9 which take an overt approach to teaching scientific inquiry.

Similarly, analyses of the analysis chapters reinforce the idea that students need to be explicitly taught particular skills. For example, Hodson [in Analysis 1] writes that students engaged in bench work need to be taught what to look for, how to look for it, and how to recognize the significance of what they see. Sibel Erduran and Jonathan Osborne [Analysis 2] suggest that we teach students how to construct scientific arguments to support or refute knowledge claims, while Jim Hewitt [Analysis 7] writes about the use of probeware technology as a way of freeing up time so that students can engage in higher order thinking skills. In Analysis 10, Larry Bencze argues for skill development as a way of ensuring students can produce as well as consume scientific and technological knowledge. Succinctly put, particular skills are necessary if students are to engage successfully in 'doing' science.

Summing it all up

This collection of personalized reflections *on* practice (Schön 1987) and the accompanying analyses chapters provide a glimpse into the complexities of charting exemplary practice. Rather than using cases as a standard against which to judge exemplariness, these accounts are used as a trigger for discussion and exploration. In other words, the accounts provide a 'leitmotif for the readers' interpretive act' (Wallace 2001: 186). George Przywolnik's reading of the cases led to the following analysis of what he coined 'deep-seated similarities' across the accounts:

> What struck me was that while each case study was profoundly different in its details, all had some deep-seated similarities. Each of the practitioners focused on what the students were doing, and how that activity influenced how the students were learning. Each provided a range of opportunities for students with different learning styles to engage with the lessons. Each tried to find connections between the material being taught and the students' worlds. And each took the time to reflect on the lessons, to separate what works from what doesn't. Perhaps these are the great commandments for science educators:
>
> - it's not what you do, it's what the *students* do.
> - vary your approach so that neither you nor your students ever feel bored.
> - students will learn what they perceive to be relevant to them; and
> - the unexamined lesson isn't worth teaching.

Up to this point, we have spent considerable time inquiring into the nature of exemplariness, and what that might look like in a science classroom. Each teacher has offered his/her story to share with others, stories that reveal individual and collective narrative histories,

stories that have been deliberately chosen. Storying and re-storying are part of teachers' lives, and often serve to stimulate personal and professional reflection and growth. In using these stories or accounts to stimulate discussion about exemplary science teaching, we are aware of the strong professional development aspects of our shared experiences. Accordingly, we now shift our focus of attention to the use of teacher accounts as a way of mediating professional development in rich and creative contexts.

Teacher accounts and professional development

As we planned the book, we were cognizant of particular principles that guided our decision making processes. We wanted to explore exemplary science practice through teachers' stories, provide various analytical lenses through which readers could interpret accounts and create a context in which educators could engage in conversations about practice. In other words, we hoped our book, by merging theory and practice, might serve as a professional development model or provide valuable professional development opportunities. Wallace (2003) describes effective teacher education as attending to the specifics of teaching, situating teaching within broader theoretical ideas, promoting quality conversations and setting up contexts in which these quality conversations can happen. Each of these points is elaborated upon in the context of our framing and writing of this book.

The specifics of teaching

Teachers' accounts are the bedrock on which this book is built. We, the editors, in framing it were deliberate in our desire to honour teachers' voices. The book reflects a belief in, and respect for, teacher knowledge and praxis. We were not interested in co-opting teachers' voices or their specific experiences, rather we hoped to capture exemplariness in science teaching through their telling and re-telling of specific teaching episodes.

The notion of particulars or specifics is key to this work. Much has been written about general principles of teaching (see, for example, Elbaz 1983; Eisner 1991; Kilbourn 1998), however, these generalized principles are rooted in multiple instances of particulars, in the overlapping stories people share. It is attention to the minutia – the detail of day to day preparation and teaching – that constitutes the lived experiences of teachers. Teachers' accounts about the particulars of their teaching render the invisible visible, and encourage readers potentially to move from pedagogy of the general to pedagogy of the specific.

Theoretical apparatus

Locating the specifics of teaching within some theoretical apparatus is fundamental to this book, and to effective professional development. Situating teaching accounts within a broader discourse about science and science education allows readers to move back and forth between the particulars of an account to speculation on broader theoretical issues. Intentionally, the first half of the book focuses on the instances of particulars (in this case exemplary science practices), while the second half of the book offers an analysis (across teacher accounts) from various theoretical lenses. Susan Yoon (Account 7) describes the relationship between the accounts and analyses with the following:

> One of the fundamental benefits of the book . . . is that it offers a framework for bridging the theory-practice gap, providing thoughtful theoretical analyses about tangible, readily applicable classroom activities that collectively represent a thorough account of the current state of science education research without a lot of unnecessary jargon.

The notion of a theory-practice gap in education is not new (Schwab 1969; Millar et al. 2000; Koballa and Tippins 2004). Indeed, it has been argued that educational theory continues to have little import on practice. However, in reading through the accounts, we are struck by the ways in which teachers' work reflects current educational research in the field. We find accounts mirroring for example, nature of science and STSE perspectives, technology-mediated instruction, issues-based curriculum, problem-based learning, open-ended inquiry, consideration of equity, and social justice. The use of theoretical apparatus then, assists us in asking the right kind of questions about practice, and making the implicit, explicit. Theory and practice work in tandem, as they should. Karen Kettle, in her reflection to us, confirms the reciprocal, dialectic relationship between theory and practice:

> Exemplary science practice does not happen by accident or in the absence of research on teaching and learning. Academic pursuits allow us to step back from the immediacy of teaching/learning interaction to build on past successes, identify current patterns, and shape future trends . . . theoretical lenses bring underlying issues such as gender, ethnicity, motivation, technology, equity, and social justice sharply into focus. They make the invisible appear. Academic writing articulates and grounds the learning process within the wider world of ideas . . . As teachers, theory assists us in reflecting upon and explaining our practice. As

academics, practice guides us toward productive areas for research. Many science teachers engaged in exemplary practice are avid consumers of research in science education and learning. Our students deserve educators with a foot in each world.

We are reminded of Somekh's (1994) use of the metaphor of a 'castle' for the different constructed worlds of the school and academy, each with their own system of values and culture. She suggests that by inhabiting each other's castles, new understandings and potential transformations among different educational communities become possible. Our journey is a strong testimony to how teachers and researchers can work together to integrate theory and practice.

Quality conversations

The notion of 'quality conversations' is central to our book, and to our shared experience. Embedded in a rich landscape of teacher accounts, we sought to generate quality dialogue between educators from teaching and research communities around questions of exemplary science teaching. Narratives about practice provided the leitmotif from which these conversations sprung.

We put a number of structures in place to enhance what we might call *internal* quality conversations of the book. For example, our use of annotated comments acts as threads that link theory and practice in both directions. These annotations are found in the teacher accounts and analyses chapters, and they are cross-referenced. Indeed, a reader may choose to begin with a teacher account, or a particular theoretical lens. It really doesn't matter where you start. We intentionally avoided a one-to-one correspondence between accounts and analyses. Teachers' stories are rich and complex, and can be viewed from a number of theoretical orientations, depending on how conversations are framed and facilitated. We wished to highlight and preserve this multiplicity and richness. Finally, as the book neared completion, teachers had the opportunity to read the entire book and send us their written responses. Their voices have been integrated into this final chapter, and in different ways they reflect what Wallace (2001) describes as 'primary' use of cases, that is, teachers directly involved in the construction of a case, and teachers writing other stories (or engaging in other conversations) in response to stories read.

It is our hope that this book inspires *external* quality conversations for educators as they engage with teachers' accounts and academic theoretical interpretations. Depending on who you are, your interests, pedagogical purposes and questions, your 'reading' of the book may take a very different direction. We draw on Wallace's (2001) distinction between secondary and tertiary uses of cases for extracting meaning from experience. In the former, 'the interpretive act is linked to evidence provided by the text – through events emphasized, downplayed or omitted, accompanying "expert" commentaries, implicitly or explicitly stated theories, focus questions, or standards of instruction' (p. 186). Direct instruction or exemplification becomes central to the user's purpose (for example, how might a teacher structure a town hall debate, or teach about the Burgess Shale). In tertiary use of accounts, the 'reader's experience and perspective takes precedence over the knowledge held in the case ... inviting layer-upon-layer of reader commentary on the case' (p. 186). In other words, accounts impel discussion and exploration (see, for example, annotations throughout the book, or teacher commentaries threaded throughout this chapter). Whichever use is employed (primary, secondary or tertiary), teachers' stories provide potential learning opportunities for those involved in the construction of the account, and for those who interact with the accounts.

Creating contexts for quality conversations

Teachers, in general, enjoy sharing stories about their teaching. However, the telling of stories in and of itself is not enough to ensure quality conversations. Quality conversations do not occur by accident. They need to be structured, focused on the specifics of teaching and situated within some theoretical and/or epistemological framework. In planning this book, we deliberately set out to showcase and celebrate teachers' stories. Their accounts framed all ensuing conversations, and provided the substance from which multiple interpretations could begin.

Involvement in other research projects and teaching in faculties of education confirm for us the importance of constructing contexts for quality conversations. In pre-service education, for example, we expose teacher candidates to interactive multimedia cases (see Bencze et al. 2001), as a way of focusing on the specifics of teaching. We provide guiding questions and tasks to be completed by our students, and facilitate group discussion about the case. In inservice situations, teachers are often encouraged to talk about their own teaching, but usually within a context of some framework or theme. Action research projects are a wonderful example of the kinds of rich contexts that support quality conversations (see, for example, our three year project 'Science and Technology in Action Research – STAR' Pedretti et al. 2003). While teacher talk may not be used as stories per se, teachers are conversing with one another about the specifics of their work, using artefacts and engaging in evidence-based discussion. Indeed, we imagine a multitude of contexts in which quality conversations can be encouraged in schools and non-school settings, teacher preparation programmes, graduate programmes and professional development activities. Our book represents one manifestation of quality conversations that we hope cascades into further fruitful dialogue.

Conclusion

We are struck by the parallels that emerge between exemplary science teaching and what we might call quality teacher education practices. First, we note that quality actions or experiences are rooted in attention to the particulars. For example, teachers expose students to a specific body of scientific knowledge and skills – recall Hodson's (1998b) framework, *learning and doing* science – while in effective teacher education (preservice or inservice), specifics of pedagogy guide teachers and facilitators. Second, these 'specifics' need to be embedded within a broader situational understanding: learners must have opportunities to develop a sense of epistemological awareness. If we are teaching students science, situational understandings might include exploration of the social cultural context of science, or the nature of laws, theories or observations (learning *about* science). Quality teacher education practices demand similar epistemological awareness and theoretical apparatus. Educators might ask: Why do I do things in a particular way? What theoretical structures inform my practice? Why do I choose to teach this topic in this particular way? Third, quality conversations, which can take many forms, play a defining role in student and teacher learning. In classrooms or professional development contexts, opportunities for dialogue enable learners to find meanings that might best serve their unique needs. Finally, we suggest that quality teaching and teacher education practices require critical reflection and careful scaffolding.

This book has taken over three years to complete, due mainly to the complex and dialectic process we devised among editors, teachers and academics. Our collaborative work reflects a level of interaction among contributing authors that we believe is rare in edited volumes. The result is an aggregation of shared stories and analyses that reflect our collective wisdom, craft knowledge and engagement with the notion of exemplary science practice.

Reflection 2
Integrating educational resources into school science praxis

Larry Bencze, Steve Alsop and Erminia Pedretti

Introduction

We conclude with reflections about this book as a form of educational research. This discussion may be of interest to anyone concerned about systematic studies of educational situations. Others may, for example, want to undertake similar investigations and report their findings to diverse audiences.

In the discussion that follows, we claim that this book is, in essence, a valid and useful representation of exemplary science teaching and learning. Its validity owes largely to the fact, for example, that the accounts of educational situations were produced by those who *participated* directly in those situations; that is, teachers and students. Its usefulness comes, to a great extent, from the fact that it contains both important generalizations about science teaching and learning and specific instances of those. As such, it is a form of *reflective practice* that teachers may use as resources for integration into their repertoires of general ideas and principles and specific strategies and techniques.

Not all readers may agree that the sort of research that generated this book is valid, however. Its approach has a particularly *qualitative* nature. Account writers, analysts and editors used their professional judgements to determine what to include and how to represent it. Some would argue that such an approach opens the door for excessive bias and indeterminate conclusions. We start, therefore, with a discussion about the extent to which the representations of exemplary science teaching in this book are valid. We then recommend ways in which teachers might best use resources available to them through this book. We conclude with suggestions for future educational research of this sort.

This book as valid educational research

Currently, educational research in general is under considerable fire. In a recent major report in the USA, for example, the authors claim that there is a

> widespread perception that research in education has not produced the kind of cumulative knowledge garnered from other scientific endeavors. Perhaps even more unflattering, a related indictment leveled at the education research enterprise is that it does not generate knowledge that can inform education practice and policy. The prevailing view is that findings from education research studies are of low quality and are endlessly contested – the result of which is that no consensus emerges about anything.
>
> (NRC 2002: 28)

In the same report, the authors advise that 'schooling cannot be improved by relying on *folk wisdom* about how students learn and how schools should be organized' (p. 12, emphasis added). Claiming that educational research should be comparable to research in the sciences, the report states that 'what unites scientific inquiry is the primacy of *empirical* test of *conjectures and formal hypotheses* using *well-codified observation methods* and *rigorous designs*, and subjecting findings to peer review' (p. 51, emphases added). On these bases, it might be tempting to conclude that the findings about 'exemplary' science teaching reported here are untrustworthy. Instead of 'well-codified observation methods and rigorous designs', we urged authors to write in personally meaningful ways about what they thought was important.

We contend that our findings about 'exemplary' science teaching have considerable trustworthiness. We suggest that much of the advice given in documents such as *Scientific Research in Education* (NRC 2002) is inappropriate. Its claim, for instance, that the sciences and educational research must be characterized by Popperian (Popper 1959) 'empirical test of conjectures and formal hypotheses using well-codified observation methods and rigorous designs' (NRC 2002: 51) is, in our view, simplistic. Many suggest, first, that a strong *empiricist* reliance on data is naïve, believing that all observation is theory laden. Indeed, there have been numerous instances in history in which theory prevailed over data, as was the case – for instance – with Galileo's studies of pendulum physics (Matthews 2001). This suggests that the sciences (and, therefore, a scientific educational research) have a strong *rationalist* flavour, a view favouring logic over data. However, both empiricist and rationalist perspectives disregard studies indicating that the sciences often have a significant *naturalistic* character – such as those illustrating influences from psycho-social factors in decision making in the sciences (e.g. Lynch 1985; Latour and Woolgar 1986; Traweek 1988; Knorr-Cetina 1995).

Although our research did have some rationalistic leanings, since we asked authors (teachers, students and academics) to write from particular perspectives and we edited this book based on our priorities and conceptions, our research also had a significant naturalistic character. Naturalistic research operates under the assumption that: 'there exist multiple realities which are, in the main, constructions existing in the minds of people; they are therefore intangible and can be studied only in wholistic [sic], and idiosyncratic, fashion' (Guba and Lincoln 1988: 81). For example, we encouraged authors to write in ways that they felt were appropriate.

Given that our research possessed notable naturalist, as well as rationalist and empiricist, elements, we felt that it was important to ensure a *moderate* level of the sort of rigour urged in documents like Scientific Research in Education (NRC 2002). For that purpose, we turned to Guba's (1981) recommendations for maintenance of trustworthiness in naturalistic research. We feel that three of his suggested strategies are particularly important in our research, that is, purposive sampling, thick description and triangulation.

Purposive sampling

Naturalistic researchers often are criticized for their inability to make generalizable claims when their data is based on small sample sizes. Naturalists respond, however, by attempting to describe *particular* cases in as much detail as possible and then assume that readers will impose their meanings on the data and the researcher's claims. Consequently, naturalistic researchers tend to use *purposive* sampling, rather than representative sampling. That is, they select individuals who might provide interesting data relating to a particular purpose. In our case, as described in the Introduction, we selected teachers and students who, by reputation, were considered 'very good' or 'exemplary'. Similarly, we selected academics who had strong publication records regarding the 'lenses' through which we asked them to analyse the case accounts.

Thick descriptions

Having selected subjects of interest, the researcher strives to provide readers with a thick (detailed) description of the context of the research. In those situations in which outside researchers study teaching, this usually involves prolonged engagement with those being studied. We addressed this, but with a difference. Our 'data' (i.e. case accounts) were collected by those involved (i.e. teachers and students) in the situations (teaching and learning) under study. This is an important contribution to validity, in that meaning is said to involve a dialectic interaction between *participation* and *reification* (Wenger 1998). Because our participants (i.e. teachers and students) were the ones reifying (e.g. representing through text and graphics) their experiences, which were relatively lengthy, our study had potentially more validity than if reifications had been developed by outsiders (e.g. researchers). According to Wenger (1998: 65) 'If reification prevails – if everything is reified but with little opportunity for shared experience and interactive negotiation [which would be the case if accounts were developed by researchers] – then there may not be enough overlap in participation to recover a coordinated relevant or generative meaning'. In other words, the reifications may be less realistic representations of participation ('reality').

Claiming to increase realism in representations through participation is not necessarily feasible, however. Because much of what teachers and students know is *tacit* (Polanyi 1967) and, therefore, inexpressible, it is not possible to fully represent participation. Moreover, attempting to realistically represent reality may not be desirable. The representation '... takes on the character of a thing and thus acquires a "phantom objectivity", an autonomy that seems so strictly rational and all-embracing as to conceal every trace of its fundamental nature ...' (Lukács 1923: 83). Avoiding such an illusion of realism in representations is also advisable for educational reasons, a view which is elaborated below (under 'Usefulness'). We believe, therefore, that it was more appropriate for the representations of exemplary teaching to be more *impressionistic* than realistic, not pretending to be exact replicas of reality. While this is not something easily judged (e.g. measured), we agreed that the case authors tended to use cursory, rather than highly detailed, representations of their experiences in teaching. Keith Hicks's description of a model of the kidney's Loop of Henle, for example, left out considerable detail: '[The Loop of Henle was] additionally illustrated by attaching a rubber hose to a tap, which was pierced with a number of holes' (p. 19).

Triangulation

In order for the claims we make about science teaching to be considered valid, one of the most important techniques we can use as qualitative researchers is to triangulate our claims. Generally, this refers to attempts to assure readers that the claims researchers make do, indeed, represent phenomena under study. Denzin (1978) suggested that there are at least four versions of this, each of which our study addresses reasonably well. In terms of *data* triangulation (using multiple data sources), our case writers used (based on their comments in the accounts) observation, listening, samples of students' work and, in two cases, visual records (i.e. Keith Hicks's digital photographs, Account 1; and Susan's video records of the town hall meeting, Account 7 [personal communication]) and interviews (Keith Hicks, Account 1). *Investigator* triangulation (using several researchers) was well addressed, in that ten academic analysts were involved and also because we asked each case writer to review all the case accounts. In terms of *theory* triangulation, we asked each academic to review all the accounts from at least one perspective, showing that this was a priority. It is also important to stress that there was considerable overlap in the academics' theoretical perspectives. This is clear, for example, in examining the various 'codes' (annotations in the margins of this text). Several authors consider the role of shared perspectives, for instance, including: Sibel Erduran and Jonathan Osborne (2.7, p. 112), Erminia Pedretti (3.5, p. 120), Jim Hewitt (7.4, p. 163) and Leonie Rennie (9.4, p. 188). Finally, in terms of *methodological* triangulation (use of various research methods), while it is difficult to completely isolate them, the analysts used unique combinations of inductive (generalizing from data, while recognizing the theory-basis of this), abductive (theorizing from data and theory) and deductive (predicting specific cases) reasoning. We noted that John Wallace, in particular, leaned greatly towards inductive/abductive reasoning with his series of categories drawn from the accounts, while Derek Hodson, for example, seemed to begin with a series of general claims about science education that he applied in his analyses. While all of this triangulation suggests a considerable degree of validity, it is important to acknowledge – given our social constructivist positions on knowledge – that it is possible that teachers, students and academic analysts were biased in certain ways, guided by their theoretical positions in their observations and propositions and hampered by possible intervening variables (e.g. their moods while reporting).

Overall, within reasonable limits (as outlined above), the case accounts and theoretical propositions associated with them (via the annotations) should be considered trustworthy and, accordingly, potentially useful for various science education contexts.

Usefulness

Given that the resources generated by our research can be trusted as reasonable and appropriate representations of exemplary science teaching and learning associated with relevant educational theory, readers may be motivated to attempt to incorporate them into science teaching and learning situations. While we acknowledge and support that readers may prefer to do this in certain ways, we offer the following guiding principles for their consideration.

Unique sets of educational resources are available

Our research generated a rich 'tapestry' of perspectives and practices that teachers may incorporate into their repertoires for a variety of teaching and learning situations. Clearly, given the organization of this book, we expect that readers will find a great variety of blends of theory and practice. As a book based on hypertext, each reader may begin (after the introductory chapter, perhaps) with one of the accounts, for example. However, as they read, they may move to one or more of the analysis chapters which, in turn, may lead to a different account before the reader returns to the section of the account at which the reading began. This process of reading short inter-connected pieces from various chapters could in principle continue, thus giving each reader a unique experience of this book. The diversity of the idiosyncratic nature of those experiences may, moreover, be increased as readers discuss ideas in the book with others and access theoretical and/or practical perspectives and prac-tices from other sources (e.g. journal articles, school textbooks etc.). In a sense, each reader's experience of this book, like any learning experience, is like swimming in a river. No two strokes will be the same. It is a highly complex activity involving simultaneous integra-tion of myriad combinations of contextual variables.

While there is always the risk of reifying (in the sense of creating an illusion of reality) teachers' experiences by providing abstract labels for what they might know, the analysis of teacher knowledge conducted by Barnett and Hodson (2001) seems useful in helping us to understand what readers might extract from this book. Based on the premise that each teacher's knowledge is a unique subset of that shared by members of any identifiable group (e.g. teachers of biol-ogy), they suggest that each teacher has a unique *pedagogical context knowledge*. This is, for each teacher, some combination – at least – of: classroom knowledge (e.g. knowledge about students, such as their different learning styles); professional knowledge (e.g. curriculum policy); pedagogical content knowledge (e.g. teaching approaches for particular science topics, such as particular teacher demonstrations for explaining physics); and academic and research knowledge (e.g. learning theories, such as constructivism) (Barnett and Hodson 2001: 443–4). Each teacher, therefore, may gain unique sets of perspectives and practices in each of the above categories by reading this book. Katherine Bellomo's account of her teaching relating to scientists' analyses of the Burgess Shale is a good case in point. It starts with a discussion of academic and research knowledge, both from Katherine Bellomo and Derek Hodson, respectively: 'The interesting thing for me was that when I read this book, I knew that it was the best example I had seen for showing science as a dynamic, changing and culturally determined practice' (Katherine, p. 46) and 'The work described in Account 5, shows that there are as many kinds of scientist as there are kinds of people, influenced in their endeavours and ambition by the same range of attitudes and emotions as other professionals' (Derek, p. 104). As a motivator, Katherine also is aware that such perspectives tend not to be supported in schools (professional knowledge): 'The science that students learn (often from a textbook) seems to have been born in the text, not in the mind, work, sweat, tears, frustrations and pleasures of the working scientist' (Katherine, p. 51). Based on these perspectives, she sets out to help students to see the theory-based nature of data analysis. In terms of pedagogical content knowledge, she chooses a range of techniques, including story-telling, lecturing and guided problem solving using artefacts (i.e. sketches of fossils and associated biological trees). Through her depiction of her implementation of this lesson in various contexts, readers gain some insights into students' reactions (classroom knowledge): 'Some students will be engaged in exploring the idea, what makes an endeavour science? While others are persistent in the notion that science, if done "properly", will yield "good" results. They are resistant to the idea that it is not a simple algorithm to be carefully followed' (Katherine, p. 50).   .

Educational resources may be *considered* for praxis

Because of the uniqueness of the set of variables affecting every educational situation, effective teaching cannot be just like constructing a building from a blueprint. Any suggestion that teachers could or should transfer pedagogical resources in this book directly into classroom practice is, therefore, misguided. Rather, we recommend that teachers consider them as they engage in *praxis* (i.e. reflective practice). In many, if not most, teaching and learning situations, teachers generate idiosyncratic gestalt reactions (Korthagen and Kessels 1999). These are complex, unconscious sets of feelings, comparable past experiences, values, role identity, outside pressures, routines, philosophical positions etc. that teachers generate in each teaching and learning context. The particular mix that teachers generate – like water flowing against a swimmer in a river – will be unique for each teaching and learning situation. These are comparable to Schön's (1987) 'reflection-in-action', which are 'gut' reactions that determine actions taken by teachers in any one teaching and learning situation. Because of their unconscious nature, these gestalt reactions are unlikely to change without more conscious reflection – that is, Schön's (1987) 'reflection-on-action'. Apparently, with reflection, individuals can generate first, more conscious schema and with persistence, more complex theories about education (Korthagen and Kessels 1999). Once generated, these conscious theories are open to challenge and possible change if teachers have access to *alternative* perspectives and practices – which they may gain by reading our book, for example. In considering pedagogical context knowledge available from this book, teachers' schema and theories may change and become part of their natural gestalt reactions, thus affecting the choices they make in a variety of teaching and learning situations. Among benefits of the case accounts in this book are that many are written as *stories* about practice. As such, they allow for prolepsis; that is, 'the representation or assumption of a future act or development as if presently existing or accomplished' (Cole 1999: 89). This allows teachers to imagine what it might be like if they were to adopt a particular perspective and/or practice.

Ways in which the pedagogical context knowledge available from this book may affect teachers' gestalts are as numerous as the number of teachers considering them. To explain this, it is helpful to think of this book as a 'boundary object', that is, an artefact that helps to 'bridge the gap' between communities of practice (Wenger 1998). Generally, each teacher who wrote a chapter in this book is a member of a particular community of practice. Teachers such as George Przywolnik, for example, are members of a subset of teachers of physics, those like him who teach in a particular way, use particular discourse practices and identify with one another in specific ways. Teachers reading his account (along with whatever other sections of this book were read) meanwhile, are likely to be members of different communities of practice, to varying degrees. Theoretically, different communities of practice need to maintain a careful balance between separation, so that they can develop deep expertise, and collaboration, so that they can grow and change to adapt to a variety of teaching and learning situations. This book represents one sort of boundary object that can enable this collaboration. Readers should be aware, however, that this book has a significant amount of reification (Wenger 1998), since it is an artefact of teachers' writing, academics' analyses and editors' choices. Although we believe this book has strong elements of teachers' participation in authentic practice (given that most of the accounts were written by them and by students), there are, invariably, many details omitted. Nevertheless, we maintain (as argued above) that this is neither unavoidable nor undesirable. We believe that the purpose of this book is not for the transfer of pedagogical context knowledge from one community of practice to another but, rather, to serve as a *resource* for teachers' praxis – that is, a set of perspectives and practices that they may consider incorporating into their gestalts. *How* their gestalts will change depends on the particular sets of contextual variables that impinge on them during reflection-on-action. Among these variables, one of the most important for us is the nature of the particular students involved. We abhor ideologies of standardization. For us education must serve, as much as is feasible, the needs, interests, perspectives and abilities of particular students to be educated, rather than those of individuals and groups who plan education and who provide educational resources (such as this book). We agree with Roth and Barton (2004: 15) when they say that 'Science [education] leads to empowerment only when it does not lead to the adoption of the reigning ideology (decontextualized truth) but if it can be used to interrogate its own ideology, that is, when science [education] becomes a contested field.'

Collaborative ongoing reflective practice is best

Given that education is like a river, that every teaching and learning situation is unique and is likely to change as myriad environmental influences change, teachers need to continue having their praxis challenged and, depending on situations, change. Teachers' gestalts are unlikely to change, even with availability of alternatives such as provided through this book, however, without significant challenges. Particularly with adults, their gestalt reactions are likely to be highly entrenched, having been established through numerous educational (and other) experiences over many years (Pajares 1992). Among approaches that may sufficiently challenge teachers to consider alternative perspectives and practices, one of the most effective is collaborative action research (Kemmis and McTaggart 2000). While practitioners (e.g. teachers) have significant control over which changes occur to their gestalts, being challenged to consider alternative perspectives and practices (some of which may be drawn from this book) by respected others (including members of their immediate community of practice and those beyond), can provide significant stimuli for change and possible action in educational situations having meaning for them. Teachers engaging in collaborative action research are likely to empower themselves, as well as their students, since such reflective practice is likely to involve *metacognition*, which means they are likely to be engaged in self-regulation of their own practices (Karpov and Haywood 1998).

With the above principles in mind, we hope that teachers find the resources in this book useful and that they benefit individual students.

Conclusions

We suggest that the contents of Parts 1 and 2 and Reflection 1 of Part 3 are trustworthy representations of exemplary science teaching from which teachers may draw in their ongoing efforts at reconsidering their praxis, hopefully in directions that will support needs, interests, perspectives and abilities of particular students in particular teaching and learning contexts. We justify the *trustworthiness* of these resources primarily through purposive sampling, thick descriptions and triangulation. Rather than thinking of this book as a collection of perspectives and practices in science teaching to be emulated, however, we commend this book as a stimulus for ongoing collaborative negotiation of praxis that leads to socially just and empowering education for every learner. 'In praxis there can be no prior knowledge of the right means by which we realize the end in a particular situation. For the end itself is only specified in deliberating about the means appropriate to a particular situation' (Bernstein 1983: 147).

References

AAAS (American Association for the Advancement of Science) (1989) *Science for All Americans: A Project 2061 Report on Literacy Goals in Science, Mathematics, and Technology*. Washington, DC: AAAS.

AAUWEF (American Association of Women Educational Foundation) (1998) *Separated by Sex: A Critical Look at Single-sex Education for Girls*. Washington, DC: AAUWEF.

Abd-El-Khalick, F. and Lederman, N.G. (2000) Improving science teachers' conceptions of nature of science: a critical review of the literature, *International Journal of Science Education*, 22(7): 665–701.

Aikenhead, G.S. (1994) What is STS science teaching? in J. Solomon and G. Aikenhead (eds), *STS education: International perspectives in reform*. New York: Teachers College Press, pp. 47–59.

Alsop (2000) Palatable biology: dimensions of affect in school science. Paper represented at the Annual Meeting of the British Education Research Association, September, Cardiff, Wales.

Alsop, S. and Hicks, K. (eds) (2001) *Teaching Science*. London: Kogan Page.

Alsop, S. and Pedretti, E. (2001) Science, technology, society, in S. Alsop and K. Hicks (eds) *Teaching Science: A Handbook for Primary and Secondary School Teachers*. London: Kogan Page, pp. 193–208.

Alsop, S. and Watts, M. (2003) Unweaving time and foodchains: two classroom exercises in scientific and emotional literacy, *Canadian Journal of Science, Mathematics and Technology Education*, 2(4): 435–49.

Angrist, J. and Lavy, V. (2002) New evidence on classroom computers and pupil learning, *Economic Journal*, 112(482): 735–65.

Arendt, H. (1958) *The Human Condition*. Chicago, IL: University of Illinois Press.

Armstrong, A. and Casement, C. (1998) *The Child and the Machine*. Toronto: Key Porter Books.

Arzi, H.J. (1998) Enhancing science education through laboratory environments: more than walls, benches and widgets, in B.J. Fraser and K.G. Tobin (eds) *International Handbook of Science Education*. Dortrecht: Kluwer, 595–608.

Aspin, D. (2002) An ontology of values and the humanisation of education, in S. Pascoe (ed.) *Values in Education*. Deakin: The Australian College of Educators.

Balmer, A. and Harnish, Q. (1998) *Mousetrapcars: A Teacher Guide*. AQ publisher.

Barab, S.A. and Plucker, J.A. (2002) Smart people or smart contexts? Cognition, ability, and talent development in an age of situated approaches to knowing and learning, *Educational Psychologist*, 37: 165–82.

Barcenal, T.L., Bilbao, P.P., Morano, L.N., Nichols, S.B. and Tippins, D.J. (2002) *Just in Case: Encounters in Science and Mathematics Teaching and Learning*. Iloilo City, Philippines: West Visayes State University Press.

Barman, C.R. (1997) Students' views about scientists and science: results from a national study, *Science and Children*, 35(9): 18–24.

Barnett, J. and Hodson, D. (2001) Pedagogical context knowledge: toward a fuller understanding of what good science teachers know, *Science Education*, 85(4): 426–53.

Barrows, H.G. and Myers, A.C. (1993) *Problem-based Learning in Secondary Schools*. Unpublished monograph. Springfield, IL: Problem Based Learning Institute, Lanphier High School and Southern Illinois University Medical School.

Beane, J.A. and Apple, M.W. (1995) The case for democratic schools, in M.W. Apple and J.A. Beane (eds) *Democratic Schools*. Alexandria, VA: ASCD, pp. 1–25.

Bell, B. and Gilbert, J. (1996) *Teacher Development: A Model from Science Education*. London: Falmer Press.

Bell, P. and Linn, M. (2000) Scientific arguments as learning arte-facts: designing for learning from the web with KIE, *International Journal of Science Education*, 22(8): 797–817.

Bencze, J.L. (2000) Procedural apprenticeship in school science: constructivist enabling of connoisseurship, *Science Education*, 84(6): 727–39.

Bencze, L., Hewitt, J. and Pedretti, E. (2001) Multi-media case methods in pre-service science education: enabling an apprenticeship for praxis, *Research in Science Education*, 31(2), 191–210.

Bentley, D. and Watts, M. (1989) *Learning and Teaching in School Science: Practical Alternatives*. Milton Keynes: Open University Press.

Bernstein, R.J. (1983) *Beyond Objectivism and Relativism: Science, Hermeneutics and Praxis*. Oxford: Basil Blackwell.

Bianchini, J.A. and Solomon, E.M. (2003) Constructing views of science tied to issues of equity and diversity: a study of beginning teachers, *Journal of Research in Science Teaching*, 40: 53–76.

Bliss, J. (1995) Piaget and after: the case of learning science, *Studies in Science Education*, 25: 139–72.

Boulter, C.J. and Gilbert, J.K. (1995) Argument and science education, in P.J.M. Costello and S. Mitchell (eds) *Competing and Consensual Voices: The Theory and Practice of Argumentation*. Clevedon: Multilingual Matters.

Bruner, J. (1986) *Actual Minds, Possible Worlds*. Cambridge, MA: Harvard University Press.

Camp, G. (1996) Problem-based learning: a paradigm shift or a passing fad? *Medical Education Online*, 1(2): 1–8.

Canadian Teachers' Federation (1992) *The Better Idea Book: A Resource Book on Gender, Culture, Science and Schools*. Ottawa, Ontario: Canadian Teachers' Federation.

Chambers, D.W. (1983) Stereotypic images of the scientist: the Draw-a-Scientist Test, *Science Education*, 67(2): 255–65.

Claxton, G. (1989) Cognition doesn't matter if you are scared, depressed and bored, in S. Adey, J. Bliss, J. Head and M. Shayer *Adolescent Development and School Science*. London: Falmer Press.

Claxton, G. (1991) *Educating the Inquiring Mind: The Challenge for School Science*. New York: Harvester Wheatsheaf.

Cole, M. (1999) Cultural psychology: some general principles and a concrete example, in Y. Engestrom, R. Miettinen and R. Punamaki (eds) *Perspectives on Activity Theory: Learning in Doing Social, Cognitive and Computational Perspectives*. New York: Cambridge University Press, pp. 87–106.

Conway Morris, S. (1998) Showdown on the Burgess Shale: the challenge, *Natural History*, 107(10): 48–55.

Cowie, H. and Rudduck, J. (1990) *Co-operative Learning Traditions and Transitions. Volume Three of Learning Together – Working Together*. London. BP Educational Service.

Cross, R. and Price, R. (2002) Teaching controversial science for social responsibility: the case of food production, in W.M. Roth and J. Desautels (eds) *Science Education as/for Sociopolitical Action*. New York: Peter Lang, pp. 99–124.

Csikszentmihalyi, M. (1988a) Literacy and intrinsic motivation, in M. Csikszentmihalyi and I.S. Csikszentmihalyi (eds) *Optimal Experience: Psychological Studies of Flow in Consciousness*. Cambridge: Cambridge University Press.

Csikszentmihalyi, M. (1988b) The flow experience and its significance for human psychology, in M. Csikszentmihalyi and I.S. Csikszentmihalyi (eds) *Optimal Experience: Psychological Studies of Flow in Consciousness*. Cambridge: Cambridge University Press, pp. 15–35.

Cuban, L. (1985) *Teachers and Machines: The Classroom Use of Technology Since 1920*. Columbia: Teachers College Press.

Curriculum Council (1998) *Western Australian Curriculum Framework*. Perth, Western Australia: Curriculum Council.

Day, C. and Leitch, R. (2001) Teachers' and teacher educators' lives: the role of emotion, *Teaching and Teacher Education*, 17: 403–15.

Denzin, N.K. (1978) *The Research Act: A Theoretical Introduction to Sociological Methods* (2nd edn). New York: McGraw-Hill.

Dewey, J. (1960) *Theory of the Moral Life*. New York: Holt, Rinehart and Winston.

Ditchfield, C. and Scott, L. (1987) *Better Science: For Both Boys and Girls* (Secondary Science Curriculum Review, Curriculum Guide 6). London: Heinemann Educational Books/Association for Science Education for the School Curriculum Development Committee.

Dobbin, M. (1998) *The Myth of the Good Corporate Citizen: Democracy Under the Rule of Big Business*. Toronto: Stoddart.

Doherty, J. and Dawe, J. (1988) The relationship between developmental maturity and attitude to school science, *Educational Studies*, 11: 93–107.

Driver, R., Leach, J., Millar, R. and Scott, P. (1996) *Young People's Images of Science*. Buckingham: Open University Press.

Driver, R., Newton, P. and Osborne, J. (2000) Establishing the norms of scientific argumentation in classrooms, *Science Education*, 84(3): 287–312.

Driver, R., Squires, A., Rushworth, P. and Wood-Robinson, V. (1994) *Making Sense of Secondary Science: Research into Children's Ideas*. London: Routledge.

Dweck, C. (1986) Motivational processes affecting learning, *American Psychologist*, 41: 1040–8.

Ebenezer, J. and Zoller, U. (1993) Grade 10 students' perceptions of and attitudes towards science teaching and school science, *Journal of Research in Science Teaching*, 30(2): 175–86.

Eichinger, D.C., Anderson, C.W., Palinscar, A. and David, Y.M. (1991) An illustration of the roles of content knowledge, scientific argument, and social norms in collaborative problem solving. Paper presented at the American Educational Research Association Conference, Chicago. 12–17 April.

Eisner, E. (1991) The art and craft of teaching. *Educational Leadership*, January: 4–13.

Elbaz, F. *Teacher Thinking: A Study of Practical Knowledge*. London: Croom Helm.

Elkind, D. (1997) The death of child nature: education in the postmodern world. *Phi Delta Kappan*, 79(3): 241–5.

Epstein, I.R. (1987) Patterns in time and space: created by chemistry. *Chemical and Engineering News*, 30: 24–36.

Fennema, E. (1987) Sex-related differences in education: myths, realities, and interventions, in V. Richardson-Koehler (ed.)

Educators' Handbook: A Research Perspective. New York: Longman, pp. 329–47.

Fenstermacher, G. (1986) Philosophy of research on teaching: three aspects, in M.C. Wittrock (ed.) *Handbook of Research on Teaching.* New York: Macmillan, pp. 37–49.

Fogarty, R. (1998) *Problem Based Learning: A Collection of Articles.* Glenview, IL: Skylight.

Gabbard, D.A. (2000) Introduction: spreading the secular gospel, in D.A. Gabbard (ed.) *Knowledge and Power in the Global Economy: Politics and the Rhetoric of School Reform.* Mahwah, NJ: Lawrence-Erlbaum, pp. xiii–xxiii.

Gallas, K. (1995) *Talking Their Way into Science.* New York: Teachers College Press.

Gardner, H. (1983) *Frames of Mind: The Theory of Multiple Intelligences.* New York: Basic Books.

Gardner, H. (1999) *Intelligence Reframed: Multiple Intelligences for the 21st Century.* New York: Basic Books.

Giancllo, L. (1988) *Getting into Gear – Gender-inclusive Teaching Strategies.* Canberra, Australia: Curriculum Development Centre.

Gilbert, J.K. and Boulter, C.J. (2000) *Developing Models in Science Education.* Dordrecht, Kluwer Academic Publishers.

Gipps, C.V. (1996) Introduction, in P.F. Murphy and C.V. Gipps (eds) *Equity in the Classroom: Towards Effective Pedagogy for Girls and Boys.* London: The Falmer Press and UNESCO Publishing, pp. 1–6.

Glasgow, N.A. (1997) *New Curriculum for New Times: A Guide to Student-centred, Problem-based Learning.* Thousand Oakes, CA: Corwin Press.

Glasser, B. and Strauss, A. (1967) The discovery of grounded theroy: Strategies for qualitative research. New York: Aldine Publishing Company.

Gould, S.J. (1989) *Wonderful Life: The Burgess Shale and the Nature of History.* New York: W.W. Norton.

Greene, M. (1995) *Releasing the Imagination: Essays on Education, the Arts and Social Change*, San Francisco, CA: Jossey-Bass.

Greening, T. (1998) Scaffolding for success in PBL, *Medical Education Online*, 3(4). http://www.Med-Ed-Online.org (accessed 20 January 2003).

Griffith, A.K. and Barman, C.R. (1995) High school students' views about the nature of science: results from three countries, *School Science and Mathematics*, 95: 248–55.

Guba, E.G. (1981) Criteria for assessing the trustworthiness of naturalistic inquiries, *Educational Communication and Technology Journal*, 29(2): 75–91.

Guba, E.G. and Lincoln, Y.S. (1988) Naturalistic and rationalistic enquiry, in J.P. Keeves (ed.) *Educational Research, Methodology and Measurement: An International Handbook*. London: Pergamon pp. 81–5.

Hanson, N.R. (1965) *Patterns of Discovery*. Cambridge: Cambridge University Press.

Hargreaves, A. (1994) *Changing Teachers, Changing Times: Teachers' Work and Culture in the Postmodern Age*. London: Cassell.

Hargreaves, A. (1998) The emotional practice of teaching, *Teaching and Teacher Education*, 14: 835–54.

Harvard Business School (2004) *The Case Method Approach*. www.hbs.edu/mba/experience/learn/thelearningmodel/thecasemethod.

Hawkins, D. (1974) *The Informed Vision: Essays on Learning and Human Nature*. New York: Agathon Press.

Hendley, D., Parkinson, J., Stables, A. and Tanner, H. (1995) Gender differences in pupil attitudes to the national curriculum foundation subjects of English, Mathematics, Science and Technology in Key Stage 3 in South Wales, *Educational Studies*, 21(1): 85–97.

Henry, M., Lingard, B., Rizvi, F. and Taylor, S. (1999) Working with/against globalization in education, *Journal of Education Policy*, 14(1): 85–97.

Herrenkohl, L., Palinscar, A., DeWater, L.S. and Kawasaki, K. (1999) Developing scientific communities in classrooms: a sociocognitive approach. *The Journal of the Learning Sciences*, 8(3 and 4), 451–93.

Hewitt, J. (2002) From a focus on tasks to a focus on understanding: the cultural transformation of a Toronto classroom, in T. Koschmann, R. Hall and N. Miyake (eds) *Computer Supported Cooperative Learning Volume 2: Carrying Forward the Conversation*. Mahwah, NJ: Lawrence Erlbaum Associates, pp. 11–41.

Hewitt, J. and Scardamalia, M. (1998) Design principles for distributed knowledge building processes, *Educational Psychology Review*, 10(1): 75–96.

Hidi, S. and Harackiewicz, J. (2000) Motivating the academically unmotivated: a critical issue for the 21st century, *Review of Educational Research*, 70(2): 151–79.

Hildebrand, G. (1989) The liver transplant committee, *Australian Science Teachers Journal*, 35(3): 70–2.

Hill, A.M. (1998) Problem solving in real-life contexts: alternatives for design in technology education, *International Journal of Technology and Design Education*, 8(3): 203–20.

Hill, A.M. (1999) Community-based projects in technology education: an approach for relevant learning, in W.E. Theuerkauf and M.J. Dyrenfurth (eds) *International Perspectives on Technological*

Education: Outcomes and Futures. Braunschweig, Braunschweig/
Ames, pp. 285–98.

Hill, A.M. and Hopkins, D. (1999) University/school collaboration
in teacher education, in M. Lang, J. Olson, H. Hansen and W.
Bunder (eds) *Changing Schools/Changing Practices: Perspectives on
Educational Reform and Teacher Professionalism*. Louvain, France:
Garant, pp. 171–82.

Hill, A.M. and Smith, H.A. (1998) Practice meets theory in technological education: a case of authentic learning in the high
school setting, *Journal of Technology Education*, 9(1): 29–41.

Hodson, D. (1993) Re-thinking old ways: Towards a more critical
approach to practical work in school science, *Studies in Science
Education*, 22: 85–142.

Hodson, D. (1996) Laboratory work as scientific method: three
decades of confusion and distortion, *Journal of Curriculum Studies*, 28(2): 115–35.

Hodson, D. (1998a) Science fiction: The continuing misrepresenta-
tion of science in the school curriculum, *Curriculum Studies*, 6(2):
191–216.

Hodson, D. (1998b) *Teaching and Learning Science: Towards a Personalized Approach*. Buckingham: Open University Press.

Hodson, D. (2003) Time for action: Science education for an alternative future, *International Journal of Science Education*, 25(6):
645–70.

Hogan, K. and Maglienti, M. (2001) Comparing the epistemological
underpinnings of students' and scientists' reasoning about conclusions, *Journal of Research in Science Teaching*, 38(6): 663–87.

http://www.hbs.edu/mba/experience/learn/thelearningmodel/
thecasemethod.html

Hughes, G. (2000) Marginalization of socioscientific material in
science-technology-society science curricula: some implications
for gender inclusivity and curriculum reform, *Journal of Research
in Science Teaching*, 37(5): 426–40.

Johnson, M. (1987) *The Body in the Mind: The Bodily Basis of
Meaning, Imagination, and Reason*. Chicago: University of Chicago Press.

Johnson, S.K. and Stewart, J. (1990) Using philosophy of science in
curriculum development: an example from high school genetics,
International Journal of Science Education, 12: 297–307.

Joyce, B. and Showers, B. (1988) *Student Achievement Through Staff
Development*. White Plains, NY: Longman.

Kahle, J. (ed.) (1985) *Women in Science: A Report from the Field*.
London: Falmer Press.

Karpov, Y.V. and Haywood, H.C. (1998) Two ways to elaborate
Vygotsky's concept of mediation: implications for instruction,
American Psychologist, 53(1): 27–36.

Kelly, G. and Bazerman, C. (2003) How students argue scientific claims: a rhetorical-semantic analysis, *Applied Linguistics*, 24(1): 53–80.

Kemmis, S. and McTaggart, R. (2000) Participatory action research, in N.K. Denzin and Y.S. Lincoln (eds) *Handbook of Qualitative Research* (2nd edn). Thousand Oaks, CA: Sage, pp. 567–606.

Kenway, J., Willis, S., Blackmore, J. and Rennie, L. (1998) *Answering Back: Girls, Boys and Feminism in Schools*. New York: Routledge.

Keys, C.W. (2000) Investigating the thinking processes of eight grade writers during the composition of a scientific laboratory report, *Journal of Research in Science Teaching*, 37: 676–90.

Kilbourn, B. (1998) *For the Love of Teaching*. London (Ontario): Althouse Press.

Knorr-Cetina, K.D. (1995) Laboratory studies: the cultural approach to the study of science, in S. Jasonoff, G. Markle, J. Peterson and T. Pinch (eds) *Handbook of Science and Technology Studies*. Thousand Oaks, CA: Sage, pp. 140–66.

Koballa, T. and Tippins, D. (2002) *Cases in Middle and Secondary Science Education: The Promise and Dilemmas*. New Jersey: Merrill/Prentice Hall.

Koballa, T. and Tippins, D. (2004) *Cases in Middle and Secondary Science Education: The Promise and Dilemmas*, 2nd edn. Columbus, OH: Prentice Hall.

Korthagen, F.A.J. and Kessels, J.P.A.M. (1999) Linking theory and practice: changing the pedagogy of teacher education, *Educational Researcher*, 28(4): 4–17.

Koslowski, B. (1996) *Theory and Evidence: The Development of Scientific Reasoning*. Cambridge, MA: MIT Press.

Kuhn, D., Shaw, V. and Felton, M. (1997) Effects of dyadic interaction on argumentative reasoning, *Cognition and Instruction*, 15(3): 287–315.

Kumar, D. and Chubin, D. (2000) *Science, Technology, and Society: A Sourcebook on Research and Practice*. London: Kluwer Academic.

Ladson-Billings, G. (2003) I used to like science and then I went to school: the challenge of school science in urban schools. Keynote Address delivered to the annual meeting of the National Association for Research in Science Teaching, Philadelphia, 12–16 April.

Lampert, M. (1985) How do teachers manage to teach? Perspectives on problems of practice, *Harvard Educational Review*, 55(2): 178–94.

Landow, G. (1996) Hypertext as collage-writing, in P. Lunenfeld (ed.) *The Digital Dialectic: New Essays on New Media*. Cambridge MA: MIT Press.

Langer, E. (1993) A mindful education, *Educational Psychologist*, 28(1): 43–50.

Latour, B. and Woolgar, S. (1979/1986) *Laboratory Life: The Social Construction of Scientific Facts*. London: Sage.

Lave, J. (1988) *Cognition in Practice: Mind, Mathematics and Culture in Everyday Life*. New York: Cambridge University Press.

Lebow, D. (1993) Constructivist values for system designs: five principles toward a mindset, *Educational Technology Research and Development*, 41: 4–16.

Lederman, N. (1992) Students' and teachers' conceptions of the nature of science: a review of the research, *Journal of Research in Science Teaching*, 29(4): 331–59.

Lock, R. (1990) Open-ended, problem-solving investigations: what do we mean and how can we use them? *School Science Review*, 71(256): 63–72.

Lortie, D. (1975) *Schoolteacher: A Sociological Study*. Chicago, IL: University of Chicago Press.

Loucks-Horsley, S., Hewson, P., Love, N. and Stiles, K.E. (1998) *Designing Professional Development for Teachers of Science and Mathematics*. Thousand Oaks, CA: Corwin Press Inc.

Lukács, G. (1923) *History and Class Consciousness: Studies in Marxist Dialectics*, trans. R. Livingstone. London: Merlin.

Lynch, M. (1985) *Art and Artifact in Laboratory Science: A Study of Shop Work and Shop Talk in a Laboratory*. London: Routledge and Kegan Paul.

McComas, W., Clough, M. and Almazroa, H. (1998) The role and character of the nature of science, in W.F. McComas (ed.) *The Nature of Science in Science Education: Rationales and Strategies*. Dordrecht: Kluwer Academic Publishers, pp. 3–39.

McLaren, P. (1994) *Life in Schools: An Introduction to Critical Pedagogy in the Foundations of Education*. New York: Longman.

McQuaig, L. (2001) *All You Can Eat: Greed, Lust and the New Capitalism*. Toronto: Viking.

Mason, L. (1996) An analysis of children's construction of new knowledge through their use of reasoning and arguing in classroom discussions, *Qualitative Studies in Education*, 9(4): 411–33.

Matthews, M.R. (1994) *Science Teaching: The Role of History and Philosophy of Science*. New York: Routledge.

Matthews, M.R. (2001) How pendulum studies can promote knowledge of the nature of science, *Journal of Science Education and Technology*, 10(4): 359–68.

Means, M.L. and Voss, J.F. (1996) Who reasons well? Two studies of informal reasoning among children of different grade, ability, and knowledge levels, *Cognition and Instruction*, 14: 139–78.

Millar, R. (1996) Towards a science curriculum for public understanding, *School Science Review*, 77(280): 7–18.

Millar, R., Leach, J. and Osborne, J. (2000) *Improving Science Edu-

cation: The Contribution of Research, Buckingham: Open University Press.

Mortimer, E. and Scott, P. (2000) Analysing discourse in the science classroom, in R. Millar, J. Leach and J. Osborne (eds) *Improving Science Education, the Contribution of Research*. Buckingham: Open University Press, pp. 126–42.

Mullet, K. and Sano, D. (1995) *Designing Visual Interfaces: Communication Oriented Techniques*. Englewood Cliffs, NJ: Prentice-Hall.

Munby, H. and Russell, T. (1994) The authority of experience in learning to teach: messages from a physics methods class, *Journal of Teacher Education*, 45: 86–95.

Noble, D.D. (1998) The regime of technology in education, in L.E. Beyer and M.W. Apple (eds) *The Curriculum: Problem, Politics and Possibilities*. Albany, NY: SUNY Press, pp. 267–83.

Nott, M. and Wellington, J. (1995) Critical Incidents in Science, Science document 14. *Teaching Science in Secondary Schools Series*. Milton Keynes: Open University Press.

NRC (National Research Council) (2000) *Inquiry and the National Science Education Standards*. Washington, DC: National Academy Press.

NRC (National Research Council) (2002) *Scientific Research in Education*. Committee on Scientific Principles for Education Research. R. J. Shavelson and L. Towne (eds), Center for Education, Division of Behavioral and Social Sciences and Education. Washington, D.C.: National Academy Press.

Ofsted (Office for Standards in Education) (2000) *Progress in Key Stage 3: Science*. London: Ofsted.

Ogborn, J. (2001) Ownership and transformation. Paper presented at Science and Technology Education Unit Seminar. London: King's College London.

OMET (Ontario Ministry of Education and Training) (1998) *The Ontario Curriculum Grades 1–8: Science and Technology*. Toronto: OMET.

Osborne, J. and Collins, S. (2000) *Pupils' and Parents' View of the School Science Curriculum*. London: King's College London.

Osborne, J., Erduran, S. and Simon, S. (2003) *Ideas, Evidence and Argument in Science*. Resource pack. London: Nuffield Foundation.

Osborne, J., Erduran, S., Simon, S. and Monk, M. (2001) Enhancing the quality of argument in science. *School Science Review*, 82(301): 63–70.

Osborne, J., Simon, S. and Collins, S. (2003) Attitudes towards science: a review of the literature and its implications, *International Journal of Science Education*, 25(9): 1049–1079.

Osborne, J., Erduran, S., & Simon, S. (2004) Ideas, Evidence and argument in Science. London: King's College London.

Pacey, A. (1992) *The Maze of Ingenuity: Ideas and Idealism in the Development of Technology.* Cambridge, MA: MIT Press.

Pajares, M.F. (1992) Teachers' beliefs and educational research: cleaning up a messy construct. *Review of Educational Research*, 62(3): 307–32.

Parker, L.H. and Rennie, L.J. (2002) Teachers' implementation of gender-inclusive instructional strategies in single-sex and mixed-sex classrooms, *International Journal of Science Education*, 24: 881–97.

Pedretti, E. (1997) Septic tank crisis: a case study of science, technology and society education in an elementary school *International Journal of Science Education*, 19(10): 1211–30.

Pedretti, E. (1999) Decision making and STS education: exploring scientific knowledge and social responsibility in schools and science centres through an issues-based approach, *School Science and Mathematics*, 99(4): 174–81.

Pedretti, E. (2003) Teaching science, technology, society and environment (STSE) education: preservice teachers' philosophical and pedagogical landscapes, in D. Zeidler (ed.) *The Role of Moral Reasoning and Socioscientific Discourse in Science Education.* Dortrecht, The Netherlands: Kluwer, pp. 219–39.

Pedretti, E., Bencze, L., Hodson, D., DeCoito, I. and DiGiuseppe, M. (2003) Building and sustaining communities of practice beyond the field: Nurturing agency and action. In J. Wallace and J. Loughran (eds) *Leadership and Professional Development in Science Education: New Possibilities for Enhancing Teacher Learning.* New York: RoutledgeFalmer, pp. 219–237.

Pintrich, P., Marx, R. and Boyle, R. (1993) Beyond cold conceptual change: the role of motivational beliefs and classroom contextual factors in the process of conceptual change, *Review of Educational Research*, Vol. 63(2): 167–99.

Polanyi, M. (1967) *The Tacit Dimension.* London: Routledge and Kegan Paul.

Pontecorvo, C. and Girardet, H. (1993) Reasoning and arguing in historical topics, *Cognition and Instruction*, 11(3 and 4): 365–95.

Popper, K. (1959) *The Logic of Scientific Discovery.* London: Hutchinson.

Ramsey, J. (1993) The science education reform movement: implications for social responsibility, *Science Education*, 77(2): 235–58.

Ratcliffe, M. (1997) Pupil decision-making about socioscientific issues within the science curriculum, *International Journal of Science Education*, 19(2): 167–82.

Rennie, L.J. (1998) Gender equity: toward clarification and a research direction for science teacher education, *Journal of Research in Science Teaching*, 35: 951–61.

Rennie, L.J. (2001) Gender equity and science teacher preparation, in D. Lavoie and W.M. Roth (eds) *Models of Science Teacher*

Preparation: Theory into Practice. Dordrecht, The Netherlands: Kluwer Academic Publishers, pp. 127–47.

Rennie, L.J. (2002) Business as usual? in J. Wallace and W. Louden (eds) *Dilemmas of Science Teaching: Perspectives on Problems of Practice.* London: RoutledgeFalmer, pp. 81–3.

Resnick, M., Berg, R. and Eisenberg, M. (2000) Beyond black boxes: bringing transparency and aesthetics back to scientific investigation, *The Journal of the Learning Sciences*, 9(1), 7–30.

Robertson, H. (1998) *No More Teachers, No More Books. The Commercialization of Canada's Schools.* Toronto: McClelland and Stewart Inc.

Robson, C. (1993) *Real World Research: A Resource for Social Scientists and Practitioner Researchers.* Oxford: Blackwell Press.

Rosser, S.V. (1990) *Female-friendly Science: Applying Women's Study Methods and Theories to Attract Students.* New York: Pergamon.

Roth, W.M. (1998) Teaching and learning as everyday activity, in B.J. Fraser and K.G. Tobin (eds) *International Handbook of Science Education.* Dordrecht, The Netherlands: Kluwer, pp. 169–81.

Roth, W.M. (2002) Phenomenology, knowledgeability and authentic science. In J. Wallace and W. Louden (eds) *Dilemmas of Science teaching: Perspectives on problems of practice.* London & New York: RoutledgeFalmer, pp. 42–48.

Roth, W.M. and A.C. Barton (2004) *Rethinking Scientific Literacy.* New York: RoutledgeFalmer.

Roth, W.M. and Desautels, J. (eds) (2002) *Science Education as/for Sociopolitical Action.* New York: Peter Lang.

Roychoudhury, A., Tippins, D.J. and Nichols, S.E. (1995) Gender-inclusive science teaching: a feminist constructivist approach, *Journal of Research in Science Teaching*, 32: 897–924.

Russell, C.L. and Hodson, D. (2002) Whalewatching as critical science education? *Canadian Journal of Science, Mathematics and Technology Education*, 2(4): 485–504.

Salomon, G. (1995) *Real Individuals in Complex Environments: A New Conception of Educational Psychology.* Draft document.

Savery, J.R. and Duffy, T.M. (1995) Problem based learning: an instructional model and its constructivist framework. *Educational Technology*, 35(5): 31–8.

Scardamalia, M. (2002) CSILE/Knowledge Forum, *Education and Technology: An Encyclopedia.* Santa Barbara: ABC-CLIO.

Schaefer, H.F. (1986) Methylene: a paradigm for computational quantum chemistry. *Science*, 231: 1100–7.

Schön, D. (1987) *Educating the Reflective Practitioner.* San Francisco, CA: Jossey-Bass.

Schreiner, C. and Sjoberg, S. (2003) *Optimists or Pessimists? How do Young People Relate to Environmental Challenges.* Oslo: Department of Teacher Training and School Development, University of Oslo, Norway.

Schunk, D. (1989) Self-efficacy and achievement indicators, *Educational Psychology Research*, 57: 149–74.

Schwab, J. (1969) The practical: a language for curriculum. *School Review*, 78: 1–24.

Schwab, J. (1973) The practical 3: translation into the curriculum, *School Review*, 31: 501–22.

Scott, P. (1998) Teacher talk and meaning making in science classrooms: a Vygotskian analysis and review, *Studies in Science Education*, 32: 45–80.

Shulman, L. (1987) Knowledge and teaching: foundations of the new reform, *Harvard Educational Review*, 57(1): 1–22.

Simpson, R., Koballa, T., Oliver, J. and Crawley, F. (1995) Research on the affective dimensions of science learning, in D. Gabel (ed.) *Handbook of Research on Science Teaching and Learning*. New York: Macmillian, pp. 211–50.

Siskin, L.S. (1994) *Realms of Knowledge: Academic Departments in Secondary Schools*. Washington, DC: Falmer Press.

Sjoberg, S. (2000) Interesting all children in science for all, in R. Millar, J. Leach and J. Osborne (eds) *Improving Science Education*. Buckingham: Open University Press, pp. 165–86.

Sjoberg, S. (2002) *Science for the Children? Report from the Science and Scientists-project*. Oslo: Department of Teacher Training and School Development, University of Oslo, Norway.

Smith, H.A. (2001) *Psychosemiotics*. New York: Peter Lang.

Solomon, J (1990) The discussion of social issues in the science classroom. *Studies in Science Education*, 18: 105–26.

Solomon, J. (1993) *Teaching Science, Technology and Society*. Philadelphia, CA: Open University Press.

Solomon, J. (1994) The laboratory comes of age, in R. Levinson (ed.) *Teaching Science*. London: Routledge in association with Open University, pp. 7–21.

Solomon, J. and Aikenhead, G. (1994) *STS Education: International Perspectives in Reform*. New York: Teachers College Press.

Solomon, J., Scott, L. and Duveen, J. (1996) Large scale exploration of pupils' understanding of the nature of science, *Science Education*, 80(5): 493–505.

Somekh, B. (1994) Inhabiting each other's castles: towards knowledge and mutual growth through collaboration. *Educational Action Research*, 2: 357–81.

Suppe, F. (1998) The structure of a scientific paper, *Philosophy of Science*, 65(3): 381–405.

Taber, K.S. (1998) The sharing-out of nuclear attraction: or I can't think about Physics in Chemistry, *International Journal of Science Education*, 20(8): 1001–14.

Taber, K.S. (2000) Chemistry lessons for universities? A review of constructivist ideas, *University Chemistry Education*, 4(2): 26–35. http://www.rsc.org/uchemed/uchemed.htm.

Taber, K.S. (2002) *Chemical Misconceptions – Prevention, Diagnosis and Cure*. London: Royal Society of Chemistry.

Taylor, L. and Whittaker, C. (2003) *Bridging Multiple Worlds: Case Studies of Diverse Communities*. Boston: Allyn and Bacon.

Thagard, P. (1992) *Conceptual Revolutions*. Oxford: Princeton University Press.

Tobin. K. (2002) Both/and perspectives on the nature of science, in J. Wallace and W. Louden (eds) *Dilemmas of Science Teaching: Perspectives on Problems of Practice*. London and New York: RoutledgeFalmer, pp. 15–18.

Tom, A.R. (1984) *Teaching as a Moral Craft*. New York: Longman.

Toulmin, S. (1958) *The Uses of Argument*. Cambridge: Cambridge University Press.

Traweek, S. (1988) *Beamtimes and Lifetimes: The World of High Energy Physicists*. Cambridge, MA: MIT Press.

Trowbridge, L. and Bybee, R. (1996) *Teaching Secondary School Science: Strategies for Developing Scientific Literacy* (6th edn). New Jersey: Merrill and Prentice Hall.

Vygotsky, L. (1978) *Mind in Society: The Development of Higher Psychological Processes*. Cambridge, MA: Harvard University Press.

Wallace, J. (2001) Science teaching cases as learning opportunities, *Research in Science Education*, 31(2): 185–90.

Wallace, J. (2003) Learning about teacher learning: reflections of a science educator, in J. Wallace and J. Loughran (eds) *Leadership and Professional Development in Science Education: New Possibilities for Enhancing Teacher Learning*. New York: Routledge Falmer, pp. 1–16.

Wallace, J. and Louden, W. (1992) Science teaching and teachers' knowledge: prospects for reform of elementary classrooms, *Science Education*, 76(5): 507–21.

Wallace, J. and Louden, W. (1997) Preconceptions and theoretical frameworks, *Journal of Research in Science Teaching*, 34(4): 319–22.

Wallace, J. and Louden, W. (2000) *Teachers' Learning: Stories of Science Education*. Dordrecht the Netherlands: Kluwer Academic Press.

Wallace, J. and Louden, W. (2002) *Dilemmas of Science Teaching: Perspectives on Problems of Practice*. London: RoutledgeFalmer.

Watts, M., Alsop, S., Zylbersztajn, A. and Maria de Silva, S. (1997) Event-Centred-Learning: An approach to teaching science technology and societal issues in two countries, *International Journal of Science Education*, 19(3): 341–51.

Wenger, E. (1998) *Communities of Practice: Learning, Meaning and Identity.* Cambridge: Cambridge University Press.

Wenger, E. (2000) Communities of practice and social learning systems, *Organization,* 7(2): 225–46.

White, H.B. (1996) Dan tries problem-based learning: a case study, in L. Richen (ed.) *To Improve the Academy Vol. 15.* Stillwater, OK: Forum Press, pp. 75–91.

Wigfield, A. and Eccles, J. (1992) The development of achievement task values: a theoretical analysis, *Developmental Review,* 12: 265–310.

Willis, S. (1996) Gender justice and the mathematics curriculum: Four perspectives, in L.H. Parker, L.J. Rennie and B.J. Fraser (eds) *Gender, Mathematics and Science: Shortening the Shadow.* Dordrecht, The Netherlands: Kluwer Academic Press, pp. 41–51.

Wiske, M.S. (1998) What is teaching for understanding? in M.S. Wiske (ed.) *Teaching for Understanding: Linking Practice and Research.* San Francisco, CA: Jossey Bass Publishers, pp. 61–86.

Woolnough, B. (1998) *Effective Science Teaching.* Buckingham: Open University Press.

Yoon, S. (2002) What children think about human-animal relationships: incorporating humane education goals in science and technology curriculum and instruction, *Canadian Journal of Science, Mathematics and Technology Education,* 2(4): 449–66.

Young, R.M. (1987) Racist society, racist science, in D. Gill and L. Levidow (eds) *Anti-racist Science Teaching.* London: Free Association Books, pp. 16–42.

Zembylas, M. (2002) Constructing genealogies of teachers' emotions in science teaching. *Journal of Research in Science Teaching,* 39(1): 79–103.

Ziman, J. (1994) The rationale of STS education is in the approach, in J. Solomon and G. Aikenhead (eds) *STS Education: International Perspectives in Reform.* New York: Teachers College Press, pp. 21–31.

Index

Contents of margin notes (*mn*) are expanded upon in adjacent text.

abilities 145, 155–7
abstract concepts 58*mn*, 128, 195*mn*, 207–8
  see also concrete learning; models
access to knowledge, skills and values 184–5, 186–7
accommodating difference/diversity 21*mn*, 43*mn*, 185, 187–9, 196*mn*
achievement goals 151–2
Acid Rain project 165–6
advocacy role of teacher 133
alternative assessment 68*mn*, 189*mn*
alternative conceptual frameworks 131
American Association for the Advancement of Science (AAAS) 197, 201
Angrist, J. and Lavy, V. 161, 169
anomaly, use of 46*mn*, 111*mn*
antidiuretic hormone (ADH), role of 20–1
apprenticeship
  accounts 42*mn*, 55*mn*, 63–8, 80*mn*, 81*mn*, 82*mn*
  analyses 101–3, 198*mn*
  see also mentoring
Arendt, H. 140
argumentation 107–9
  anomaly 46*mn*, 111*mn*
  contrasting 46*mn*, 110–11
  criteria 85*mn*, 86, 111*mn*
  defining 73*mn*, 110
  evaluation of 46*mn*, 74*mn*, 110*mn*, 111*mn*
  group discussions 16*mn*, 54, 112–13, 112*mn*
  nature of 110–11
  quality of 111
  role play 23*mn*, 41*mn*, 55*mn*, 112*mn*
  scaffolds 42*mn*, 47*mn*, 57*mn*, 121*mn*
  supporting strategies 112–14
artwork 40, 45, 104
Aspin, D. 120, 121
astronomy 23–4
audience 44, 45, 135
authentic tasks, problem-based learning (PBL) 139–40
autonomy 32*mn*, 34–5, 67*mn*, 152*mn*

Ayyavoo, G. (Account 9) 71–5, 76–8, 80

Barnett, J. and Hodson, D. 222
Bell, P. and Linn, M. 108
Bellomo, K. *see* Burgess Shale fossils (Account 6/Bellomo)
Bernstein, R.J. 226
best solution choice, mousetrap car design 86–7
Bianchini, J.E. and Solomon, E.M. 186
bias 46*mn*, 47*mn*, 49*mn*, 104*mn*
biographical materials 43, 45, 104
  see also Burgess Shale fossils (Account 6/Bellomo); drama, scientists' lives (Account 5/Kettle)
biological classification 48–9, 98–9, 110
biotechnology 75–6, 77, 78, 119–20
brainstorming 43, 50, 65, 72, 86
Bray, W. 100
breaking down material 67*mn*, 73*mn*, 128*mn*
building confidence 31, 43*mn*, 155–6, 190*mn*
Burgess Shale fossils (Account 6/Bellomo) 46–52
  argumentation 110–11
  central themes 172, 175, 177, 179, 181
  challenging traditional views 98–9, 104–5
  conceptual development 131, 133
  contextualized learning 145
  inclusivity/democratic education 183, 186–7, 190–1, 192, 196, 199
  motivational beliefs 154, 157, 158
  reflections 206, 207–8, 215, 222–3
  STSE education principles/practice 118–19, 121, 122, 124–5
business model *see* consumerist orientation

cameras 24, 28, 164, 167*mn*
Cartesian diver 73, 184
CD-ROMs 31, 33
centrality of content 34*mn*, 80*mn*, 174–5
chemistry
  biotechnology project 75–6, 77, 78, 119–20

chemical reaction rates 68
e-learning (SCOT) project 33, 34, 35–6
see also organic chemistry (Account 3/Ellis)
classroom environments 151–2, 156
Claxton, G. 146, 147, 197, 201
cognition
    'cognitive conflict situation' 26–7, 133
    conflict-solving strategies 156
    emotions and 146–7
    metacognition 141, 225
Cole, M. 224
collaboration
    learning through 20*mn*, 163*mn*
    mastery orientation 54*mn*, 152*mn*
    reflective practice 225
    team teaching 35–6
    vs competition 152
communication technology 165–7
    see also specific types
community discourse 121–2
community-based projects 57*mn*, 139, 140*mn*
community/ies of practice 101–3, 198–9, 224
competition
    mousetrap car design 90
    science fair projects 71–83
    vs collaboration 152
computer modelling/animation 34*mn*, 81, 101, 162*mn*, 167*mn*
conceptual change 46*mn*, 132–3
conceptual development 127–35
conceptual integration 86*mn*, 132–3
concrete learning
    accounts 18*mn*, 30*mn*, 58*mn*, 76*mn*, 89*mn*
    analyses 113, 128*mn*, 161–4, 195*mn*
confidence
    students 31, 43*mn*, 155–6, 190*mn*
    teachers 150
conflict-solving strategies 156
constructivism
    conceptual analysis 130
    framework and principles 137–8
    PBL 32*mn*, 33*mn*, 138*mn*
consumerist orientation 194–5
    strategies to counter 196–202
content of science 127
    centrality of 34*mn*, 80*mn*, 174–5
    patterns in 29*mn*, 127*mn*
contexts 142–5
    abstract concepts 58*mn*, 195*mn*
    classroom environments 151–2, 156
    learner abilities 145
    pedagogical context knowledge 222–3
    quality conversations 215–16
    role play 40*mn*, 55–6*mn*, 118*mn*
    socio-cultural 40–1, 104
contrasting arguments 46*mn*, 110–11
controls, positive and negative 78
Corry, A. *see* inquiry mentoring (Account 8/Corry)
cost cutting 34*mn*, 44*mn*, 156*mn*
creative approaches 207–8
creative consultant role of teacher 43, 156

creative productivity 39, 42
criteria, use in argumentation 85*mn*, 86, 111*mn*
critical analysis 39*mn*, 41*mn*, 58*mn*, 59*mn*, 120*mn*, 123*mn*
Cross, R. and Price, R. 122–3
Csikszentmihalyi, M. 134, 158–9
Cuban, L. 168
cue cards 64
'culminating performance' 176
cultural capital 194
culture
    learning mediated by tools of 33*mn*, 73*mn*
    location of science in 42*mn*, 51*mn*, 105*mn*, 208–9
    of science 185–6, 189–91, 192
    stories from indigenous people 68
    see also entries beginning socio-cultural
curriculum
    elements 6, *7*
    individualization/differentiation 32–3, 34–5, 187*mn*
    naturalistic 39*mn*, 200*mn*
    rationalization of expectations 38–9, 200*mn*
    see also inclusive science curriculum
Cutchicchia, J. 79, 80, 81

data collection *see* observation
data interpretation *see* interpretation
decision-making 41*mn*, 58*mn*, 122–3
deduction *vs* induction 18*mn*, 24*mn*, 68*mn*, 85*mn*, 195*mn*
democratic education 194–202
Descartes' dream 157–8
Dewey, J. 136, 207
diagrams 16–17, 18, 19, 163
    'tree of life' 48, 49, 110–11
dialogue, teaching styles 108
difference/diversity
    accommodating 21*mn*, 43*mn*, 185, 187–9, 196*mn*
    curriculum 32–3, 34–5, 187*mn*
    group work 35*mn*, 62*mn*, 188*mn*
    promoting 200–1
    see also learning styles
digital cameras 24, 28
digital multimedia 34, 36, 99, 129, 188
disguise of dilemma 50*mn*, 54*mn*, 179–80
dissection of kidney 17–19, 98
distribution, across situations and groups 43*mn*, 144
diversity *see* difference/diversity
Doherty, J. and Dawe, J. 148, 153
doing science 82, 209–11
    vs learning science 34*mn*, 99*mn*
    see also mentoring; physical activity; theory, and practice links
drama, scientists' lives (Account 5/Kettle) 38–45
    argumentation 112
    central themes 175
    challenging traditional views 104–5
    conceptual development 130, 132, 134
    inclusivity/democratic education 189–90, 191, 196, 197, 199, 200
    motivational beliefs 153
    problem-based/contextualized learning 142, 144–5

reflections 206, 207, 209, 213–14
STSE education principles/practice 118
Driver, R. et al. 106, 108, 111, 131

e-learning *see* SCOT project (Account 4/Rennie and
    Edwards)
Ebenezer, J. and Zoller, U. 148, 153
economic model *see* consumerist orientation
educational research 218–21
educational resources 221–5
Eichinger, D.C. et al. 108, 112
email 32, 33–4, 45, 165, 167
embodied learning
    accounts 17*mn*, 19*mn*, 25*mn*, 30*mn*, 56*mn*
    analysis 143–4
emotions and cognition 146–7
    see also motivation
empiricist *vs* naturalistic research 218–19
empowerment
    accounts 45*mn*, 49*mn*, 61*mn*, 79*mn*, 124*mn*
    analysis 123–5
enlightenment, promoting 199–200
enthusiasm
    students 38, 45*mn*, 49*mn*, 61*mn*, 79*mn*, 124*mn*
    teachers 31, 149–50, 208
    see also knowledge, relationship to
environmental issue *see* town hall debate (Account 7/
    Yoon)
epistemology
    awareness 216
    discourse 49*mn*, 122
    expedience of 51*mn*, 63*mn*, 176–7
    goals 106
    nature of science perspectives 47*mn*, 119*mn*
equity *see* democratic education; inclusive science
    curriculum
essays/scripts 42–3, 134, 142
evaluation
    of argumentation 46*mn*, 74*mn*, 110*mn*, 111*mn*
    survey by SCOT project students 36, 37, 138
Evans, D. 82
examination revision 21–2, 31
exemplary practice, concept of 2, 4–5, 206–7
Exemplary Science and Mathematics (ESME),
    Australia xvi–xvii
experiments 99–101
    data interpretation 24*mn*, 28*mn*, 100*mn*
    design checklist 66–7, 102
    theoretical framework 28*mn*, 49*mn*, 78*mn*, 99, 100–1
expert mentoring 79–82
external quality conversations 214–15

faculty facilitated PBL 142
flow, state of 20*mn*, 22*mn*, 134*mn*
fossils *see* Burgess Shale fossils (Account 6/Bellomo)
framework development, mousetrap car design 86

Gabbard, D.A. 193
Gallas, K. 158
games
    biological classification 48–9

'who am I?' 40
Gardner, H. 145
gender issues 148, 185, 187
genetic research 80, 81–3, 103
Gestalts 224–5
    see also patterns in science content
Goncalves, J. 81
Gould, S.J. 46, 47, 48, 50, 110, 190, 208
Greene, M. 1
group(s)
    discussions 16*mn*, 54, 112–13
    learning distributed across situations and 43*mn*, 144
    presentations 20–1
    restructuring 35*mn*, 36, 113*mn*
    work 20*mn*, 35*mn*, 62*mn*, 74*mn*, 85, 111, 142*mn*,
        188
Guba, E.G. 219–21
    and Lincoln, Y.S. 218
'guided inquiry' 176

Hanson, N.R. 97
Hargreaves, A. 146, 182
Hendley, D. et al. 148
Herrenkohl, L. et al. 108–9
Hicks, K. *see* kidney function/dysfunction (Account 1/
    Hicks)
higher order reasoning skills 59*mn*, 152*mn*
Hill, A.M. 139, 140
    and Smith, H.A. 143, 144, 145
historical approach
    humanizing science 38*mn*, 47*mn*, 118*mn*
    STSE education 118
    see also drama, scientists' lives (Account 5/Kettle)
Hodson, D. 6, 96–105, 147, 175, 178, 198, 199, 203,
    208, 209, 210–11, 216, 221, 222–3
Hogan, K. and Maglienti, M. 107, 108
Howes, M. 82
humanizing science 41*mn*, 42*mn*, 104*mn*, 189*mn*,
    208–9
    historical approach 38*mn*, 47*mn*, 118*mn*
    relating science to people 24*mn*, 38*mn*, 48*mn*, 123–5,
        153*mn*
    scientists are real people 51*mn*, 103–5, 153–4, 186*mn*
hypothesis development 65–6, 73–4

immediacy of input 64*mn*, 84*mn*, 173–4
implementation, mousetrap car design 87–9
impressionistic *vs* realist representation 220
inclusion *see* democratic education; inclusive science
    curriculum
inclusive science curriculum 183
    accounts 183, 186–91, 195–6, 209
    components 184–6
incremental learning 132–3
individuality *see* difference/diversity; learning styles
induction *vs* deduction 18*mn*, 24*mn*, 68*mn*, 85*mn*,
    195*mn*
information
    processing/limitations 128–9
    utilizing channels 129
informed decision-making 41*mn*, 58*mn*, 122–3

inquiry journals 72
inquiry mentoring (Account 8/Corry) 63–70, 98,
    113–14, 130, 147, 165, 173, 174–5, 176–7, 181,
    189, 197, 198
inquiry skills 64*mn*, 165*mn*
interest 153–4
internal quality conversations 214
Internet 32, 45, 166, 167
interpretation
    of experimental data 24*mn*, 28*mn*, 100*mn*
    of observation 98–9, 104–5
investigations mentoring (Account 9/Ayyavoo) 71–5,
    76–8, 80
investigator triangulation 221
issues-based approach, STSE education 119–20
iterative problem-based learning 89*mn*, 140, 141*mn*

Johnston, J. *see* mousetrap car design (Account 10/
    Johnston)

Kettle, K. *see* drama, scientists' lives (Account 5/Kettle)
kidney function/dysfunction (Account 1/Hicks) 15–22
    central themes 172, 173, 175, 178, 180–1
    challenging traditional views 98
    conceptual development 128, 130, 133–4, 135
    inclusivity/democratic education 188–9, 195, 196,
        197, 201
    motivational beliefs 149, 153, 155, 157
    problem-based/contextualized learning 139, 140,
        141, 142, 143–4
    reflections 220–1
    technologies 162–3
knowledge
    access to 184–5, 186–7
    construction 49*mn*, 190*mn*
    consumers 194–5, 196
    development, proactive perspectives 19*mn*, 44*mn*,
        197*mn*
    negotiated 50*mn*, 75*mn*, 101*mn*
    pedagogical context 222–3
    prior 21*mn*, 30*mn*, 45*mn*, 129*mn*, 130*mn*, 131, 132–3
    relationship to 31*mn*, 36*mn*, 38*mn*, 51*mn*, 150*mn*,
        154*mn*
    restructuring 46*mn*, 133*mn*
    and skill acquisition 18*mn*, 27*mn*, 86*mn*, 142*mn*
    tacit 220
    transfer 15*mn*, 51*mn*, 128*mn*
Knowledge Forum project 166–7
Koballa, T. and Tippins, D. 206
Koslowski, B. 107
Kuhn, D. 107
    et al. 108

laboratory, legacy of the 64*mn*, 178–9
Ladson-Billings, G. 184–5
Landow, G. 11
Langer, E. 120, 155
language 21*mn*, 65*mn*, 134*mn*
laptop computers 32, 36
Lave, J. 101–2
learners

abilities 145, 155–7
    developing opinions of selves 54*mn*, 156*mn*
    motivational factors 150–7
    see also group(s); participation; peer(s); student(s)
learning autonomy 32*mn*, 34–5, 67*mn*, 152*mn*
learning quanta 67*mn*, 73*mn*, 128*mn*
learning styles 30–1, 34*mn*, 36*mn*, 68*mn*, 77*mn*, 129*mn*
    digital multimedia 34, 36, 99, 129, 188
learning *vs* doing science 34*mn*, 99*mn*
legacy of the laboratory 64*mn*, 178–9
logarithmic decibel scale 26–7, 133, 164
Lukás, G. 220

McComas, W. et al. 96–7
McLaren, P. 194
mastery orientation
    collaborative environment 54*mn*, 152*mn*
    higher order reasoning skills 59*mn*, 152*mn*
    learning autonomy 32*mn*, 67*mn*, 152*mn*
    and performance orientation goals 29*mn*, 31*mn*,
        151–2
Matthews, M. 104
measurement, in physics 26–7, 133, 164, 167*mn*, 187
memory 128, 129
mentoring (Accounts 8 & 9) 63–70, 71–83
    argumentation 110, 111, 113–14
    central themes 173, 174–5, 176–7, 180, 181
    challenging traditional views 98, 100, 101, 102–3
    conceptual development 130
    inclusivity/democratic education 189, 197, 198, 199
    motivational beliefs 147, 152
    problem-based/contextualized learning 141, 142
    STSE education principles/practice 119–20, 123
    technologies 165, 166, 167*mn*
    see also apprenticeship
'messing about' 175–6
metacognition 141, 225
methodological triangulation 221
micro-array analysis 81–2, 103
Millar, R. et al. 9
mini-projects 74
models 19–21, 27–8, 29–30, 34, 76–7, 81
    analyses 101, 130, 134, 161–2, 163, 167*mn*
    computer 34*mn*, 81, 101, 162*mn*, 167*mn*
    help comprehension 30*mn*, 161*mn*
    scientists use of 29*mn*, 77*mn*, 81*mn*, 101*mn*
    see also role play
molecules
    collisions 25–6
    isomerism 29–30, 134, 161–2
    vibrations and waves 24–5
morality, motive of 23*mn*, 31*mn*, 63*mn*, 75*mn*, 180–1
Mortimer, E. and Scott, P. 121, 122
motion
    computer animation 34*mn*, 162*mn*, 167*mn*
    measurement 27, 164, 167*mn*
motivation 146–59
    classroom environments 151–2, 156
    excitement/engagement 45*mn*, 49*mn*, 61*mn*, 79*mn*,
        124*mn*
    project work/science fairs 72, 79

promoting self-motivation 197, 201
motive of morality 23*mn*, 31*mn*, 63*mn*, 75*mn*, 180–1
motor memory 129
mousetrap car design (Account 10/Johnston) 84–91
  argumentation 111
  concept development 130
  democratic education 198
  problem-based/contextualized learning 140, 141, 144
movie clips 34
multiple viewpoints 39*mn*, 41*mn*, 58*mn*, 59*mn*, 120*mn*,
  123*mn*
Muskat, B. 80, 103
mutational conceptual change 133

narrative/story approach 67–8, 209, 211–12, 215–16,
  224
National Research Council (NRC) 218, 219
National Science Education Standards (NSES), US
  xvii
National Science Teachers Association (NSTA), US
  xvi
naturalistic curriculum 39*mn*, 200*mn*
naturalistic *vs* rationalistic research 218–19
nature of science 96–7, 118–19, 199
  see also Burgess Shale fossils (Account 6/Bellomo)
negotiated knowledge 50*mn*, 75*mn*, 101*mn*
negotiated meaning, problem-based learning (PBL)
  74*mn*, 141, 142*mn*
nephron *see* kidney function/dysfunction (Account 1/
  Hicks)
news conference 44
Ngai, D. (Account 9) 78–83, 100, 101, 103, 119–20,
  147, 198, 199
Noble, D.D. 193

objectification, science is more than 51*mn*, 158*mn*
observation 63–5, 97–9
  has to be taught 18*mn*, 58*mn*, 64*mn*, 98*mn*
  theory laden 24*mn*, 26*mn*, 48*mn*, 58*mn*, 98*mn*
Ofsted 149
open-ended inquiry 209–10
optical illusions 64, 98
organic chemistry (Account 3/Ellis) 29–31
  argumentation 113
  central themes 174, 175, 178, 180
  conceptual development 128, 129, 130, 132–3, 134
  contextual learning 144
  inclusivity/democratic education 187, 195
  motivational beliefs 150
  reflections 201–2, 207–8
  technologies 161–2
Osbourne, J.
  and Collins, S. 148
  et al. 112, 114, 147–8, 158
outdoor education centre 55, 57–8, 123
oxy-acetylene welding 87–8

Pacey, A. 136
Parris, J. 81
participation
  gender differences 187

and mix skills 20*mn*, 188*mn*
and reification 219–20
in relevant solution development 51*mn*, 62*mn*,
  125*mn*
patterns in science content 29*mn*, 127*mn*
  see also Gestalts
pedagogical context knowledge 222–3, 224
peer(s)
  editing essays/scripts 42, 43, 134, 142
  interaction 16*mn*, 30*mn*, 113*mn*
  prompters/coaches 44
performance
  'culminating performance' 176
  orientation goals 29*mn*, 31*mn*, 151–2
personalization *see* humanizing science
philosophical approach *see* nature of science
photographs 21
  vs diagrams 16–17
physical activity 20*mn*, 84*mn*, 133–5, 139–40
  manipulation of apparatus 30*mn*, 86*mn*, 129*mn*
physics (Account 2/Przywolnik) 23–8
  central themes 172, 181
  challenging traditional views 99
  conceptual development 131, 133, 134
  inclusivity/democratic learning 187, 195–6, 201
  motivational beliefs 149, 153
  problem-based/conceptual learning 139, 140, 144
  reflections 207–8, 211
  technologies 164
Pintrich, P. et al. 150, *151*, 153, 154, 155
plural accounts 108, 109
plurality of pedagogy 17*mn*, 31*mn*, 39*mn*, 175–6,
  175*mn*
political aspects *see* culture; humanizing science
Popper, K. 218
post-school mentoring (Account 9/Ngai) 78–83, 100,
  101, 103, 119–20, 147, 198, 199
posters 21
PowerPoint 20–1
practical learning *see* physical activity; theory, and
  practice links
praxis/reflective practice 223–5, 226
prior knowledge 21*mn*, 30*mn*, 45*mn*, 129*mn*, 130*mn*,
  131, 132–3
proactive perspectives, knowledge development 19*mn*,
  44*mn*, 197*mn*
problem identification 15–16, 85
problem solving *see* problem-based learning (PBL)
problem-based learning (PBL) 136–45, 209–10
  grounded in constructivism 32*mn*, 33*mn*, 137–8
  iterative 89*mn*, 140, 141*mn*
  knowledge and skill acquisition 18*mn*, 27*mn*, 86*mn*,
    142*mn*
  negotiated meaning 74*mn*, 141, 142*mn*
  practical activity 20*mn*, 84*mn*, 140*mn*
problematize science 41*mn*, 51*mn*, 196*mn*
professional training/development 114–15, 215–16
purposive sampling 219

qualitative approach 217
quality

of argumentation 111
conversations 214–16
of problem-based learning (PBL) 141
question-and-answer sessions 19, 21–2, 44

Ratcliffe, M. 123
rationalist *vs* naturalistic research 218–19
rationalize expectations 38–9, 200*mn*
realism 16*mn*, 23*mn*, 55*mn*, 81*mn*, 119*mn*, 187*mn*
    contexts 57*mn*, 84*mn*, 85*mn*, 139, 140*mn*
    object representation 19*mn*, 163*mn*
    STSE education 26*mn*, 39*mn*, 51*mn*, 56*mn*, 77*mn*,
        117, 199*mn*
    vs impressionistic representation 220
reasoning ability 107
    higher order skills 59*mn*, 152*mn*
    see also argumentation
recognition of diversity *see* difference/diversity; learning
    styles
redirected science 61*mn*, 105*mn*
reflection 89–90, 141
    and discussion 44–5, 189*mn*
    on other students' work 74*mn*, 111*mn*
reflective practice/praxis 223–5, 226
reinforcement 19*mn*, 24*mn*, 59*mn*, 129, 129*mn*
relevance
    participation in solution development 51*mn*, 62*mn*,
        125*mn*
    of science 45*mn*, 51*mn*, 72*mn*, 77*mn*, 154*mn*, 179
    to prior knowledge 21*mn*, 130*mn*
    see also utility value
Rennie, R. and Edwards, K. *see* SCOT project
    (Account 4/Rennie and Edwards)
reporting 67–8, 103
Resnick, M. et al. 164–5
rewarding activity 20*mn*, 22*mn*, 134*mn*
rocket science 27–8, 164*mn*
role play
    argumentation 23*mn*, 41*mn*, 55*mn*, 112*mn*
    contexts 40*mn*, 55–6*mn*, 118*mn*
    multiple viewpoints/critical analysis 39*mn*, 59*mn*,
        120*mn*
    in physics 23–6, 195–6
    see also drama, scientists' lives (Account 5/Kettle);
        town hall debate (Account 7/Yoon)
Roth, W.M. 178–9, 205
    and Barton, A.C. 225
    and Desautels, J. 122
    and Wallace, J. xviii

Salomon, G. 169
Savery, J.R. and Duffy, T.M. 137–8, 140
scaffolds 30*mn*, 42*mn*, 54–5, 131–2
    affective realm 156
    argument development 42*mn*, 47*mn*, 57*mn*, 121*mn*
    writing frames 57*mn*, 65*mn*, 113–14
Schaefer, H.F. 100
Schön, D. 2, 211, 223
school setting 84*mn*, 85*mn*
school-based mentoring (Account 9/Tzau) 75–8, 100,
    101

Schunk, D. 156
Schwab, J. 7, 9
Science Class of Tomorrow *see* SCOT project (Account
    4/Rennie and Edwards)
science fair projects 71–83
science, technology, society and environment (STSE)
    116–26
    realism 26*mn*, 39*mn*, 51*mn*, 56*mn*, 77*mn*, 117,
        199*mn*
scientific knowledge *see* knowledge
scientific observations *see* observation
'scientific revolutions' 133
scientists
    characteristics, student list 50
    real people 51*mn*, 103–5, 153–4, 186*mn*
    social context 40–1, 104
    status and theory acceptance 48*mn*, 99*mn*
    stereotypes 40*mn*, 45, 104*mn*, 153, 157*mn*, 189
    see also drama, scientists' lives (Account 5/Kettle)
SCOT project (Account 4/Rennie and Edwards) 32–7
    argumentation 113
    central themes 174, 181
    inclusivity/democratic education 187–8, 196
    motivational beliefs 157
    problem-based/contextualized learning 138
    technologies 162, 165
Scott, P. 108, 134
Search for Excellence in Science Education (SESE) xvi–
    xvii
self, sense of 158–9
self-efficacy 155, 156
self-motivation 197, 201
sensors 164–5
Simpson, R. et al. 157
situatedness 38*mn*, 48*mn*, 144–5
Sjoberg, S. 148, 153, 154–5
    Schreiner, C. and 155
skills 23, 73–4, 198, 210
    access to 184–5, 186–7
    acquisition 18*mn*, 27*mn*, 86*mn*, 142*mn*
    higher order reasoning 59*mn*, 152*mn*
    inquiry 64*mn*, 165*mn*
    mix 20*mn*, 188*mn*
Smith, H.A. 145
social justice 194–202
social learning 43*mn*, 79*mn*, 198–9
socio-cultural construction of science 50–2, 190*mn*
socio-cultural context 40–1, 104
socio-cultural meaning 74*mn*, 142*mn*
socio-cultural subgroups *see* difference/diversity
Somekh, B. 214
sound measurement 26–7, 133, 164, 167*mn*, 187
sound software 34
special educational needs *see* town hall debate (Account
    7/Yoon)
special interest groups (SIGs) 55–6, 57–8, 59–62
staff adviser programme 54, 55
status and theory acceptance 48*mn*, 99*mn*
stereotypes 40*mn*, 45, 104*mn*, 153, 157*mn*, 189
stopwatches 26, 27*mn*, 164*mn*, 167*mn*

story/narrative approach 67–8, 209, 211–12, 215–16, 224
structured learning *see* scaffolds
structured problems 140–1
STSE *see* science, technology, society and environment
student accounts *see* organic chemistry (Account 3/Ellis); post-school mentoring (Account 9/Ngai); school-based mentoring (Account 9/Tzau)
student(s)
  centred problem-based learning (PBL) 141–2
  challenging expectations 27*mn*, 40*mn*, 64*mn*, 133*mn*
  conceptual analysis 131
  conferencing 74–5
  confidence building 31, 43*mn*, 155–6, 190*mn*
  evaluation survey (SCOT project) 36, 37, 138
  participation *see* participation; peer(s)
  reactions 50–1, 154
  tenacity of ideas 24*mn*, 50*mn*, 131*mn*
  theatrical performances 39–40
  see also group(s); learners; participation; peer(s)

Taber, K.S. 128, 130
tacit knowledge 220
talk, shared perspectives/articulations 43*mn*, 61*mn*, 121*mn*
task mastery 29*mn*, 31*mn*, 151–2, 151*mn*
teacher(s)
  enthusiasm 31, 149–50, 208
  Gestalts 224–5
  relationship to subject 31*mn*, 36*mn*, 38*mn*, 150*mn*
  roles 43, 133, 156
  successful practice 3–4
  therapeutic practitioner 34*mn*, 44*mn*, 156*mn*
  training/professional development 114–15, 215–16
  transformation 63
teaching
  science and technology 5–6, 7
  specifics of 212–16
  styles 108
  tenacity of 17*mn*, 23*mn*, 47*mn*, 172–3
team teaching (SCOT project) 35–6
'technocentric mindset' 168–9
technology
  design projects 143
    see also mousetrap car design (Account 10/Johnston)
  instructional 160–70
    see also SCOT project (Account 4/Rennie and Edwards); *specific types*
templates 64–5, 102, 113–14
tenacity
  of student ideas 24*mn*, 50*mn*, 131*mn*
  of teaching 17*mn*, 23*mn*, 47*mn*, 172–3
textbooks 49, 162–3
theory
  framework for experiments 28*mn*, 49*mn*, 78*mn*, 99, 100–1
  and practice links 9–11, 213–14, 217–26
  triangulation 221
therapeutic practitioner 34*mn*, 44*mn*, 156*mn*
thick descriptions 219–20

time issues
  constraints 20, 21, 69
  intervention 69*mn*, 102*mn*
  memory formation 129
Tomorrow-98 initiative, Israel 161
topic choice 72–3, 81
Town Hall Council Chair (Sumeet) 59, 60, 61–2
Town Hall Council Members 56, 57, 61
town hall debate (Account 7/Yoon) 53–62
  argumentation 112, 113
  central themes 173, 179–80, 181
  challenging traditional views 98, 105
  conceptual development 134
  inclusivity/democratic education 188, 197, 198, 199–200
  motivational beliefs 149, 152, 157
  problem-based/contextualized learning 139, 144
  reflections 213, 221
  STSE principles/practice 119, 120–2, 123, 124
triangulation 220–1
trustworthiness of educational research 218, 219–21
Tzau, V. (Account 9) 75–8, 100, 101

understanding, promoting 201–2
unique perspectives 222–3
usefulness of educational resources 221–5
utility value 63*mn*, 154–5
  see also relevance

values
  access to 184–5, 186–7
  and mindfulness 120–1
vibrations and waves, physics 24–5
video 16, 24–5, 28, 40, 43, 44, 62, 74
  animation 130
  camera 164, 167*mn*
  vs real-life objects 162–4

Walcott, C. 46, 47–9, 50, 98, 99, 105, 110, 190
wall displays 21
Wallace, J. 211, 212, 214–15, 221
  and Louden, W. 3–4, 171, 174, 180
Watts, M. et al. 119
Wenger, E. 198–9, 219–20, 224
Western Australia Curriculum Framework (Curriculum Council) 184
Wigfield, A. and Eccles, J. 154, 156
'wireless network' 32
Wittington, Briggs and Conway Morris 48, 49, 98, 158, 190
Woolnough, B. 149–50
word processors 162
working memory 128, 129
Writers in Electronic Residence (WIER) 166
writing frames 57*mn*, 65*mn*, 113–14

Young, R. 104

Zembylas, M. 146
Ziman, J. 117, 119